Jörg Rogge (ed.)
Cultural History in Europe

Mainz Historical Cultural Sciences | Volume 5

Editorial

The **Mainzer Historische Kulturwissenschaften** [Mainz Historical Cultural Sciences] series publishes the results of research that develops methods and theories of cultural sciences in connection with empirical research. The central approach is a historical perspective for cultural sciences, whereby both epochs and regions can differ widely and be treated in an all-embracing manner from time to time. The series brings together, among other things, research approaches in archaeology, art history and visualistic, philosophy, literary studies and history, and is open for contributions on the history of knowledge, political culture, the history of perceptions, experiences and life-worlds, as well as other fields of research with a historical cultural scientific orientation.
The objective of the **Mainzer Historische Kulturwissenschaften** series is to become a platform for pioneering works and current discussions in the field of historical cultural sciences.

The series is edited by the Co-ordinating Committee of the Special Research Group Historical Cultural Sciences (HKW) at the Johannes Gutenberg University Mainz.

JÖRG ROGGE (ED.)
Cultural History in Europe
Institutions – Themes – Perspectives

[transcript]

The Conference on Cultural History in Europe was sponsored by the DFG.
The Print was sponsored by the Research Focus Historical Cultural Sciences
(HKW).

Bibliographic information published by the Deutsche Nationalbibliothek
The Deutsche Nationalbibliothek lists this publication in the Deutsche Nationalbibliografie; detailed bibliographic data are available in the Internet at http://dnb.d-nb.de

© 2011 transcript Verlag, Bielefeld

All rights reserved. No part of this book may be reprinted or reproduced or utilized in any form or by any electronic, mechanical, or other means, now known or hereafter invented, including photocopying and recording, or in any information storage or retrieval system, without permission in writing from the publisher.

Cover layout: Kordula Röckenhaus, Bielefeld
Proofread by Cathleen Sarti, Mainz
Typeset by Justine Haida, Bielefeld
Printed by Majuskel Medienproduktion GmbH, Wetzlar
ISBN 978-3-8376-1724-5

Contents

Welcome Address 7
ULRICH FÖRSTERMANN

Traditions, Topics and Trends in Cultural History
in Europe—an Introduction 11
JÖRG ROGGE

From Ethnology and Folklore Studies to Cultural History
in Scandinavia 31
ANNE ERIKSEN

Traditions of Cultural History in Finland, 1900-2000 45
HANNU SALMI

The Practice of Cultural History in Britain 63
LUDMILLA JORDANOVA

The Cultural History MA at the University of Aberdeen,
1986-2011: a personal reflection 79
NICK FISHER

Perspectives of the Cultural History in Latvia:
The 20th century and beyond 91
MĀRTIŅŠ MINTAURS

A would-be science?
A History of Material Culture in Poland
before and after the year 1989 125
IGOR KĄKOLEWSKI

**Achievements and Contradictions in the Writing and
Teaching of Cultural History in Hungary** 141
ANDREA PETŐ

Beyond the Alpine Myth, Across the Linguistic Ditch
Cultural History in Switzerland 157
CHRISTOF DEJUNG

What's new about the *New Cultural History*?
An exemplary survey of the Austrian academic community 171
CHRISTINA LUTTER

We've only just begun
Cultural History in Germany 191
ACHIM LANDWEHR

Cultural History in Spain
History of Culture and Cultural History:
same paths and outcomes? 211
CAROLINA RODRÍGUEZ-LÓPEZ

Cultural History in Italy 239
ALESSANDRO ARCANGELI

Contributors 257

Welcome Address

ULRICH FÖRSTERMANN, VICE-PRESIDENT FOR RESEARCH,
JOHANNES GUTENBERG-UNIVERSITY, MAINZ

This volume presents the papers of the International Conference on *Cultural History in Europe*, which took place in Mainz from March 17th till 21st 2010. It was the first international conference of the Collaborative Research Focus on *Historical Cultural Sciences* of the Johannes Gutenberg University.

This Research Focus investigates the distinctive nature of cultural circumstances within their respective individual historical context. It is one of the seven Research Foci of our University, which were selected in a competitive process for their specific potential for interdisciplinary research. The selection occurred with external expertise under the auspices of our very own Gutenberg Research College. Financially supported by the State of Rhineland-Palatinate from 2008 to 2013, the Research Focus *Historical Cultural Sciences* aims at developing a specific historical-cultural profile within the University's general academic portfolio.

Please, allow me to explain this concept: The Research Focus combines several departments and different academic disciplines within our University, thereby interconnecting and stimulating research within the cultural sciences. The Focus combines empirical work and profound theoretical and methodological considerations in a historical perspective.

Overall, the internationally competitive research at the Johannes Gutenberg University is characterized by a broad variety of disciplines. As an international research location, we resolutely pursue a strategy of promoting excellence in science and the Humanities, hosting eight Collaborative Research Centers, ten Research Groups, and eight Graduate Schools (all funded by the German Research Foundation), as well as numerous research initiatives funded by other sources, both public and private.

The conference and this subsequent volume is a prime example for the successful efforts of our scholars and their efficient international cooperation

with other research groups. It intends to comprehensively take stock of cultural history in Europe: Participants from over ten European countries will:
- report on the state of cultural history in their respective countries,
- consider in which way cultural history, as an academic discipline, is incorporated into the structured system of their own Universities, research institutes or other institutions,
- ascertain which questions and topics are particularly in demand in certain countries or have already been dealt with to a large extent,
- identify (presumed) future fields of research,
- examine the opportunities and the limits of financial support from Universities and/or (state) governments, and
- consider the relationship of cultural history to other parts of historical science and to cultural studies in a wider sense.

Historical Cultural Sciences have a long tradition at our University—not only in the social sciences but in all of the humanities—a special research library is currently being established on our campus. Furthermore, our colleagues invited several outstanding scholars in the field of *Theories and Methods of Historical Cultural Sciences* to Mainz as Fellows of our Gutenberg Research College. In this context, they also:
- organize interdisciplinary research symposia three to four times each semester in order to increase synergies between the different academic disciplines,
- publish a new historical-cultural book series called *Mainzer Historische Kulturwissenschaften* (*Mainz Historical Cultural Sciences*), the first four volumes are already published, and
- initiate a project to develop a manual on key concepts of the Historical Cultural Sciences.

In short, Historical Cultural Sciences here in Mainz are pursuing a path of excellence, which, we hope, will eventually also be acknowledged in the upcoming Federal Excellence Initiative.

By bringing together young and established scholars from all over the world, this conference was a shining example for the way our University actively participates in the global academic community and contributes to our overall goal of continuing internationalization of academic programs and research. Our University gains much from such exchanges, and we greatly appreciate the contacts we have been able to make and maintain.

Let me say "thank you" to the many supporters and organizers: First and foremost Jörg Rogge and his team, who have done a wonderful job in organizing the conference and editing this volume. They received considerable help, I hear, by our colleagues from the Medieval section of our Department of History. Last but not least I would like to thank the German Research Foundation (DFG) for their generous support of the conference.

Traditions, Topics and Trends in Cultural History in Europe—an Introduction[1]

JÖRG ROGGE

In the debates about the theory and methods of European historical science in the past thirty years, cultural historical approaches and formulations of questions played and do play an outstanding role. The interest in this was stimulated by the changing prevailing political and social conditions, on the one hand, and an increasing dissatisfaction with the dominant historical-scientific concepts on the other. Thus at the beginning of the 1980s in the Federal Republic of Germany, criticism of Social History or Historical Social Science interested in socio-economic structures and processes, which paid hardly any attention to the cultural meaning dimensions of historical reality, was the starting point for the newly awakening interest in culture and the people who had produced their respective culture. The invitation given by historical science to pay more attention again to the actors—admittedly not to the *great men*—corresponded to the attitude that the individual in his respective place could or must contribute towards changing social and political conditions. Because it was the people themselves who created the world they lived in by acting and interpreting; they were not simply at the mercy of anonymous structures, but invited, e.g. to demonstrate against the nuclear industry and environmental pollution, to stand up for peace and security or also to demand equal rights for men and women, and thus overcome traditional gender roles.

With the political watershed of 1989/90 and the experiences of the Germans in and with the GDR, the sensibility for the diversity of the pasts experienced by human beings increased further. Precisely the experiences which people make,

---

1 Many Thanks to John Michael Deasy, Kristina Müller-Bongard and Cathleen Sarti for their manifold support during the editing process of this volume.

contribute to their behaviour and are the basis for their interpretation of their world. People were (and are) linked together and with their environment by social practices and various forms of communication. The historical actors express their opinion on their opposite numbers and the environment; they thus generate meanings and give their (living) world a meaning.[2]

Against this background, a new form of cultural history developed in Germany, differing from the old cultural history of the closing years of the 19th and early part of the 20th century. In disassociation from social history, one let oneself be influenced above all by everyday and mentality history—the concepts of the *Annales* primarily[3] - as well as historical anthropology.[4] In addition came gradually French, but above all Anglo-American concepts and methods, such as the *New Cultural History*, methodological approaches of gender history[5] and in part also of cultural studies. But in Germany, older key players in cultural studies in the 19th and 20th centuries (Karl Lamprecht, Eberhard Gothein, Ernst Cassirer, Max Weber) were also rediscovered and used in the development of current cultural study concepts. However, the forbears' ideas and concepts have been treated mainly up to now with a view to their potential for a historical cultural science and have not yet been exploited for empirical research.[6] Even if the works of older German cultural history have been read again in the last few years, it is rather the works of European and American historians, which have in the meantime acquired the status of classics, that have gained a model character for German cultural historians.[7]

The publication of the results of cultural historical works after the turn of the millennium, both in the German-speaking area and in Europe, supplied the basis for first summaries of the discussion of methods and theory,[8] introductions to a European cultural history[9] and cultural historical syntheses for individual centuries.[10] These publications prove that cultural history is on the way to estab-

---

2 On this cf. ROGGE, 2010.
3 RAPHAEL, 1994.
4 DÜLMEN, 2001; TANNER, 2004; WINTERLING, 2006.
5 Methodologically pathbreaking was SCOTT, 1986. See also OPITZ, 2005.
6 On this for instance the works by OEXLE, 2000, and OEXLE, 1996.
7 These are e.g. GINZBURG, 1980; DAVIS, 1984, DARNTON, 1989, BURKE, 2002.
8 GREEN, 2008; TSCHOPP/WEBER, 2007; POIRRIER, 2008; TSCHOPP, 2005, ARCANGELI 2010.
9 LANDWEHR/STOCKHORST, 2004, MAURER, 2008.
10 SALMI, 2008.

lishing itself as a conception for research into the past alongside other methods of access in historical science.

However, that has not been made easy for it—especially not in Germany. There cultural history was and is not undisputed. It has been criticised by representatives of historical-scientific conceptions for whom diversity was (and is) a synonym for arbitrariness.[11] Admittedly, the advocates of cultural historical approaches have fostered this criticism to a certain extent by leaving open what exactly cultural history is meant to be and is.[12] Therefore the notions of what cultural history is meant to be with regard to methodology and concept range from cultural history as a sectoral discipline of historical science, like technological or economic history, through the view that cultural history is a specific method of historical science, to the position that history as a whole should be conceived as a historical cultural science. At all events, an increasingly widely held consensus, objects and topics were thus intended to be examined from a cultural historical point of view, too, which—like politics and law—which previously lay outside the focus of cultural historians. Topics, on which the traditional form of cultural history had explicitly turned its back.[13]

But one of the distinguishing features of cultural history is at all events its claim to reflect its own activity—the research concepts, topics and fields. Because the result, not only of cultural historical research, is ultimately a construction by historians who are influenced by their respective current social and cultural circumstances. This view is—so at any rate the cultural historical credo—the prerequisite for the fact that the research results are based on a scientific-rational gain of knowledge.[14] This process of self-reflection is an integral part of cultural historical work and therefore it is important that this reflection be made the object of consideration. The discussion about the objects and fields of work, as well as about methodological access and operationalisation is to be continued, just as questions must be asked about the achievements of cultural history and its capability in comparison with other concepts. This applies *grosso*

---

11 Perhaps the most prominent German critic is Hans-Ulrich Wehler; see e.g. his review of Ute Daniel's *Kompendium Kulturgeschichte*, WEHLER, 2003, cf. KOCKA, 1999. For the defendants' arguments see e.g. MEDICK, 2001.

12 DANIEL, 2006; MAURER, 2008.

13 At the centre of this perspective are above all processes of communication by which social, political and legal institutions are first created; see for instance STOLLBERG-RILINGER. 2005. A survey of the history of cultural historiography by the collection of essays compiled and commented by TSCHOPP, 2008.

14 TSCHOPP, 2008, p. 32 and DANIEL, 2006.

Jörg Rogge

modo for all European countries in which cultural history is pursued and where it is more or less installed at universities and research institutions.

For this reason, I asked colleagues from twelve European countries to sketch out the respective current basic conditions—scientific-political and social assessment of cultural history—or also the historical development of these basic conditions for cultural historical research in their countries. The contributors give, in part from very personal perspectives and on the basis of their experience with the subject of cultural history in their countries and in Europe as a whole, an assessment of institutions, topics and perspectives of cultural history. In addition, they outline their assessments of the further development of topics and fields of work in their countries, whereby the degree of institutionalisation of cultural history at universities, research institutes and other institutions is dealt with in varying evaluation, typical national traditions are presented, important current research topics and formulations of questions are touched on, and a look is taken at the perspectives and the relationship to other concepts of historical science and to cultural studies.

ANNE ERIKSEN presents the common tradition of cultural history in the Scandinavian countries Denmark, Sweden and Norway, the common roots of which go back to the 19th century. Eriksen emphasised that the development of ethnology and folklore in these countries was closely connected with the process of modernisation and nation building in Scandinavia. In the countries studied by her, cultural history developed in the recent past out of the disciplines European ethnology and folklore which, according to Eriksen, can be described as a *special way* in European comparison. She illustrates this by the example of the University of Oslo where, in 2003, both disciplines were combined into the subject *Cultural History*. She describes the relationship to cultural studies as being relaxed and productive. There is no strict differentiation between cultural history and cultural studies, as they developed from the same disciplines and thus have a common history.

HANNU SALMI sketches out, on the one hand, the development of cultural history in Finland since the end of the 19th century, dealing on the other hand with its integration into research institutions. First of all an Institute for Cultural History was founded at the Swedish-speaking Åbo Akademi in Turku in 1953. The research conducted there was, however, for the most part ignored by Finnish-speaking cultural historians. On the other hand, at the Finnish-speaking University founded in Turku in 1919, it took until 1972 before cultural history became institutionalised as a discipline in the form of the *Department for Cultural History*. Today the department is among the most important university institutions in the country working on cultural history, both in teaching and research, with an influence also in Scandinavia. Salmi sees in semiotics, structuralism and British Cultural Studies important stimuli for the methodological-theoretical development of cultural history in present-day Finland.

LUDMILLA JORDANOVA emphasises the institutionally problematical situation of cultural history in England. Although there are certainly historians working on cultural history in England—such as e.g. Peter Burke—cultural history as a subject is not very present in teaching and research institutions, hardly institutionalised and organised there in departments of its own. One reason for this is that until the 1970s, in research practice, social and cultural history were dealt with together, enjoying in principle equal rights. Under the influence of historical anthropology, as well as cultural sociology and increasingly also the Warburg Institute, a newly conceived cultural history then diverged from social history of the classical kind. According to Jordanova, this new cultural history differs from older social history through its interdisciplinarity and from cultural studies through its more pronouncedly theoretical, polymorphous, flexible and open approach.

NICK FISHER reports on his personal experiences with the institutionalisation of the subject at the University of Aberdeen. He and his colleagues had understood cultural history as an opportunity to free themselves from the conventional boundaries of disciplines. It was also a reaction to the first financial cuts in the mid-1980s and an attempt to make the location Aberdeen attractive for students. Since 1989, the course of studies recorded a continuous rise in the numbers of students. Fisher shows how, despite or on account of its successes, cultural history was criticised both by the administration and within its own university on account of its contents. An example of the difficulties of consolidating interdisciplinary, new directions in studies institutionally in the long run. Finally, the successful programme of studies fell victim to the restructuring in the University in 2002. The until then independent subject was connected more closely again to the Department of History, losing as a result not only its autonomy, but also staff posts. After the course of studies had in this way been made unattractive, the numbers of students fell dramatically, leading ultimately to the cessation of the course with the last graduate in 2011.

In contemporary Latvia, cultural history is hardly institutionalised—apart from the Academy of Culture founded in 1990—and has therefore only poor possibilities for developing. MĀRTIŅŠ MINTAURS attributes this finding above all to Soviet rule under which Latvian historiography was ideologically controlled and to a large extent isolated from external influences. Although these restrictions no longer applied after 1991 and access to new methods and approaches has been easily possible since then, political history dominates Latvian historiography. That is a reflex of the new political independence. However, since the mid-1990s, some works of the French *Annales*, gender history and social anthropology have been translated into Latvian. Mintaurs sees the reorganisation of research and teaching in Latvia as still not yet complete and emphasises the importance of exchange programmes with which the latest methods and theories of cultural history could be imported into Latvian research institutions and universities.

IGOR KĄKOLEWSKI concerns himself above all with the Institute for the History of Material Culture of the Polish Academy of Sciences (IHMC PAN) founded in 1953/54 because different varieties of cultural history were institutionalised there. After the establishment of Communist rule, the methodological reconstruction and centralisation of the sciences took place. The central issue for research work after 1956 was material culture and, above all, the means and techniques of production which became the starting point for research into culture as a whole—above all of the Middle Ages and the early Modern Period.[15] The research programme was developed further until the 1970s: the topics and fields of work were everyday life, communication and travels. These works had their methodological foundation above all in the French *Annales* school that in addition was the *window on the world* for Polish historiography until the end of the 1960s. In the 1970s and 1980s, a general opening towards international approaches to cultural history took place in Poland, above all outside of the IHMC. In 1992, the IHMC was renamed the Institute of Archaeology and Ethnology. At present, both theoretical-methodological topics are dealt with and empirical research is conducted on concrete questions. In the current debate on methods—under different conditions from those in the 1960s and 1970s—the question of the importance of material artefacts for the world people lived in plays a great role, and linked with that the question how a methodological access to that can be developed.

In Hungary after the First World War, a cultural history was written under national auspices. According to ANDREA PETŐ, the tendency of historical science before the Second World War was best described by Cooper's statement "empires produced a strong empire-centred imagination"[16]. In the interwar period in Hungary, a trend of cultural history dominated in Hungary, with the Department of Cultural History at the University of Budapest, that had been established in 1898 as its centre, in which culture was closely linked with nation. The objective was to at least emphasise its own cultural superiority after Hungary had lost political dominance in the Carpathian region after 1920.[17] After 1945/50, historical materialism with its understanding of culture as a superstructure phenomenon of the

---

15 KĄKOLEWSKI in this volume, p. 132.
16 COOPER, 2005, p. 23; here from PETŐ, in this volume, p. 144.
17 PETŐ, in this volume, p. 147.

material basis did, it is true, dominate, but in the 1970s, as in Poland, the *Annales* with their concept of culture as a unity gained influence. In addition, the concepts of older German cultural history were adopted,[18] until finally in the mid-1980s a general opening for further western historical scientific concepts took place. Pető states that after 1989 a conceptional and methodological modernisation of Hungarian historical science failed to materialise for the most part. Interestingly enough, even historians of the new generation have hardly concerned themselves with cultural history. In addition, the institutionalisation of cultural history in Hungary has been greatly hindered by financial bottlenecks at the state universities and the Bologna process, because in education the classical fields, such as political, economic and social history dominate. Therefore in Hungary, the privately financed Central European University in Budapest with its decidedly cultural historical orientation is the great exception.

CHRISTOF DEJUNG emphasises the importance of the "Swiss cliché" and multilingualism for cultural history in Switzerland. The main fields of focus in Swiss cultural history are currently national identity, the history of mentality, economy and knowledge. One characteristic of cultural history there is its relatively close co-operation also with Swiss academics at foreign research institutions. Cultural history in Switzerland is also promoted outside of the universities by numerous private foundations. Dejung is of the opinion that the work on and with cultural history has only just begun and that in particular works on the history of the body and national identity are to be expected from Swiss cultural history in the next few years.

CHRISTINA LUTTER opens her article with a theoretical-methodological situation analysis, starting out from Lynn Hunt's and Roger Chartier's reflections, of what had characterised *New Cultural History* since the 1980s. Then she explains cultural historical and, in a wider sense, cultural studies research activities and opportunities in Austria, taking the University of Vienna in particular into consideration. Lutter observed that cultural historical research in Austria, in comparison with other European countries, with the exception of Germany, has a strong presence at universities, but particularly also at non-university research institutions[19] and networks. One important reason for this was the *younger generation's* increased interest in international, theoretically informed and interdisciplinary cultural studies research, particularly with reference to the political cultural

---

18 PETŐ, in this volume, p. 148.
19 Among the internationally well-known institutions is the IFK in Vienna. Admittedly its scope for action is jeopardised on account of the current interventions in extra-university research institutions by the Austrian government.

concept of British cultural studies. The abundance of existing research activities and results, particularly at the *micro level*, of individual institutes and research networks corresponds only in part with the research objectives of the large universities and institutions for the promotion of research. This incongruence becomes especially clear through the fact that there are still hardly any institutionalised programmes of study for cultural studies or cultural history at Austrian universities.

ACHIM LANDWEHR assesses that cultural history in Germany is, on the one hand, already well established institutionally. Cultural historical research programmes are being conducted in research centres, research groups, projects and excellence clusters (e.g. Heidelberg, Münster, Berlin, Konstanz and Mainz). On the other hand, this finding should not obscure the fact that cultural history is being conducted, up to now, first and foremost in projects and institutions for limited periods of time. With regard to the establishment of *New Cultural History*, Landwehr recalled that in the 1980s it was felt by the representatives of social and political history to be a provocation, if not indeed a threat to the history established at the universities. In the meantime, however, cultural history in Germany is regarded as a recognised method of approaching the past. According to Landwehr, the New Cultural History sees itself more as a method or a specific perspective and is less fixed on certain topics or fields of research. Despite these comparatively good institutional conditions, it is, however, also true that in fact this just marks the beginning of intensive work in cultural history.

In Spain, too, cultural history is in great demand at present. As in Germany, there, too, cultural history was at first conducted by historians specialising in the Middle Ages and Early Modern Period. CAROLINA RODRÍGUEZ-LÓPEZ explained this by Spain's imperial position in the Early Modern Period, on the one hand, and the instrumentalisation of this *brilliant epoch* in Spanish history during Franco's rule until 1975 on the other. However, the conception and implementation of a modern cultural history using the international discussion only became possible in the post-Franco era. Since 1989 there have been research groups, institutions and academic programmes dealing in particular with Spanish cultural history. The starting point for cultural history in Spain was above all the social history of the labour and trade union movement. A further important influence for the conception of modern Spanish cultural history was the history of ideas and research into the importance of Spanish intellectuals who had also fought politically against Franco and the authoritarian regime.

ALESSANDRO ARCANGELI states that cultural history is not established at Italian universities. In his estimation, this is because cultural historical approaches appear first and foremost as *imports* from France and Britain in Italy and one contents oneself with their reception. In addition, cultural history is seldom studied as a main subject at universities. Therefore it is difficult to develop one's own approaches or indeed to implement them in the Italian university system. Currently, historians still refer for the most part to the approaches embodied in traditional Italian historical science approaches. On this basis, special research works, e.g. on the history of the book, nutrition, or even the genders have been produced which are, however, seldom understood as being in a greater context. Arcangeli observes that cultural history is being conducted now and then, without being designated or reflected as such. But precisely the lack of reflection hinders the establishment of a theoretically and methodologically sound, independent cultural history; such as, for example, in Germany. The main focus of cultural historically oriented research in Italy is to be found at present in Pisa, Bologna and Venice, with chronological emphasis on the Modern Period and early Modern Period.

On the basis of these observations and descriptions, influences, traditions and interactions can be recognised which have shaped the development and form of cultural history practised in each case in the countries considered here, and still shape them today. It shows which countries have traditions in common in cultural studies, but also what differences exist with regard to how cultural history is conceived in each case, what approaches are preferred in the countries and for what political purpose cultural history was and is employed. As a result, the basic political conditions for the adaptation of cultural history are addressed. In addition, perspectives can be named which the contributors see for cultural history in their countries and as a trend in Europe. Thus in the survey of the contributions from twelve European countries, a more exact—even if not complete—picture of the current situation of cultural history in Europe results, and topics and perspectives for the future of cultural history become apparent.

Cultural studies traditions and influences

There is a trend towards several important lines of tradition to be recognised which have considerably influenced cultural historical research in Europe in the past 20 to 30 years. The most important traditions and influences mentioned in the papers are summarised briefly here below. There is a strand of tradition in European cultural history that has its methodological and theoretical roots in intellectual history and the history of ideas, as well as the older German cultural history of the 19th century, such as in Austria, Germany, Italy, Spain and the Baltic countries. The French *Annales* establish a second line of tradition. Their representatives and concepts did not only have considerable influence in Western Europe, but also supplied conceptional and theoretical input to historical science in Poland and Hungary during communist rule.

With regard to Switzerland, it has to be added that since the late 19th century the development of cultural history was shaped by three approaches.[20] On the one hand, Jacob Burckhardt's concept, in which art and religion are emphasised as the most important aspects of culture, in which the singularity of a historical epoch (e.g. the Renaissance) is reflected. Burckhardt is, it is true, still invoked today as an important reference for cultural history, but his approach is hardly present any more in current European cultural history. Secondly, in Fribourg academics have tried to show the cultural binding force of Catholicism, in order to be able to use it politically as an important means for securing federalism in the modern national state. However, the recognisably greatest influence on current concepts of cultural history in Switzerland has emanated from the University of Zurich where cultural anthropology and ethnology were established institutionally. These subjects were interested above all in the everyday culture of ordinary people. In England, a social history had a great influence on historical scientific concepts that was more profoundly influenced by anthropology than by sociology or other social sciences.[21] A social history dominated which, in contrast for instance to that in Germany, was less greatly interested in economic and social structures as the impulse for historical developments. People's notions and convictions interested British social historians who, with recourse to concepts of social or cultural anthropology, examined, for example, systems of belief as cultural systems with their own integrity. On account of the reception of anthropological approaches by British social historians, in research practice, the limits to topics and fields of work, which are regarded as a cultural historical alternative to social and political history in other countries, have been open. Thus there was no need—unlike, for instance, in the German-speaking academic area—to draft and institutionalise a cultural history separate from social history. The cultural history practised in Britain shows points in common with Norway and Sweden with regard to the central importance of family and gender history, as well as the *Post Colonial Studies*. Because the Empire was (or is?) of outstanding importance in Britain for her national identity. Only recently have French concepts, such as the history of mentality or discourse, been received without, however, the approaches, e.g. of Roger Chartier or Philippe Ariès being directly continued.[22]

---

20 DEJUNG, in this volume, p. 159.
21 JORDANOVA, in this volume, p. 66.
22 JORDANOVA, in this volume, p. 7: "[...] apart from France, the cultural-historical methods and approaches of European countries are rather little known in the UK."

The third great line of tradition to be named for the conception of current cultural historical trends are—as already mentioned for Switzerland—folklore and ethnology. Formulations of questions and methods from these disciplines have had a powerful effect, not just in Switzerland, but also for the conception and research practice of cultural history in Scandinavia and Finland. This is shown by the fact that a main focus of cultural historical research is the people's material culture and everyday life.

Political significance and function of cultural history in the 19th and 20th centuries

Cultural history had the function of elaborating the cultural bases of the way nations see themselves in many countries in the 19th century and until the middle of the 20th century. As shown by the contributions in this volume, that is true for Finland and Scandinavia, but also for the Baltic states and Central East European countries during the interwar period and after 1989/90. In 1809, Finland became part of the Russian Empire and, in the following decades, the call for political independence was substantiated by the reference to the Finns' cultural independence. Their own language, literature and culture were invoked whereby German influence (Johann Gottfried Herder) was of considerable importance. Even after Finland had become an independent state in 1917, the Finns defined themselves as a nation more through their history and culture than through statehood.[23] In Norway, Sweden and Denmark, the folk culture became part of the compensation process in the transformation of monarchies into national states in the 19th century. In Norway the specific folk culture was a legitimation factor for the national state.[24] It was stated that the language, customs and mentality had become clearly distinct from those in Denmark or Sweden and had existed since the Middle Ages, even in times when there was no Norwegian state. This was substantiated by means of fairy tales, poetry, but also the material culture of ordinary people. One result of this work was the 12-volume series *Everyday Life in the North of the 16th Century* which appeared in 1879-1893. A detailed picture of the people's life was given in this.[25]

The political utilisation of cultural history in Poland, Hungary and Latvia results from the special development of their statehood and political indepen-

---
23 SALMI, in this volume, p. 46.
24 ERIKSEN, in this volume, p. 31.
25 ERIKSEN, in this volume, p. 35.

dence in comparison with Western European countries. The contributions make it clear that in these three countries cultural history—regardless of how it was conceived from a methodological-theoretical point of view in each case—was employed as an instrument for shaping the current social and political conditions in each case. In the history of these countries, which had, of course, only experienced comparatively short phases of sovereignty until 1989/90, there were again and again periods in which recourse to cultural history, mostly understood as the history of their respective own culture, was of political relevance. Thus in Latvia in the interwar period, the main task of cultural history was seen as being to prove continuity of the Latvian nation since the 13th century, at the same time showing the differences of the genuine indigenous Latvian culture from that of the immigrant Baltic Germans.[26] And after 1989/90, cultural historical work was under the maxim that the cultural history of the Latvians is part of the history of the Latvian nation. Cultural unity and identity with the help of scholarship was invoked and will always be so in times in which no state of their own exists.[27]

In Hungary after 1989/90, one turned to the cultural historiography of the interwar period which offered a starting point for finding the nation. After decades under Soviet dominance, which was covered up as *internationalism*, it was a matter of safeguard or again uncovering the historical roots of the nation. One means for this was the *Cultural History of Hungary* which was published between 1939 and 1942 and was often reprinted in 1990/91. One thus had at the same time—whether consciously or unconsciously—also established intellectual contacts with the Horthy era again (Miklós Horthy, Regent of Hungary 1920-1944). In Andrea Pető's opinion this became the basis for the new conservative historiography in Hungary.[28]

---

26 MINTAURS, in this volume, p. 99-101.
27 This applies admittedly also for Scandinavia, Italy and Germany in the 19th century.
28 PETŐ, in this volume, p. 196. But in the 1970s, in Hungary and also in Poland the concepts of the *Annales* (Braudel, Chaunu) and the old German cultural history were the methodological tools in order to get round the dominant materialistic view of history (according to Pető remarkably many young conservative to national-right historians as sympathisers of Premier Viktor Orbán, who advocates authoritative and national positions).

Institutionalisation

Cultural history is institutionalised at universities and extra-university research institutions. In addition, relevant research is conducted in project-related activities for limited periods. In Germany and Austria, in comparison with other European countries, such as Britain, Italy and Spain, cultural history is not only present at universities, but also relatively well institutionalised. Thus, for instance, at German universities in the form of M.A. courses of studies. However, it is also noticeable that until today it is only firmly integrated institutionally in the form of chairs and departments at a few universities. Among the exceptions are the university in Frankfurt an der Oder, where cultural history is established under cultural studies, the University of Augsburg with a chair and an Institute of European Cultural History, as well as the University of Jena with a professorship of cultural history and the university of Potsdam with a proffessorship for cultural history of the modern era. Extra-university institutions of great importance in Germany and Austria are the Cultural Studies Institute in Essen, the International Research Centre for Cultural Studies in Vienna and the Max Weber College in Erfurt. All in all, institutional locations for limited periods at present dominate cultural historical work: The graduate schools and excellence clusters at the universities in Giessen, Heidelberg, Berlin, Münster and Konstanz.[29] In addition, there are still university research centres for a limited period, such as the FSP Historical Cultural Sciences in Mainz or the Historical Cultural Sciences Research Centre at the University of Trier.[30]

Therefore, it can hardly be stated that cultural historical approaches have been sustainably institutionally established in the structures at German universities—even if names have been replaced.[31] At the University of Mainz, in the course of the reorganisation of the faculties a few years ago, a *Faculty of History and Cultural Studies* was established. However, just like elsewhere, a budgeted established post for cultural history was not included.[32]

---

29 LANDWEHR, in this volume, p. 198.
30 http://www.historische.kulturwissenschaften.uni-mainz.de/, 01.03.2011 and http://www.hkfz.uni-trier.de/, 01.03.2011.
31 Lutter in this volume on the situation in Austria.
32 There is no chair of cultural history in Western Germany that is filled by a historian. Silvia Serena Tschopp in Augsburg is a literary specialist by training. Even historians who see themselves firmly as cultural historians, such as Ute Daniel (Braunschweig, Professor of Modern History), Achim Landwehr (Düsseldorf, Professor of

This result nevertheless proves a comparatively well institutionalised cultural history, as the articles on Italy, Hungary, Spain and Britain as well as Latvia show. Finland is an institutional exception with the Department of Cultural History at the University of Turku in southern Finland. But in order that cultural history can exist in the long term and make its contribution for contemporary societies, it needs an appropriate institutional basis at universities and research institutions. Merely because only thus does it give at least minimal prospects of a university career for some of the up-and-coming academics now being trained at graduate schools and clusters.

In Scandinavia, apart from the universities, above all museums are still to be made out as important places for cultural historical research. At the end of the 19th century, museums were established in Sweden and Norway (1891 Nordic Museum in Stockholm, 1894 Nordic Museum in Oslo) which are important institutions for imparting and researching into cultural history to the present day. The basic idea with the establishment of the museums at that time was that anyone who knows the material folk culture, would also know the national history. However, in Norway in the meantime, the presentation of culture in museums is being reviewed in order to adapt it to present conditions. Norwegian national culture is challenged by migration and multiculturalism. There, as in other European countries, too, there is no longer a uniform culture, however one may like to define it. Therefore, it is intended to research into how cultural diversity can be exhibited at and with the museums in Norway.[33] In Finland, cultural history was institutionalised by the establishment of chairs at the universities. After the Second World War, Åbo Akademi, as well as since the 1970s the Department of Cultural History at the University of Turku became the most influential institutions for cultural history in Finland, because chairs and departments were established there. Teaching and research were thus able to be well combined.[34] In Britain, cultural history, unlike social history is hardly apparent institutionally. Professor Jordanova observes "cultural history is remarkably uninstitutionalised in formal, structured ways".[35] There is a lack of a specific tradition such as e.g. that at the museums and universities of institutionalised folklore in Scandinavia and Finland which could—as happened for example in Oslo—be further developed into departments of cultural history. Just as little were there recognisable

History of the Early Modern Period) or in Austria Christina Lutter (Vienna, Professor of Austrian History) do not hold nominally cultural historical chairs.
33 ERIKSEN, in this volume, p. 41.
34 SALMI, in this volume, p. 51.
35 JORDANOVA, in this volume, p. 64.

cultural historical schools in Britain around which interested parties could gather. Traditionally, classical and possible topics and questions of cultural history are also pursued outside of historical science in other disciplines.[36]

In the German-speaking part of Switzerland, cultural history has been developing in parallel to social history since the 1960s and has since then been an undisputed and accepted approach for historical analysis. On the other hand, the situation in the French-speaking part of Switzerland is different where, until the 1980s the history of ideas and literary history dominated, before anthropologically oriented cultural history succeeded in finding its feet there too.[37] Admittedly, Dejung observes that in contrast to the German-speaking part of Switzerland, historians in the French-speaking region of the country are still hardly touched by the *cultural turn*.[38] Dejung describes the Research Centre for Asia and Europe (Main focus *Postcolonial Studies*, cultural transfer) in Zurich as one of the most important research institutions dealing with cultural history in Switzerland. The University in Lucerne has been working on cultural historical-cultural studies image building for about 15 years, also linking research and teaching through interdisciplinary collaboration.

In Italy, according to Arcangeli's observations, there have only been endeavours to establish cultural history more firmly at the universities since recently. An appropriate academic network has been established at the Universities of Bologna, Padua, Pisa and Venice since 2009. In addition, seminars with international speakers are being held and a book series *Cultural studies. Concepts and practices* has been planned. Until now in Italy, cultural historical (individual) projects have dominated which are financed by state—in particular by the National Council of Research—and private promotional institutions. One main focus here is the saving and archiving of material in databases,[39] another cultural contacts in the Mediterranean area. In Hungary departments of cultural history were at least founded at the universities in Pécs in 2000 and Miskolc in 1995. Admittedly, according to Pető, the Central European University in Budapest has the most logically consistent cultural historical orientation in the country.

In the European perspective, further organisational forms and formats are to be perceived in cultural historical research practice. There are interdisciplinary centres at universities, such as the Centre for Cultural Studies (Graz) and university interdisciplinary study groups, such as the *Cultural Studies Working Group*

---

36 JORDANOVA, in this volume, p. 73.
37 DEJUNG, in this volume, p. 160.
38 DEJUNG, in this volume, p. 166.
39 ARCANGELI, in this volume, p. 248.

in Vienna or the *Group for Cultural History Studies* in Madrid (University Carlos III). And then there are research centres, such as the Historical Cultural Sciences Research Centre in Mainz at which historians have a platform for cultural historical problems. In addition, there are research networks, spread over several universities in a country, such as the new network already mentioned between Bologna, Padua, Pisa and Venice. In addition, there are formats transcending national borders, such as the international networks of up-and-coming academics of the German Research Community, or cooperation agreements between two or more universities, such as e.g. the *Group de Recherche sur L'histoire des Intellectuels* at the Universities of Paris VIII (St Denis) and Barcelona. Finally, since 2007, the *International Society for Cultural History* regularly offers cultural historians the opportunity for cooperation and the development of new ideas for joint projects in the cultural historical field of work with annual conferences and the claim to involve all continents.[40] These research formats—which are in part also used in training students working for a doctorate—are currently the best possibilities for implementing the methodological approaches of cultural history on an interdisciplinary and inter-country basis.[41]

However, in the majority of cases in the articles it is argued that cultural history needs a firm place at universities as the prerequisite for a longer-term existence as a separate research movement. Only in this way can cultural history also influence the necessary training of the rising generation of academics. Both in research and in teaching, cultural history is distinguished by the fact that international cooperation and network-forming are cultivated. In addition, in the articles you find a plea for work with flexible cultural studies concepts which are distinguished by openness and are intended to avert the danger of getting caught in academic impasses.

In addition, cultural history obtains its relevance as a means of defending positions of the humanities in the ever fiercer competition for financial resources. Whereby—as the controversies in Scotland and Germany in particular prove—it has to be noted that new perspectives and research approaches always lead to fierce discussions. Successful new directions of research are claimed to be a threat

---

40 www.abdn.ac.uk/isch/, 01.03.2011. Since 2007, conferences have taken place in Aberdeen, Gent and Turku. Oslo is following in 2011, then Nancy in 2012 and Istanbul in 2013.

41 The general problem of academic policy is to promote great plans and activities instead of supporting the "genuine" projects at working level, LUTTER, in this volume, p. 186.

to established scholarship as they—apart from financial and personnel aspects—
might potentially decide what the subject matter of historical science was.[42]

Problems, perspectives and potentials

Salmi and Eriksen emphasise that cultural history offers a special perspective of
the past. One important question is how did people in the past form the world
they lived in and how did they communicate with their environment.[43] In addition, Eriksen stresses that cultural history has been a reaction to dominant trends
in historical science and can be regarded as a corrective to these trends.[44] Since
the 1990s, in her opinion, two *turns* have influenced cultural history in Scandinavia: The *reflective turn*, by which it became clear that through their work on
a phenomenon, e.g. people and folk culture in Norway, researchers themselves
contributed to the existence of this phenomenon. The subject of investigation by
cultural historians does not exist in itself, but is jointly constituted by the choice
of method and conception. Then there was the *anthropological turn*, according
to which culture is understood as a universe of meanings, symbols and as the
result of communication.

The observations made on the Norwegian example can be applied to European cultural historical research. Cultural history should not fall behind these
two heuristic basic assumptions. The research field (national) identity is still
topical as, for example, Dejung reports for Switzerland, where it is difficult to
achieve such an identity given the linguistic and geographic diversity, as well
as the federal constitution. In Italy, too, great attention is devoted to identity.
Research is conducted into the identities of late medieval burghers and also
that of the inhabitants of the Mediterranean area in the 19th and 20th centuries.
European cultural history has currently a further point of focus in the history of
knowledge together with the academic culture and its central medium of book
production, the study of academic institutions and the formation of an elite.
It is also becoming apparent that research into collective and communicative
memories will still play a role, and also the occupation with bodies as well as
the culturally coded gender and behavioural attributions will produce further

---

42 These controversies did not take place in this intensity in Italy and Spain. There was
   and is no intensive discussion of method, rather for certain topics one reverts pragmatically to cultural historical approaches.
43 SALMI, in this volume, p. 55. ERIKSEN, in this volume, p. 42-43.
44 ERIKSEN, in this volume, p. 37.

important insights. In addition, cultural transfer and cultural exchange play an important role in current works and *Postcolonial Studies* are applied in country contexts.

Apart from the fields of work already mentioned, for the further development of the content of cultural history, the contributors estimate that artefacts and material culture will play an important role. In this connection, questions are asked both about the symbolic significance of the artefacts, as also about their materiality as such and the way in which they were worked. Or put differently: How do objects function in cultural contexts?

How financial support will develop will also be of great importance for the further development of cultural history in Europe. Thus for example in Finland, after a phase of institutional expansion of cultural history at the University in Turku, the question will be how the further development of studies and teaching can be safeguarded if further cuts are made in the academic budget after 2010 and universities expect budget losses. In Italy, Arcangeli discerns a trend towards cultural history among young researchers, but he has doubts whether these scholars will find a place in the Italian university and research scene and fears further emigration. In Germany, we must wait and see what success cultural historical formats will have in the competition for excellence staged by the Federal and state authorities. In Sweden, the trend is towards social sciences and contemporary history, with the cultural inheritance being further cultivated in the museums. In Copenhagen, on the other hand, cultural history has a strong position. In Norway there is the movement of *Cultural Studies* mainly oriented towards contemporary societies (University of Bergen) and Cultural History (University of Oslo) with projects on the cultural representation of minorities in museums after the end of the great national narratives or the history of knowledge.[45] The future development of cultural history will depend anyway on its succeeding in asserting the significance of its cognitive possibilities and research results compared with those of *Cultural Studies* in academic and social competition.

---

45 ERIKSEN, in this volume p. 39-40.

Literature

ARCANGELI, ALESSANDRO (ed.), La storia culturale: una svolta nella storiografia mondiale?, Verona 2010.

BURKE, PETER, Papier und Marktgeschrei. Die Geburt der Wissensgesellschaft, Berlin 2002.

DANIEL, UTE, Kompendium Kulturgeschichte, 5th ed., Frankfurt/Main 2006.

DARNTON, ROBERT, Das große Katzenmassaker. Streifzüge durch die französische Kultur vor der Revolution, München 1989.

DAVIS, NATHALIE ZEMON, Die wahrhaftige Geschichte der Rückkehr des Martin Guerre, München 1984.

DÜLMEN, RICHARD VAN, Historische Anthropologie: Entwicklung, Probleme, Aufgaben, Köln 2001.

GINZBURG, CARLO, Der Käse und die Würmer—die Welt eines Müllers um 1600, Berlin 1980.

GREEN, ANNA, Cultural History, New York 2008.

KOCKA, JÜRGEN, Historische Sozialwissenschaft. Auslaufmodell oder Zukunftsvision? in: Oldenburger Universitätsreden 107, Oldenburg 1999.

LANDWEHR, ACHIM/STOCKHORST, STEFANIE, Einführung in die europäische Kulturgeschichte, Paderborn 2004.

MAURER, MICHAEL, Kulturgeschichte. Eine Einführung, Köln 2008.

MEDICK, HANS, Quo vadis Historische Anthropologie? in: Historische Anthropologie 9 (2001), p. 78-92.

OEXLE, OTTO GERHARD, Geschichte als Historische Kulturwissenschaft, in: Kulturgeschichte Heute, ed. by WOLFGANG HARDTWIG/HANS ULRICH WEHLER, Göttingen 1996, p.14-40.

ID., Kultur, Kulturwissenschaft, Historische Kulturwissenschaft, in: Das Mittelalter 5 (2000), p. 13-33.

OPITZ, CLAUDIA, Um-Ordnungen der Geschlechter, Einführung in die Geschlechtergeschichte, Tübingen 2005.

POIRRIER, PHILIPPE (ed.), L'Histoire culturelle: un "tournant mondial" dans l'historiographie?, Dijon 2008.

RAPHAEL, LUTZ, Die Erben von Bloch und Febvre. Annales-Geschichtsschreibung und nouvelle histoire in Frankreich. 1945-1980, Stuttgart 1994.

ROGGE, JÖRG, Historische Kulturwissenschaften, in: Historische Kulturwissenschaften. Positionen, Praktiken und Perspektiven, ed. by JAN KUSBER et al., Bielefeld 2010, p. 351-379.

SALMI, HANNU, Nineteenth-Century Europe. A Cultural History, Cambridge 2008.

SCOTT, JOAN W., Gender. A useful category of historical analysis, in: American Historical Review 91 (1986), p. 1053-1075.
STOLLBERG-RILINGER, BARBARA (ed.),Was heißt Kulturgeschichte des Politischen? Berlin 2005.
TANNER, JAKOB, Historische Anthropologie zur Einführung, Hamburg 2004.
TSCHOPP, SILVIA SERENA (ed.), Kulturgeschichte, Stuttgart 2008.
ID., Einleitung. Begriffe, Konzepte und Perspektiven der Kulturgeschichte, in: Kulturgeschichte, ed. by ID., Stuttgart 2008, p. 9-32.
ID., Die Neue Kulturgeschichte—eine (Zwischen-)Bilanz, in: Historische Zeitschrift 289 (2009), p. 573-605
ID./WEBER, WOLFGANG E. J., Grundfragen der Kulturgeschichte, Darmstadt 2007.
WEHLER, HANS-ULRICH, Kursbuch der Beliebigkeit: Das "Kompendium" der "Neuen Kulturgeschichte", in: ID., Konflikte zu Beginn des 21. Jahrhunderts. Essays, München 2003, p. 177-184.
WINTERLING, ALOYS (ed.), Historische Anthropologie, Stuttgart 2006.

http://www.historische.kulturwissenschaften.uni-mainz.de/, 01.03.2011
http://www.hkfz.uni-trier.de/, 01.03.2011
http://www.abdn.ac.uk/isch/, 01.03.2011

From Ethnology and Folklore Studies to Cultural History in Scandinavia

ANNE ERIKSEN

This article presents a northern perspective on cultural history, that of the Scandinavian countries Denmark, Sweden and Norway. Within the two disciplines of ethnology and folklore studies, these countries share a tradition in cultural history dating back to the 19th century. Once closely related to the projects of nation-building and the idea of national culture, these disciplines have slowly been transformed into modern cultural history. Since Peter Burke coined the term "the discovery of the people" in his now classic study, numerous works have provided detailed knowledge on how this discovery was closely related to the processes of modernisation.[1] Burke's perspectives have been elaborated on and criticised in a flood of studies discussing the role of folk culture in nation-building in Europe and elsewhere. One issue of major theoretical pertinence has been how this discovery of a domestic version of the noble savage—the European peasant—influenced reflexive thinking on culture. In the same way as we see in the encounter with the "exotic" culture of other continents, the realisation that groups of people in Europe were in possession of cultural forms and expressions which were largely unknown to the elite fuelled discussions on culture and cultural value *per se*. The discovery of the people and the subsequent use of folk culture in nation-building, as well as the significance given to such projects in the broader modernisation processes, is a rather general phenomenon. Within the general frames, we find many and considerable local variations with respect to the impact of folk culture on national culture and its political pertinence, as well as the duration and academic impact of the interest in the cultural forms of ordinary people.

---

1 BURKE, 1978.

In Scandinavia, the "discovery of the people" was not merely a short-lived romantic affair of the late 18th and the early 19th centuries. The awakened interest also led to more serious and long-lasting relationships. In Denmark, Sweden and Norway the archives and collections that followed from the initial discovery survived the first stages of antiquarianism, romantic philology and ardent nation-building. Out of this initial enthusiasm grew the two academic disciplines European ethnology and folklore studies. During the 20th century they gradually liberated themselves from their romantic and nationalistic foundations and, have been the basis for a new interest in developing cultural history as a modern discipline during the last two or three decades.

Discovery of the people in Scandinavia—19th century

Political contexts were important reasons for the discovery of the people having such an impact in Scandinavia, but the implications were not the same in all three countries. At the beginning of the 19th century both Denmark and Sweden faced the future as dramatically diminished states with reduced political influence. Traditional rivals, both states had been influential European powers during the 16th and 17th centuries. Both monarchies were also multi-ethnic and multi-lingual. Denmark included Iceland, the Faroe Islands, Norway and the duchies of Slesvig and Holstein. To Sweden belonged Finland and during the period of the empire (1611-1718) also some possessions in the Baltic region. Scania, long a Danish possession, became part of Sweden in 1658. However, both countries gradually lost influence and adopted approximately their current sizes. Sweden suffered a decisive blow with the loss of Finland in 1809. Denmark was massively reduced by the loss of Norway, which gained national independence after the Napoleonic wars. After some months of freedom in the summer of 1814 Norway was forced into a union with Sweden but allowed to keep its newly composed Constitution and the recognition as a state. In the 1860s Denmark suffered another blow with the loss of the duchies of Slesvig and Holstein to Germany.

Hence, the three countries had different reasons for embracing the enthusiasm for folk culture which became so popular all over Europe. Denmark and Sweden turned to folk culture as part of the process of compensating for the loss of external political power through the development of a more acute sense of internal national unity. When the old conglomerate monarchies were to be replaced by new nation states, a common national culture was needed and folk culture became an important element in this construction work. In Norway, while the situation was different, the interest in folk culture was just as strong. With the freshly gained political independence it was important to demonstrate the legitimacy of the new state and folk culture served this end. It gave the impression of demonstrating a continuity spanning from the middle ages to the present. This implied focusing on the period when Norway was the stronger of the Scandinavian states and reigned over large possessions in the North Sea region. Postulating close connections between present-day folk culture and that of the Middle Ages—including the Norse saga literature—was a way of claiming a cultural continuity of *Norwegianess* through periods when no state had existed. Moreover, folk culture was thought to demonstrate the existence of a culture, mentality and language clearly different from the Danish and specifically Norwegian.

As a general phenomenon, the early interest in folk culture mainly concentrated on oral folklore, more particularly on poetry and fairy-tales. In Sweden, the first collection of folk ballads was published in 1814-1818 by Geijer and Afzelius, while in Denmark, Svend Grundtvig published an extensive collection of medieval ballads in the 1850s.[2] The work of the German Grimm brothers had great influence on collectors of legends and fairy-tales in Scandinavia. In Norway, Andreas Faye published a book of legends in 1833 after an early visit to Germany. P.Chr. Asbjørnsen and Jørgen Moe's collection of fairy-tales from 1841 onwards also drew heavily on Grimm and earned their warm praise. For the second edition of the book, appearing in 1852, Moe wrote an introduction that is generally considered to be the first scientific text on Norwegian folk tales. One of the main aims was to point out the distinctive national features of the narratives. The work of the Norwegian collectors was in turn an inspiration to the Swede Olof Hyltén-Cavallius in his work on legends and beliefs during the 1850s and '60s, and to the Dane Evald Tang Christensen, who published his tales and legends in the 1890s.

These men were archive-builders who laid the ground for collections that still exist today, such as the Danish collection of folklore at the National Library in Copenhagen and the Norwegian Folklore Archives at the University of Oslo. During the last decades of the 19th century, folklore studies grew into an university discipline. Svend Grundtvig was not only a collector of ballads, but also became the first Danish professor in folklore studies. Molten Moe, son of the collector Jørgen Moe, became the first professor as well as the heir to his father's great collection, which was bequeathed to the University of Oslo upon his death in 1913.

---

2 STRÖMBÄCK et al., 1971.

Open-Air Museums and early research

The activities presented so far would have been part of the history of philology and not of cultural history, if other elements such as an interest in material folk culture and the social life of the common people had not been included. This interest was expressed in part through the open-air museums, and in part through some important research works. The first open-air museum in Scandinavia was established at Skansen, in Stockholm Sweden, in 1891, as an extension of the Nordic Museum, a collection dating back to 1873. The man behind the project was Arthur Hazelius, an avid collector of folk art and antiquities from both Sweden and Norway, hence the name *The Nordic Museum*. From the very beginning Skansen became renowned for not merely exhibiting old buildings, but also showing realistic interiors and domestic scenes—initially populated by mannequins, but quite soon replaced by real people and living animals.[3]

Only three years later, in 1894, Norsk Folkemuseum opened in Oslo, Norway. The museum was laid out as a park on the peninsula of Bygdøy. Its origin was a small collection of peasant's houses and a stave church, belonging to King Oscar II.

An important motivation behind the establishment of the museum was to stop Hazelius from exporting Norwegian objects to Sweden. A more positive assessment of this rivalry will note that popular material culture was becoming a highly valuable part of national history at this time, worthy of care and preservation. The leading ideologue behind the museum in Oslo was the professor in folklore studies, Moltke Moe. In his inaugural speech he declared that:

> "The aim of this collection is to give the Norwegian people a picture of the life that was lived in Norway down through the centuries, our fathers' ways of building houses, their furniture, their tools and utensils, their dress, in short the entire environment in which they moved and lived, and of which the memory now is gradually fading."[4]

Moe considered it self-evident that knowing material folk culture meant knowing national history. Judging by the success of the museum, many agreed with him. From the 1890s and well into the 20th century, open air-museums sprang up around the country, conceived as expressions of cultural identity. A new wave of national enthusiasm swept over the country from 1905 when the union with

---

3 HILLSTRÖM, 2006.
4 AALL, 1920, bilag 1, translated here.

Sweden was dissolved, up to 1914, the centenary of the Constitution, leading to the establishment of many new museums.

The most monumental Danish contribution to the Scandinavian tradition of cultural history is without doubt Troels Frederik Troels-Lund's work *Dagligt Liv i Norden i det sekstende Aarhundrede* (Everyday life in the North in the 16th century), originally published in twelve volumes from 1879 to 1893. One could say the aim of this exploration was exactly the same as Moltke Moe's description for the museum: To give an exhaustive picture of the way of the lives of the people.

Troels-Lund approached his task very systematically. The separate volumes of his work are given to such topics as food (vol. 5), dress (vol. 4) and annual feasts (vol. 7). One entire volume is on childbirth and baptism. Two volumes treat buildings and construction. The first is about the houses of common men, the second about castles and fortresses. A look into the first of these two volumes reveals a number of subtopics. The chapters dealing with houses in towns and cities also comprise texts on the cleanliness of the streets, stray dogs, epidemic diseases and night watchmen; the chapters on the interiors of the same houses deal with such topics as different kinds of beds and bedding, the temperature in the houses and ways to keep warm.

Troels-Lund's work was immensely popular, and has been reprinted numerous times to this day. But was it history? This question was posed in an extremely irate article by the German history professor, Dietrich Schäfer, who published his *Das eigentliche Arbeitsgebiet der Geschichte* in 1888, and then repeated his question in 1891. Troels-Lund's answer was the text *On cultural history* from 1893, which has been printed as a foreword to all subsequent editions of his work, and which can still be read as a kind of manifesto on the worth and significance of cultural history.[5] The Schäfer/Troels-Lund dispute was partly the result of the contemporary political situation, not least of the recent wars between Germany and Denmark, ending with Denmark losing the duchies of Slesvig and Holstein. Nonetheless, it also has a more general relevance for the history of cultural history. As a representative of the German historical school, Schäfer's point of view was that the state, its expansion and political life were the real objects of historical studies. Hence, he expressed his concern over the growing interest in such lower themes as the everyday life of the masses and all those "dark necessities belonging to the animal part of the human race".[6] The only excuse for treating such topics at all, according to Schäfer, must be that in a small and

---

5 TROELS-LUND, 1914/1893.
6 Quoted in TROELS-LUND, 1914/1893, p. XXXVI.

powerless state such as Denmark, which was not given any "national mission",[7] there was not much else to write about. Cultural history was an expression of political impotence and perhaps a natural reaction after a confrontation with the Prussian state and its war machinery. But it was not history.

Troels-Lund did not see things this way, which is abundantly clear in his answer to Schäfer. Even he related his work to the war, but he considered a patriotic duty to demonstrate through his scholarly work that even though Denmark had lost political power, there still existed a Danish culture to be proud of. Perhaps more interesting today is his general defence of cultural history as a discipline. Troels-Lund makes it very clear that writing about everyday life means writing about the most important dimensions of human development: Those aspects of change occurring slowly over the centuries, which involve us all, but where the differences are so small and so gradual that they can only be studied by means of the details of everyday life—the way we eat and dress, live and die. He is equally clear that in these very fundamental historical processes, the births, lives and deaths of common people are just as important as those of the elite. He has made his choice, he declares, to study history "not from the top of the cone, in its full, flowing sunshine, but from the wide and solid bottom, upon which the cone rests."[8]

I do not suggest that European ethnology and folklore studies, as they emerged in Denmark, Sweden and Norway in the late 19th century, represented a full-fledged version of modern cultural history. My argument is that this development has supplied a kind of Scandinavian *Sonderweg* to the modern field of cultural history and that it fundamentally defines our approach even today. Apart from the fact that cultural history has been institutionalised and thus has existed as a continuous strand of knowledge and research, this Scandinavian tradition has some distinctive features of its own. One of them is the interest in popular culture, the culture of peasants, working people and commoners. The original concept of folk culture (as the core of national culture) put a heavy emphasis on peasants—people living so far away from cities, foreigners and all consequences of modernity that they could be believed to have preserved the true, ancient culture of their nation. Later, the ideas about an archaic folk culture were replaced by a broader and more general interest in popular culture. Even today, *ordinary people* and everyday life are key issues in our research, while studies of elite culture are less frequent, though not absent. Another important feature, probably connected to the first, is the idea of cultural history as a critical, even

---

7 Id.
8 Id., p. 7.

oppositional discipline. The interest in everyday life and the experiences of the non-elite have been linked to the wish to have more democratic perspectives on history and the claim that history is more than merely the study of economic and political change. The Danish cultural historian Palle O. Christiansen goes so far as to define cultural history as such. In the introduction to his book *Kulturhistorie som opposition* (Cultural History as Opposition, 2000), he states that the history of cultural history can only be understood in relation to other developments within the discipline of history. Cultural history has always been a "reaction against dominant ideas about history and historic reality."[9] Rather than presenting a narrative of continuous development, Christiansen structures his history of cultural history as a collection of *answers* to positions and issues within mainstream history from the mid 19th century to the present. While on the one hand this gives cultural history a position on the periphery, Christiansen emphasises the critical potential, and portrays cultural history as a running corrective for other forms of history.

Twists and turns

Among the numerous *turns* in cultural theory during recent decades, two are particularly relevant for understanding how the Scandinavian tradition of ethnology and folklore studies has evolved into cultural history in the modern sense. The first is the reflexive turn. New and more acute ways of thinking about how scholarly work not only creates knowledge on phenomena already existing in the world, but also itself contributes to the existence of these phenomena, has had profound impact on the self-understanding of these two disciplines. New and critical perspectives on the history of ethnology and folklore studies as parts of the processes of nation-building emerged from within the disciplines themselves.[10] Ethnologists and folklorists of the 19th century studied folk culture and helped to *discover* it. To many of them, their work represented a mixture of scholarly and political interest. With the reflexive turn, the interest in the political agendas of these founders of the disciplines became more prominent and a critical history of the disciplines became an object of study in itself in the late 20th century. An understanding that studying and *discovering* popular culture also contained elements of construction became part of this reflexive and deconstructive perspective.

---

9   CHRISTIANSEN, 2000, p. 7. See also CHRISTIANSEN, 2008, p. 65.
10 E.g. ERIKSEN, 1993.

To scholars of the 19th century, the more general processes of modernity also justified their work with popular culture: It was important to gain knowledge on traditional forms of culture before they disappeared. The reflexive perspective made it clearer that such ideas in themselves are integral parts of modernity. The act of describing specific cultural forms, expressions or even whole ways of living as *traditional* or *ancient* in itself means that a threshold is inserted between then and now, between what is and what has been. Such a process defines tradition, but also defines what is contemporary. Our endeavours to save or investigate tradition makes the modern stand out more clearly.[11]

Greater insight into the ways scholarly work contributes to the existence of what is being investigated created a much keener theoretical awareness within the two existing disciplines. Most specifically, it meant a definite liberation from old political projects, and more generally, it created an interest in such theoretical issues as cultural representations and conceptual history. On a more concrete level, the same insight has led to studies in, for instance, museology and collective memory, in both cases raising questions on how past experience is conceptualised, given cultural form and communicated.

The *anthropological* turn had an impact on ethnology and folklore studies in several ways. Thanks to the influences of Mary Douglas, Edmund Leach, Clifford Geertz, Victor Turner and others, the study of carnivals, witch hunts, magic, popular medicine, the list goes on, became the work of historians. In ethnology and folklore studies, these topics were not new; they had been the staple of these disciplines since their origins. Nonetheless, up to then they had contributed to the reputation of the two traditions as being more about curiosities than real history and had created an image of ethnologists and folklorists as the true heirs to the antiquaries of earlier centuries. The anthropological turn changed this, transforming old topics of ethnology and folklore studies into important issues in new forms of historical enquiry. The material collected in the 19th and early 20th centuries became a goldmine for studying world-views and mentalities of past ages, and old studies based on this material gained new relevance.

As inspiring as this development might have been, another aspect was even more important. Behind the new interest in rituals, carnivals, witches and so on was a new understanding of culture that focused on meaning and symbols and on communication and representations. In ethnology and folklore studies, this new way of thinking about culture led away from an interest in forms, motives and lines of traditions alone. The anthropological turn was decisive for the refashioning of ethnology and folklore studies into a discipline that invested

---

11 BAUMAN/BRIGGS, 2003.

in representations and construction of meaning and was less preoccupied with studying the wanderings of historical forms and morphologies. During the 19th century, popular culture had been collected and archived as objects or items. It the late 20th century it re-emerged as elements in communication and constructions of meaning.[12]

Recent Work

At present, the Scandinavian tradition of ethnology and folklore studies seem, to be developing in two directions. One part understands itself and cultural history in the modern sense, while the other has chosen to fashion itself more in the direction of cultural studies or social science. These distinctions are not always very clear, but may be discerned as trends, for instance to be read out of the names of departments, occurring in study programmes and so on. The general trend seems to be that the majority of ethnologists have turned to social science and undertake contemporary studies in Sweden. A smaller proportion works as cultural historians. The post-graduate education, which evolved at Nordiska museet in Stockholm is important here, as is the University of Gotland with its emphasis on cultural heritage studies. In Denmark, the cultural history tradition holds a stronger position. At the University of Copenhagen, a historical perspective is deeply integrated in the work of such scholars as Bjarne Stoklund, Tine Damsholt and Signe Mellemgaard.[13]

In Norway, the situation is mixed. At the University of Bergen, ethnology and folklore studies were renamed Cultural Studies some years ago. Cultural studies programmes are also offered at some of the university colleges. The University of Oslo has chosen to go in the other direction. Seven years ago, in 2003, ethnology and folklore studies were combined to the cultural history course of studies, which is now the official name of the discipline. Starting as a patchwork of projects and courses based in ethnology and folklore, a more integrated tradition of cultural history has been established.

Courses in cultural history are now offered at both the bachelor's and master's levels. At present, there are about 75 students in the bachelor's programme and 50 in the master's programme. A separate master's programme in museology was opened in 2010. At present nine there are also Ph.D. students, some working on individually designed projects and others engaged in projects initiated

---

12 E.g. PALMENFELT, 1993; ANTTONEN, 1997.
13 STOKLUND, 2003; DAMSHOLT, 2000; MELLEMGAARD, 1998.

by senior scholars. The main source for project funding outside the universities is the Norwegian Research Council. Recently, a programme on cultural values has funded some quite substantial projects in cultural history at the University of Oslo and has also improved the possibilities to build international networks.

Together with its history as a product of the two older disciplines, these projects define the profile of cultural history at the University of Oslo at present. One of them, entitled *Patterns of Cultural Evaluation* and headed by Saphinaz Naguib, studies museums of cultural history in an epoch after the collapse of grand national narratives. The aim is to analyse representations of diversity in Norwegian museums of cultural history and to explore the dialectics between historical narratives and perceptions of culture and belongingness, and the ways these narratives are conveyed visually in exhibitions. The notion of diversity is used to encompass a great number of complex issues pertaining to ethnicity, religion, social class, education, economy, gender, age and lifestyle. The project examines how exhibitions draw upon and reproduce older models and stereotypes about the nation and Norwegianess, how new visions and paradigms are introduced and which visual and aesthetic schemes are applied in exhibitions. The project is also highly interested in the ways in which ethnic groups and minorities represent themselves in their own museums. In this project, the notion of citizenship is vital, both as an analytical tool and as a concept to be investigated: At present, the idea that the task of museums is to contribute to an experience of citizenship is very strongly expressed in European political rhetoric.

While the above-mentioned project focuses on cultural representation, the other project is based on an interest in the history of knowledge. Entitled *Animals as Objects and Animals as Signs* and headed by Liv Emma Thorsen, the project explores how nature—animals—is turned into knowledge. The project aims to explain the processes that make animals into representations for scientific purposes and for social practices. It will also look into the connection between natural history representations and a more general aestheticisation of animals. Objects on display in museums of natural history are a major example. They do not only have a history of their own, as animals, but also as museum exhibits and scientific items. The animals represent ways of seeing nature, of transforming nature into knowledge and of communicating that knowledge to others by means of very definite strategies. Hence, this part of museology is very closely related to yet another field, that of the cultural history of science.

Another important field in cultural history in Oslo is museology. Contrary to what might be believed, it does not originate from the open-air museums, but rather reflects an interest in the history of knowledge and a study of cultural representations. Museums and collections represent ways of organising knowledge, and these ways have changed historically. Refusing to equate museums with the great public institutions that were established during the 19th century, based on a predominantly historical and often national way of thinking, the studies of museums reach back into early modern collections and work their way up to the present. Today, the grand narratives of national culture that were the basic premise of museum building in the 19th century are being challenged both by migration and multiculturalism, by new modes of communication and by the new media.

Material culture is another strong field, not only in Oslo but as a general feature in the Scandinavian tradition of cultural history. To early scholars like Troels-Lund and the museum founders, material culture was of great significance. The open-air museums were mainly collections of artefacts from premodern, peasant society: tools, utensils, textiles and costumes, and not least buildings. The early research focused on the function, history and typologies of this type of artefact. In more recent years, inspiration from international material culture studies has transformed the field and given it theoretical premises of its own. Within this large cross-disciplinary field, at least three approaches can be discerned that have influenced the work on material culture within Scandinavian cultural history. The first of these was a new interest in the symbolic meaning of artefact, leading to a predominantly semiotic approach. In cultural history, this led to greater interest in the artefacts of mass culture, which until then had not been regarded as worthy of research interest. This changed when attention turned from the objects themselves to the cultural meaning ascribed to them. The second approach was inspired by phenomenology and focused on the experience of materiality rather than the objects *per se*. From this followed studies of, for instance, artisan skills and the tacit knowledge forming the basis of practical competences. The latest perspectives, inspired by the actor-network theory of Bruno Latour, study the interaction that takes place between humans and their artefacts.[14] Taken together, these new perspectives have widened the field of study from the (frequently handmade) artefacts of traditional society to materiality *per se*. The focus is no longer exclusively on the objects, but on their workings in a cultural context.

Competence in the field of traditional popular culture in Scandinavia continues to be strong. The Norwegian Folklore Archives are still a part of cultural history at the University of Oslo, and extensive digitalisation projects have made them accessible for research in new ways in recent years. Large parts of the material are now available to scholars through the web. Just as important, the

---

14 STOKLUND, 2003; DAMSHOLT et al., 2009.

new technology opens the way for a different type of question than before, as it is now possible to work with a larger amount of material. The search options also create new ways of combining information. At present, a large range of Norwegian court cases on witchcraft are available online; about 650 cases can be accessed. The material tells of witchcraft and magic from the 16th to the 18th centuries. On a more general level, the material is also a source for the investigation of early modern mentality and world-views. Supplementing this, a collection of magic books is also available online. The books, in the vernacular known as *svartebøker* (black books), were cloaked by an aura of mystery in folk tradition. They contained recipes and instructions on how to cure diseases in humans and animals. Aided by the books, the wise men and women who once owned them could also find thieves, tell fortunes and secure desired love partners. The majority of the books in existence are from the 19th century, but some date back all the way to the 15th century. Great collections of traditional oral poetry and narratives are also available online. Large parts of the archives on fairy-tales, popular legends and medieval ballads can be accessed. This part of the collection mainly stems from the 19th and early 20th centuries.

The last field to be mentioned in this presentation of cultural history in Oslo encompasses collective memory, heritage studies and the notion of history. The book *Det var noe annet under krigen* (Things were different during the war)[15] introduced studies in collective memory in Norwegian academia. The book is an exploration of how a broad tradition of knowledge on Norway during the German occupation (1940-1945) has served as the foundation of the modern Norwegian identity. Based on extensive detailed historical research, the tradition is found to have a highly realistic basis and is devoid of serious factual errors. However at the same time it is an extremely heroic narrative, which means that important aspects of what actually took place have been omitted and also that the included events are ascribed a significance they might not at all have had. Not reserved merely to scholarly genres, this tradition has been and still is communicated through monuments and memorials, in museums, films, textbooks for schools, literature and so on. The general message is to tell all Norwegians that they (or their parents and grandparents) contributed heavily to the allied victory and that they did so mainly by being good Norwegians. Taking this work as their point of departure, a number of young scholars have then further developed the study of the collective memory of World War II.[16] Our work in the field of collective memory has developed into studies of uses of the past and the idea

---

15 ERIKSEN, 1995.
16 ESBORG, 1995; KVERNDOKK, 2000, 2007; SEM, 2008.

of history. The general point of departure here is the assumption that cultural history is not defined by its subject matter but rather by its approach. Cultural historians study productions of meaning in past societies. An important field in production of meaning, however, is the past itself. In modern societies, the past is conceived as history, today even as *heritage*. How was it conceived and conceptualised before the 19th century paradigm of history? How did people negotiate the past to make it meaningful and relevant without understanding history as change, uncontrolled events and temporal processes, but rather as a spatial unfolding of constant elements like human vice and virtue?[17] Even more important to the discipline of cultural history are the questions of epistemology: Are we as historians able to study history as a culturally specific way of lending meaning to the past, or have we so completely naturalised this way of thinking that it is impossible for us to apply analytical perspectives on it? I think the answers to these questions hinge on how much cultural history understands itself as simply a history of culture (as the production of meaning) and how much it allows itself to be informed by a more theoretical approach.

Literature

AALL, HANS, Norsk folkemuseum 1894-1919. Trekk av dets historie, Kristiana 1920.
ANTTONEN, PERTTI, Transformations of a murder narrative. A case in the politics and history of history and heroisation, in: Norveg 2 (1997), p. 3-28.
BAUMAN, RICHARD/BRIGGS, CHARLES L., Voices of Modernity. Language Ideologies and the Politics of Inequality, Cambridge 2003.
BURKE, PETER, Popular culture in early modern Europe, London 1978.
CHRISTIANSEN, PALLE OVE, Kulturhistorie som opposition. Træk af forskellige fagtraditioner, Copenhagen 2000.
ID., L'expérience et la vie quotidienne: L'historie culturelle en Scandinavie, in: L'histoire culturelle: un "tournant mondial" dans l'historiographie, ed. by PHILIPPE POIRIER, Dijon 2008, p. 65-78.
DAMSHOLT, TINE, Fædrelandskærlighed og borgerdyd. Patriotisk diskurs og militære reformer i Danmark i sidste del av 1700-tallet, Copenhagen 2000.
DAMSHOLT, TINE et al. (eds.), Materialiseringer. Nye perspektiver på materialitet og kulturanalyse, Århus 2009.

---

17 ERIKSEN/SIGURÐSSON, 2009.

ERIKSEN, ANNE, Den nasjonale kulturarven—en del av det moderne?, in: Kulturella perspektiv 1 (1993), p. 16-25.

ID., "Det var noe annet under krigen". 2. verdenskrig i norsk kollektivtradisjon, Oslo 1995.

ID., The Murmur of Ruins. A Cultural History, in: Ethnologia EuropaeaEthnologia Europaea 36, 1 (2007), p. 5-20.

ERIKSEN, ANNE/SIGURÐSSON, JÓN VIÐAR (eds), Negotiating Pasts in the Nordic Countries. Interdisciplinary Studies in History and Memory, Lund 2009.

ESBORG, LINE, "—Og så var vi alle gode nordmenn—" Fortellinger om den symbolske motstanden under okkupasjonen av Norge 1940-45. Master's thesis, University of Oslo 1995.

HILLSTRÖM, MAGDALENA, Ansvaret för kulturarvet. Studier i det kulturhistoriska museiväsendets formering med särskild inriktning på Nordiska museets etablering 1872-1919, Linköping 2006.

KVERNDOKK, KYRRE, "De kjempet, de falt, de gav oss alt". Om den rituelle bruken av norske krigsminnesmerker. Master's thesis, University of Oslo 2000.

ID., Pilegrim, turist og elev. Norske skoleturer til døds- og konsentrasjonsleirer, Linköping 2007.

MELLEMGAARD, SIGNE, Kroppens natur. Sundhedsopplysning og naturidealer i 250 år, Copenhagen 1998.

PALMENFELT, ULF, On the Understanding of Folk Legends, in: Telling Reality. Folklore Studies in the Memory of Bengt Holbek, ed. by MICHAEL CHESNUTT, Copenhagen/Turku 1993, p. 143-167.

SEM, LEIV, "For oss er Falstad det norske holocaust". Ein diskursanalytisk studie av debatten om krigsminnestaden Falstad i 2003-2004, Ph.D. thesis, University of Oslo 2008.

STOKLUND, BJARNE (ed), Tingenes kulturhistorie. Etnologiske studier i den materielle kultur, Copenhagen 2003.

STRÖMBÄCK, DAG et al. (eds), Leading folklorists of the North. Biographical studies, Oslo 1971.

TROELS-LUND (T.F.), Dagligt Liv i Norden i det sekstende Aarhundrede. Copenhagen 1879/1914.

Traditions of Cultural History in Finland, 1900-2000

HANNU SALMI

A recent book *L'histoire culturelle: un 'tournant mondial' dans l'historiographie?*, edited by Philippe Poirrier in 2008, creates a comparative, transnational view on how cultural historical research has developed and pays attention to, for example, Australia and Brazil as well as Mediterranean and Scandinavian countries. The case of Finland is covered by Palle Ove Christiansen's article that describes the developments of Scandinavian cultural history. Finland is included in its scope but, in the end, it receives only passing, marginal attention. The article concentrates mainly on Danish, Norwegian and Swedish examples.[1] An obvious reason for this emphasis is the fact that Finnish historical research has long remained behind the language barrier: in fact, there are almost no articles or books on Finnish historiography in other languages. Swedish is the second domestic language in Finland, but still much of research is published only in Finnish.

However, Christiansen mentions two features that distinguish Finnish cultural history from other Nordic countries. Firstly, Finland started to institutionalize this particular field of research by founding chairs in cultural history, which is something completely different from, for example, what happened in Sweden at the same time. Secondly, Finnish historians were the first in Scandinavia to publish a comprehensive cultural history of their country. The four-volume *Suomen kulttuurihistoria* (Cultural History of Finland) was published in 1933-1936.[2] *Norsk kulturhistorie* (Cultural History of Norway) and *Svenska folket genom tiderna* (Swedish People through the Ages) were both initiated in 1938, at

---

1 CHRISTIANSEN, 2008.
2 After the Second World War, two other series titled *Suomen kulttuurihistoria* have been published: in 1979-1982 (3 Vols) and in 2002-2004 (5 Vols).

the eve of the Second World War. The Swedish project was completed in 1940, the Norwegian during the German occupation in 1942.³

Scandinavian historians have often wondered why the position of cultural history has been so strong in Finland.⁴ There are obviously many explanations for this. For the Finnish political thought and debate, *culture* has been an essential concept since the 19th century, and its meaning became crucial right after 1809, when Finland was detached from Sweden and became part of the Russian empire.⁵ At that time, influences were especially absorbed from Germany: Johann Gottfried Herder's (1744-1803) thinking, in particular, offered inspiration for those nationalists who emphasized the significance of language, literature, history and education. A recent volume *Herder, Suomi, Eurooppa* (Herder, Finland, Europe) points out how the enthusiasm for Herder flourished especially in areas where the fashionable French culture, or civilization, had not gained a foothold and where connections to ancient cultures were relatively thin.⁶ Finland was one of these areas, and the notion of *culture* became strongly tied with the German understanding of *Bildung*.

The cultural approach was highlighted during the 19th century when Finland was the autonomous Grand Duchy of the Russian Empire. Scholars, authors and poets focused on establishing and grounding Finland as a nation, as a culture in its own right. In the prevailing political circumstances, the importance of studying the history of the people not the state was emphasized. This particular emphasis did not disappear after the Finnish independence in 1917. The small nation state continued in defining itself in cultural terms.

Cultural Historical School

During the 19th century, German thinking had a profound influence on Finnish intellectuals. While the country had only one university before the First World War, it was also common to study abroad, and Germany offered several potential sites of learning for Finnish students and scholars. No wonder that also the cultural approach to historical research was influenced by Germany. In the end of the 19th century, many young historians were especially fascinated by Karl Lamprecht's (1856-1915) disputed ideas. Lamprecht was a renowned fig-

---

3 CHRISTIANSEN, 2008, p. 74, 76.
4 HAAPALA, 2007, p. 51.
5 RANTALA, 2010, p. 21.
6 OLLITERVO/IMMONEN, 2006, p. 8-9.

ure throughout Europe and advocated the study of collective phenomena, larger cultural and psychological trends, conformities and historical laws. Lamprecht's idea of *Volksseele* has often been argued to have influenced Annales School and its views on mentalities.[7]

Lamprecht's thought-provoking arguments were discussed in *Historiallinen Aikakauskirja*, the Finish academic journal for historians, which started its publication in 1903. Lamprecht's name was already mentioned in the first issue of the journal.[8] Also the Finnish Historical Society discussed Lamprecht in 1895 when U. L. Lehtonen, a history student at the time, spoke on the first three volumes of *Deutsche Geschichte*.[9]

The most famous Finnish historian of his generation was Gunnar Palander (1876-1933, after 1906 known as Gunnar Suolahti), who actually studied in Leipzig in 1898-99. Together with his colleague U. L. Lehtonen he followed Lamprecht's lectures.[10] The timing was favourable in the sense that the controversial historian had just published his essay *Was ist Kulturgeschichte?*, inspired by Wilhelm Wundt's psychological theories. For Lamprecht, *Kulturgeschichte* was an overarching research agenda that was interested in the collective rather than the individual and allowed the study of, amongst others, natural conditions, economic and social factors, legal issues, language… The dispute between collective and individual historiography was heated at the time of Suolahti's visit to Leipzig.[11]

Suolahti was by no means uncritical towards *Kulturgeschichte*: he wanted to construct his own type of cultural history where, in addition to collective phenomena, also singular perspective and individual experience could have more value.[12] Suolahti's interest in the individual becomes especially obvious in a critique of Arvède Barine's two-part biography of *la Grande Mademoiselle* (1626-1693) in *Historiallinen Aikakauskirja*. The book on "a minor and historically rather insignificant princess" receives much appreciation from Suolahti, as cultural history in the form of a biography.[13]

---

7 On Lamprecht's notion of Volksseele, see CHICKERING, 1993, p. 135.
8 Lyhyitä tiedonantoja, 1903, p. 32. On Lamprecht, see also PALANDER, 1904; SALOMAA, 1915.
9 SUOLAHTI, 1947, p. 67. On Lehtonen's later understanding of cultural history, see LEHTONEN, 1925.
10 Including, for example, the lecture course *Deutsche Verfassungs-Wirtschaft in Kulturgeschichte*. See SUOLAHTI, 1947, p. 68.
11 SUOLAHTI, 1947, p. 71-73.
12 See, for example, KLINGE, 1993, p. 469-470.
13 SUOLAHTI, 1905, p. 225.

Suolahti shared Lamprecht's view that historians should pay more attention to the mental or spiritual life (in Finnish, *sielunelämä*) of the past. For Suolahti, cultural history should also cover, as he wrote in 1905, "the history of instincts, emotions and thoughts".[14] As Suolahti's review on Barine's biography reveals, he aimed at recognizing the general within the singular and here emotions would be an essential focal point. His interest in *historical characters* or *types* led to some of his most fluent cultural historical essays, such as *Keimailijat* (Coquets), published in 1913.[15] In addition to historical types or characters Suolahti argued that cultural history should also pay attention to epochs and their characteristics. In this sense, there was, if not a morphological view of cultures, at least an idea that each historical period was a culture of its own and had particular features that historians should try to track down. Later, the idea that historical periods had a particular character became popular in Finland through Egon Friedell's *Kulturgeschichte der Neuzeit*, which was published as a Finnish translation between 1930-1933 under the title *Uuden ajan kulttuurihistoria*.[16] Suolahti did not go as far as Friedell in his literary efforts, but aimed more at understanding the past as a lived and experienced world.

Gunnar Suolahti himself studied gentry, especially clergy, and its way of life; his most popular book was the two-volume *Elämää Suomessa 1700-luvulla* (Life in the Eighteenth-Century Finland, 1909, 1917) which is still used as a course book. Suolahti also made exercises in short, essayistic form and published a collection *Vuosisatain takaa: kulttuurihistoriallisia kuvauksia 1500-1700-luvuilta* (Beyond the Centuries: Cultural Historical Descriptions from Sixteenth to Eighteenth Centuries, 1913).[17]

During the late 19th and early 20th century, academic life in Finland was centered on Helsinki and Suolahti became an influential figure within the limited academic circles. The centrality of an influential cultural historical approach in Finland at the turn of the century can be connected to the fact that Suolahti personally was the heart of Finnish historical research. He was one of the founders of *Historiallinen Aikakauskirja*, the most important scholarly journal for historical research and he was also its first editor-in-chief in 1903-10. Since 1918, he was professor of Finnish history and since 1929 professor of Finnish and Scandinavian history at the University of Helsinki.[18]

---

14 ID., p. 226.
15 SUOLAHTI, 1993, p. 149-168.
16 FRIEDELL, 1930-1933.
17 JUTIKKALA, 2000; SUOLAHTI, 1993.
18 JUTIKKALA, 2000.

Suolahti's activity as a cultural historian can be crystallized in the four-volume work *Suomen kulttuurihistoria* (Cultural History of Finland), published in 1933-1936. Suolahti died in 1933 and saw only the first part of his work. The series was completed by his students, such as Pentti Renvall and Eino Jutikkala who later became eminent figures in Finnish historical research up to the 1960s and early 1970s. Some of Suolahti's disciples went on to social sciences, like Heikki Waris who became professor of social politics and Esko Aaltonen who made a career as professor of sociology. It seems obvious that the influence of the Cultural Historical School, as it was called, extended to social sciences and gave an impetus for Finnish historical sociology and social history.

The publication of *Suomen kulttuurihistoria* started 16 years after the Finnish independence, and it is astonishing that it completely ignored the political periodization. As the editors state in the Preface, they understood culture so widely that it covered "the different phenomena of both material and spiritual life from business and trade and social conditions, from the everyday life of lower and upper classes to the highest expressions of the human mind, art, science and religion".[19] It seems that the Lamprechtian agenda was still at stake, in particular in respect to the understanding of cultural history as an overarching perspective that went above other fields of historical research, such as economic or social history. On the other hand, it seems that the book series lacked many of those sensitive, essayistic features that were typical of Suolahti's own work. *Suomen kulttuurihistoria* was the final blooming of the Finnish Cultural Historical School that soon, especially after Suolahti's death in 1933, started to disperse.

Obviously, there were several background factors for the cultural history boom of the early twentieth-century Finland. At the end of the autonomous period, during the years of Russification, there was no need to use *culture* as an exclusive concept. Instead, the inclusive notion remained through the turbulence of independence and the Civil War. Perhaps in the end the Civil War of 1918 even intensified the need to highlight cultural issues instead of political ones and contributed to seeing culture as a unifying principle.

Cultural Histories in the Shadow

The Cultural Historical School saw the concept of culture in a wide sense. Still, its major effort *Suomen kulttuurihistoria* aroused criticism. Two years after the last volume in 1938, *Historiallinen Aikakauskirja* published a critique by Rag-

---

19 SUOLAHTI et al., 1933, p. 5.

nar Rosén, simultaneously unveiling time how things had changed. The author drew on the political events of his day and referred to the rising totalitarianism: "the shaking events around us emphasize the individual again, with profound consequences". In the contemporary situation, Rosén argued that there would be no sense in concentrating only "on the activities of the masses and on the averages" and forgetting the historical role of leaders and politicians.[20]

Rosén also questions the notion of Finland and notices that there is much less on the developments of Eastern than Western Finnish culture. Another aspect, not mentioned by Rosén, is the obvious connection of the Cultural Historical School to the rising Finnish-language culture and to the political movement called the Fennomans. The language feud had settled down during the 1930s, but it laid its impact on the academic scene. Suolahti had followed Scandinavian research and was very much interested, for example, in the work of T. F. Troels-Lund in Denmark.[21] Suolahti was probably irritated by the ways the language feud influenced universities and tried to find reconciliation.

At the turn of the century, exceptionally interesting research was done by Swedish-language scholars. The most renowed Finnish academic outside Finland, the philosopher, sociologist and social anthropologist Edvard Westermarck became world-famous in 1891 with his book *The History of Human Marriage*, published by Macmillan in London. Already then Westermarck's approach could have anthropologically influenced Finnish cultural history, but his thoughts seem not to have reached the members of the Cultural Historical School, or if they did, they were regarded to be historically problematic.

The language feud was etched into the Finnish university structure. Up to 1918, the University of Helsinki had been the only university in the country, but soon after the independence it got two rivals, both from Turku. In fact, Turku had hosted the old Swedish Royal Academy, founded in 1640, but the academy had moved to Helsinki after the Great Fire of Turku in 1827. In the wake of the language feud, Turku became the host town for both the Swedish-language university, Åbo Akademi, and the Finnish, the University of Turku. Åbo Akademi was finally founded in 1917 and the University of Turku three years later. Edvard Westermarck became the leading figure of Åbo Akademi and served as its first rector in 1918 and as a professor of philosophy up to 1932.

The Turku universities in particular became the influential sites of cultural historical research in Finland after the Second World War. They both even sought to institutionalize this field of research; while cultural history was only

---

20 ROSÉN, 1938, p. 323-324.
21 See the review of Troels-Lund's *Lifsbelysning*, PALANDER, 1903, p. 25-26.

one branch of historical research promoted by Suolahti and his disciples at the University of Helsinki, the establishment of chairs and departments started to take place in Turku. In 1920, Åbo Akademi founded the chair that was defined to the *cultural history and folk life studies*. It seems that, according to the outline of the chair, cultural history referred to high culture, but that the professor should also emphasize the study of folk life. The first appointed professor was Gabriel Nikander (1884-1959) who actually had been docent of Nordic cultural history at the University of Helsinki since 1917 and later wrote several chapters for *Suomen kulttuurihistoria*. Nikander's production lacks a *magnum opus* but he wrote several articles, for example, on the history of agriculture, fishing, mining industry and technology.[22]

After Nikander's retirement, Åbo Akademi even founded an institute of cultural history (*Kulturhistoriska institutionen*) in 1953 under the leadership of Nikander's follower Helmer Tegengren (1904-1974). Tegengren was the scholar of rural life in Ostrobotnia, but also addressed the distant culture of the Sámi in the Kemi Lapland. Although Tegengren himself published highly appreciated books on local history, the Institute was in practice a department of ethnology and concentrated on the study of folk culture.[23] After Tegengren's death in 1974, the institute finally changed its name into the Department of Ethnology.

Another institution worth mentioning in this connection is the Donner Institute which is a private research centre as part of the Åbo Akademi Foundation and was established in 1959 as a result of a large donation made by Uno and Olly Donner. The aim was "to encourage scholarly research in religious and cultural history". The institute is mainly known for its contribution in religious studies and maintains one of the most valuable Nordic libraries of the field, the Steiner Memorial Library.[24]

After the Second World War, the institutes of Åbo Akademi remained rather small units, but they supported cultural historical research at a time when social sciences and new structural approaches wiped over the Finnish academia.

Curiously enough, at the same time many of Suolahti's students in Helsinki had continued their work in social sciences. It seems also that the concept of culture lost its explanatory power during the turmoil of the Second World War and its aftermath. If the First World War had been succeeded by the debate on a

---

22 JUTIKKALA, 2001. See also VUORELA, 1977, p. 54.
23 On TEGENGREN, see PALOPOSKI, 1974, p. 160-161.
24 WIDÉN, 1993, p. 180-182. See also Donnerska institutet, http://web.abo.fi/instut/di/, 23.02.2011.

cultural crisis[25], similar tones can be detected in the late 1940s. Culture was very much seen as a matter of values. At the same time, however, the concept became more and more used as a dividing practice in the contemporary discourse. In the 1950s, the gap between high and low culture was perhaps deeper than ever before. This tension was clearly intensified by many new forms of popular culture, from rock music to television.

If there were clear signs of institutionalization to be distinguished in Turku, the role of cultural history at the University of Helsinki remained ambiguous and unstable. During the Second World War many historians have found themselves in the propaganda units of the Finnish army where their services were used for political purposes. The early twentieth-century interest in collective phenomena in the scholarly agenda remained not only in social sciences but also in historical research, where economic and social aspects gained more popularity. The crisis of cultural history in Helsinki is reflected by the fact that Gunnar Suolahti's nephew, Eino E. Suolahti (1914-1977), was the docent of cultural history at the University for 25 years (1947-1972), but earned his living outside the academia, first as the literary director of Werner Söderström Publishing Company in 1951-1966 and later as the director of the Academic Bookshop between 1966-1976.[26]

Still, Eino E. Suolahti made a strong impact on the Finnish understanding of cultural history. During the Second World War he was one of the few that followed international discussions of the field, especially the work of Johan Huizinga. His three essays on Huizinga in *Historiallinen Aikakauskirja* are among the best commentaries of the famous Dutch historian in Finland. The first of them, published in 1941, concentrated especially on Huizinga's *The Autumn of the Middle Ages* and on its interpretation of medieval history.[27] Suolahti continued his Huizinga presentations in 1943 and 1945, and was informed of Huizinga's untimely death just before finalizing the last essay.[28] Interesting in these texts is Suolahti stressing the importance of combining analytical rigout with the touch of synthesis. Furthermore, Suolahti uses Huizinga to emphasize the role of art and literature in analysing the cultural modes of the past. This, on the other hand, makes his approach different from the more ethnologically oriented cultural history that was underlined in Åbo Akademi at the same time.

As a publisher, Eino E. Suolahti continued his work as a proponent of cultural history. In the late 1940s and 1950s he participated in the publication of

---

25 On the Finnish debate on cultural crisis, see MIKKELI, 1996.
26 LEIKOLA, 2007.
27 SUOLAHTI, 1941.
28 SUOLAHTI, 1943; SUOLAHTI, 1945.

some key works of classical cultural history. His own company, Werner Söderström, published Johan Huizinga's *Homo ludens* as *Leikkivä ihminen* in 1947, *The Autumn of the Middle Ages* under the title *Keskiajan syksy* in 1951 and *Erasmus* in 1953; the latter as his own translation from the German language. The project continued with Jacob Burckhardt's *The Civilization of the Renaissance in Italy* (Italian renessanssin sivistys) in 1956. Suolahti himself translated also Burckhardt's *Reflections on History* (Maailmanhistorian näköaloja), but the book came out through the rivaling publication company Otava in 1951.[29]

Towards the Cultural Turn

There is historical irony in the fact that at the time when the Institute of Cultural History at Åbo Akademi was renamed as the Department of Ethnology, the other university in the town, the University of Turku, started the process of establishing its own chair in cultural history. In fact, the process had already started at the turn of the 1960s and 1970s and was connected to a larger change in the Finnish university system. There was a huge expansion of education in Finland when the baby boom generation entered the scene new universities were opened, for example, in Oulu in 1958 and in Joensuu in 1969.

History departments usually had two chairs, one for Finnish and one for general history. After the Second World War, however, special chairs and departments were established to enrich the field and widen the educational options. Contemporary history got its chair in the 1950s and economic and social history in the 1960s, both at the University of Helsinki. In the 1970s, history of science and ideas was established at the University of Oulu and cultural history at the University of Turku. There seems to be a particular division of labour, although this development probably evolved without any overall plan.

After initial difficulties, the chair in cultural history was finally founded in 1972 at the University of Turku and not only a chair but also a department, thus making it possible to study cultural history as a majoring subject both on

---

29 NB. The Finnish translations of Huizinga and Burckhardt came in the 1940s and 1950s. Still, both authors were known by Finnish academics before the Second World War through Swedish translations and German originals. Jacob Burckhardt's name was mentioned in Finland already in a newspaper advertisement of his *Handbuch der Geschichte der Malerei* in 1861. See *Finlands Almänna Tidning*, 19 June 1861. Huizinga's *Autumn of the Middle Ages* was sold in Academic Bookshop in Helsinki in 1927 as a Swedish translation. See *Historiallinen Aikakauskirja* 4 (1927), p. 338.

MA and PhD levels. This emphasis was a major turn in the institutionalization process of cultural history in Finland. Eventually, it proved to be difficult to find a professor who would have fit the profile of the new chair. The outline of the professorship tried to diverge from both the Lamprechtian and ethnological traditions and emphasize also on the history of art, science and religion.

In 1978, the first professor Veikko Litzen (1933-2011) was finally appointed.[30] Litzen had defended his doctoral theses *A War of Roses and Lilies: The Theme of Succession in Sir John Fortescue's Works* in 1971 and had also published a text book on medieval cultural history under the title *Keskiajan kulttuurihistoriaa* (Cultural History of the Middle Ages, 1974). Although the chair was originally outlined to focus on high culture, Litzen soon redefined the points of departure. Instead of seeing culture as sector of social life, the new department started to emphasize cultural history as a perspective into the past.

In 1981, Litzen defined his discipline in a way that stressed culture as communication:

> "Culture is comprised of those solutions and ways of action that people of the past have developed as answers to the challenges posed by their environment (social environment included). These habitual reactions, patterns of the answers as well as the answers themselves—both tangible and intangible—create the whole that is called culture."[31]

This definition was repeated by Litzen in his lectures, but already in 1982 he was appointed the director of the Finnish Institute in Rome, Villa Lante. Litzen's successor Keijo Virtanen (born 1945) continued to cultivate an open, inclusive understanding of culture and became the architect of the success of cultural history in Turku. The wider understanding of culture was exemplified by his interest in the study of popular culture. At the time this was unusual, since popular culture was not on the agenda of academic research in Finland, at least not in history departments.[32] In 1993 Virtanen defined cultural history as a discipline that studies "those plans, habits and deeds, through which people of the past formed their relationship with their lives and through which they communicated with their environment".[33]

---

30 On the nomination process, see Turun yliopiston kulttuurihistorian professorin virka, 1979, p. 58-59.
31 LITZEN, 1981, p. 8.
32 VIRTANEN, 1984.
33 VIRTANEN, 1993, p. 11.

In the 1980s, in addition to classical cultural history, influences came from German cultural research and social sciences, like Walter Benjamin, Georg Simmel and Max Weber, but also from the Annales School, from the work of Marc Bloch, Lucien Febvre, Michel Vovelle, Fernand Braudel, Roger Chartier, Emmanuel Le Roy Ladurie and many others. Also Swedish ethnological research was noted, and especially Jonas Frykman and Orvar Löfgren's *Den kultiverade människan* (The cultured human, 1979) was used as a course book for years. Gunnar Suolahti's works were also used and read through the 1980s and 1990s, but otherwise the new department no longer saw much continuum to the tradition of cultural history in Finland. The gap, left presumably by the success of social sciences in the 1960s and 1970s, was too wide to cover. On the other hand, the idea of being a pathbreaker was important for the identity of the small academic unit in the 1980s. There was an apparent interest in digesting influences from different international traditions and also from other fields of research within humanities. Litzen's interview from November 1982 reveals that already at that time the popularity of cultural history among students had risen so much that the number of teachers seemed inadequate.[34] The steady growth continued through the 1980s and 1990s.

It seems obvious that the Department of Cultural History had taken a keen interest in defining itself. During the 1980s and 1990s, several books were published on the nature of cultural history. In 1981 *Mitä kulttuurihistoria on?* (What Is Cultural History?) was edited by Kari Immonen (born 1945), future professor of cultural history himself. The most important work was Keijo Virtanen's *Kulttuurihistoria—tie kokonaisvaltaiseen historiaan* (Cultural History: towards a Comprehensive Understanding of History), published in 1987, which aimed at positioning the Turku department in relation to contemporary debates on cultural research. Also in 1991, a small booklet *Mitä kulttuurihistoria on?* (What Is Cultural History?) by Timo Tarmio was produced for open university courses.[35] An important addition to the conceptual basis of cultural history was offered by Kari Immonen in 1996 in his book *Historian läsnäolo* (The Presence of the Past) which, drawing on the idea of *Geschichtskultur*, stressed the active nature of historical knowledge and the importance of studying how history exists in the present day.[36]

The article collection *Kulttuurihistoria: Johdatus tutkimukseen* (Cultural History: Introduction to Research, 2001) summarized the development of the 1990s. The book included essays on gender history, history of the senses, history

---

34 Mies puolipäivässä, 2009, p. 19-21.
35 IMMONEN 1981; VIRTANEN, 1987; TARMIO, 1991. See also SALMI, 1987, p. 228-229.
36 IMMONEN, 1996. See also IMMONEN, 1993, p. 19-33.

of death, history of cinema and popular culture, history of family, childhood and sexuality and also essays on the methodology of micro-history and the history of mentalities. Research activities laid particular emphases on medieval and early modern history, on late nineteenth- and early twentieth-century history as well as the history of popular culture. There were also active research groups on the history of modernity, technology, gender and material culture.

During the 1980s, the Department of Cultural History was a small unit compared to its related departments, Finnish History and General History; but the amount of students rose steadily during the 1990s and soon Cultural History grew into a unit with two professors and three other positions. In retrospect, it seems that the depression of the early 1990s also influenced in the education sector, and cultural history became a popular field in the open university. By the end of the decade almost a thousand students had studied the basic courses in cultural history all over Finland through distance learning.

The 1990s were characterized by a clear enthusiasm for cultural studies in Finland, and it is obvious that more cultural historical research was conducted in every university than ever before. Markku Peltonen has estimated that almost half of the PhD's in history, completed in Finnish universities after 1989, can be classified into a broad category of cultural history, intellectual history and the history of ideas.[37] Still, the Turku department serves not only as an illuminating example of the cultural turn, it also participated in constructing the change in Finland.

The consequences of the cultural turn become discernible in the figures on the Turku department's educational output. Table 1 shows the numbers of MA graduates per year. It demonstrates that the 1990s was a decade of gradual growth, and after the year 2000, the annual number of graduates has settled down to 20-25 (however 2009 was an exceptional year with 41 MA's). It is interesting to compare this development with the Cultural History MA in Aberdeen (cf. Nick Fisher's article in this book). In Finland, cultural history took on institutionalized forms which enabled long-term development. It remains to be seen how the new university policy, and those economic fluctuations it seems to involve, will influence this development in the 2010s.

---

37 PELTONEN, 2009, p. 85.

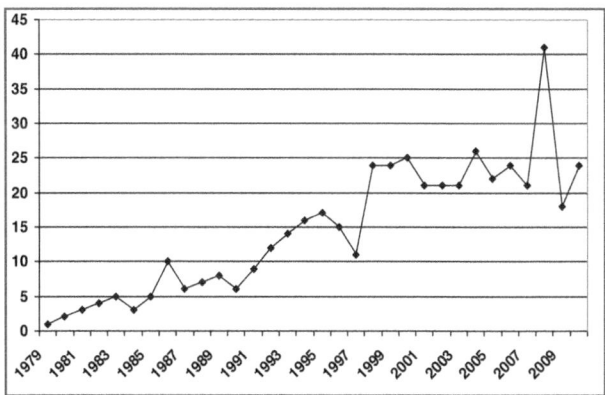

Table 1: MA Theses (per year) in Cultural History, University of Turku 1979-2010

In addition to annual MA graduates, it is important to look at doctoral dissertations that tell more about research activities. A similar rising curve can be observed in the amounts of PhD theses. The first doctoral dissertation, Luigi de Anna's *Conoscenza e immagine della Finlandia e del settentrione nella cultura classico-medievale* was completed in 1988, fairly late considering that the department had started in 1972.[38] Table 2 shows how the library of doctoral dissertations has increased. A total of 35 completed between 1988-2009. During the same period the country produced just under 500 new doctors of history. Approximately 7% of them come from the Department of Cultural History and 16% from the University of Turku. During the last ten years the percentages are marginally higher, 9% and 17%.

Table 2 reveals that the rise has been particularly sharp after 1999. There are many explanations for this development. One reason is the increase of research funding in Finland after the depression of the 1990s which benefited also humanities and provided opportunities for young scholars. On the other hand, more and more talented students were interested in continuing their studies. Also in 1997, department's PhD education was reorganized around research groups, which seems to have given an extra impetus for scholarly efforts and also widened the professional basis for supervision. General background factors cannot explain the growing interest in cultural history, as the increase in figures has been more moderate in other departments. Table 3 shows how PhD education has devel-

---

[38] The complete list of doctoral dissertation can be viewed at http://www.hum.utu.fi/oppiaineet/kulttuurihistoria/jatko-opinnot/vaitos/vaitoskirjat.html, 23.02.2011.

oped in relation to other history departments of the University of Turku: here also Art History as well as the Department of Contemporary History is listed, which is situated in the Faculty of Social Sciences. The table seems to refer to a similar development in the two new departments, Cultural and Contemporary History.

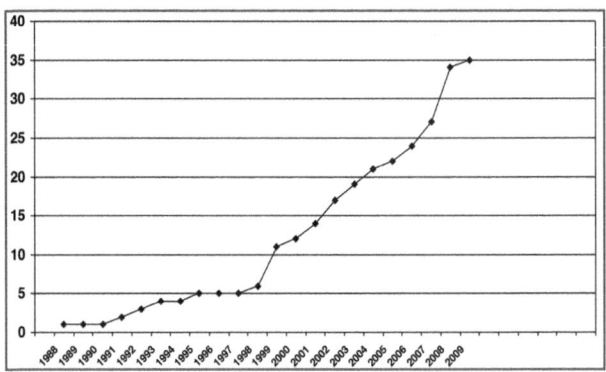

Table 2: PhD Theses in Cultural History, University of Turku 1988-2009

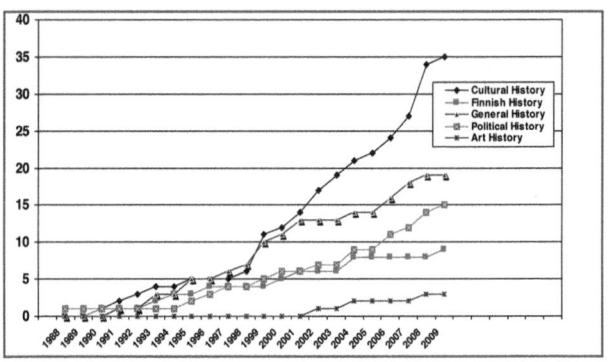

Table 3: PhD Theses in History, University of Turku, 1988-2009

In conclusion, it is evident that there is a century-long tradition of cultural history in Finland and that the concept of culture has had explanatory powers in historical research. However, it is just as evident that there were two periods of particular interest in cultural history. In a recent analysis, based on all doctoral dissertations in history completed in Finland, Markku Peltonen has drawn a similar conclusion. Peltonen notes that the first upheaval of cultural history was in the 1930s and 1940s. Many of the PhD theses, inspired by the Cultural History

School before the war, were completed in the 1940s. The second boom started in the 1990s and is still underway.[39]

In Finnish historical research of the late 1960s and early 1970s, historians rarely described themselves as cultural historians. Back in the 1980s this began to change gradually. The development of the Department of Cultural History is an epitome of those profound changes Finnish historical research has gone through. The Department started as a tiny, often neglected unit with only a few students, but it experienced a huge expansion in the 1990s and was suddenly at the centre of attention as, at the same time, historical research in general increasingly opened up to the so-called new histories and the *cultural turn*.

Literature

CHICKERING, ROGER, KARL LAMPRECHT: A German Academic Life (1856-1915), Leiden 1993.

CHRISTIANSEN, Palle Ove, L'Expérience et la vie quotidienne: L'histoire culturelle en Scandinavie, in: L'histoire culturelle: "un tournant mondial" dans l'historiographie?, ed. by PHILIPPE POIRRIER, preface by Roger Chartier, Dijon 2008, p. 65-178.

FRIEDELL, EGON, Uuden ajan kulttuurihistoria 1-3, translated by Erik Ahlman, Porvoo 1930-33.

HAAPALA, PERTTI, Kulturgeschichte i den finländska historieskrivningen, in: Den dubbla blicken. Historia i de nordiska samhällena, ed. by HARALD GUSTAFSSON et al., Lund 2007, p. 51-61.

IMMONEN, KARI (ed.), Mitä kulttuurihistoria on?, Turku 1981.

ID., Mennyt nykyisyytenä, in: Metodikirja. Näkökulmia kulttuurihistorian tutkimuksee, ed. by MARJO KAARTINEN et al., Turku 1993, p. 19-33.

ID., Historian läsnäolo, Turku 1996.

JUTIKKALA, EINO, GUNNAR SUOLAHTI (1876-1933), in: Kansallisbiografia, 2000 http://www.kansallisbiografia.fi/, 20.10.2010.

ID., Gabriel Nikander (1884-1959), in: Kansallisbiografia, 2001 http://www.kansallisbiografia.fi/, 20.10.2010.

KLINGE, MATTI, Gunnar Suolahti epookkia ja tyyppiä etsimässä, in: Suolahti, Gunnar, Vuosisatain takaa. Kulttuurihistoriallisia kuvauksia 1500-1800-luvuilta, Helsinki 1993, p. 464-480.

---

39 PELTONEN, 2009.

LEHTONEN, U. L., Mitä on kulttuurihistoria, in: Historiallinen Aikakauskirja 2 (1925), p. 129-134.

LEIKOLA, ANTO, Suolahti, Eino Edvard (1914-1977), in: Kansallisbiografia, 2007 http://www.kansallisbiografia.fi/, 20.10.2010.

LITZEN, VEIKKO, Kulttuurihistoria on kokonaisvaltaisuutta korostava historia, in: Mitä kulttuurihistoria on?, ed. by KARI IMMONEN, Turku 1981, p. 7-17.

ID./VIRTANEN, KEIJO, Kulttuurihistoria, in: Historiallinen Aikakauskirja 1 (1983), p. 17-20.

Lyhyitä tiedonantoja, in: Historiallinen Aikakauskirja 0 (1903), p. 30-32.

Mies puolipäivässä. Veikko Litzénin haastattelu 19.11.1982. Haastattelija Leena Rossi. Turku 2009.

MIKKELI, HEIKKI, Kulttuurikriisi sotienvälisessä Suomessa—mikä oli kriisissä?, in: Historiallinen Aikakauskirja 2 (1996), p. 122-140.

OLLITERVO, SAKARI/IMMONEN, KARI, Johdanto, in: Herder, Suomi, Eurooppa, ed. by SAKARI OLLITERVO/KARI IMMONEN. Helsinki 2006, p. 7-21.

PALANDER, GUNNAR, Lamprechtin mietteet nykyajan historiasta, in: Historiallinen Aikakauskirja 4 (1904), p. 97-107.

ID., Historiallista kirjallisuutta: Troels-Lund Lifsbelysning, in: Historiallinen Aikakauskirja 0 (1903), p. 25-26.

PALOPOSKI, TOIVO J., Helmer Tegengren, in: Historiallinen Aikakauskirja 2 (1974), p. 160-161.

PELTONEN, MARKKU, Aate-, oppi- ja kulttuurihistoriallinen tutkimus Suomessa 1908-2006, in: Historia eilen ja tänään. Historiantutkimuksen ja arkeologian suunnat Suomessa 1908-2008, ed. by SINI KANGAS et al., Helsinki 2009, p. 83-93.

RANTALA, HELI, Kulttuurin juurilla: kulttuurin käsite varhaisessa suomalaiskeskustelussa, in: Kulttuurihistoriallinen katse, ed. by HELI RANTALA/SAKARI OLLITERVO, Turku 2010, p. 19-40.

ROSÉN, RAGNAR, Suomen Kulttuurihistoria, in: Historiallinen Aikakauskirja 4 (1938), p. 319-325.

SALMI, HANNU, Kulttuurihistoria—tie keskusteluun?, in: Historiallinen Aikakauskirja 3 (1988), p. 228-229.

SALOMAA, J. E., Karl Lamprechtin historianmetodi, in: Historiallinen Aikakauskirja 2 (1915), p. 113-146.

SUOLAHTI, GUNNAR, Historiallista kirjallisuutta (Arvéde Barine. La jeunesse de la Frande Mademoiselle, 1627-1652, ja Louis XIV et la Frande Mademoiselle, 1652-1683), in: Historiallinen Aikakauskirja 6 (1905), p. 225-228.

ID. et al. (eds.), Suomen kulttuurihistoria I, Jyväskylä 1933.

ID., Vuosisatain takaa. Kulttuurihistoriallisia kuvauksia 1500-1800-luvuilta, ed. by MATTI KLINGE, Helsinki 1993.

SUOLAHTI, EINO E., Gunnar Suolahti: ihminen ja tutkija, Porvoo 1947.

ID., Keskiajan kuva Johan Huizingan näkemänä, in: Historiallinen Aikakauskirja 2 (1941), p. 85-98.

ID., Kulttuurihistorian näköaloja, in: Historiallinen Aikakauskirja 3 (1943), p. 174-178.

ID., Kulttuurihistoriallisia esseitä, in: Historiallinen Aikakauskirja 3 (1945), p. 268-271.

TARMIO, TIMO, Mitä kulttuurihistoria on? Turku 1991.

Turun yliopiston kulttuurihistorian professorin virka, in: Historiallinen Aikakauskirja 1 (1979), p. 58-59.

WIDÉN, SOLVEIG, Åbo akademi 1918-1993: forskning och institutioner, Åbo 1993.

VIRTANEN, KEIJO, Kulttuurin käyttäjäkunnan laajeneminen: eliitti-/populaarikulttuuri 200 vuoden perspektiivinä, in: Historiallinen Aikakauskirja 4 (1984), p. 269-276.

ID., Kulttuurihistoria—tie kokonaisvaltaiseen historiaa, Turku 1987.

ID., Kulttuurihistoria humanistisena tieteenä, in: Metodikirja. Näkökulmia kulttuurihistorian tutkimukseen, ed. by MARJO KAARTINEN et al., Turku 1993, p. 9-18.

VUORELA, TOIVO, Ethnology in Finland before 1920, Helsinki 1977

Donnerska institutet, http://web.abo.fi/instut/di/, 23.02.2011.
http://www.hum.utu.fi/oppiaineet/kulttuurihistoria/jatko-opinnot/vaitos/vaitoskirjat.html, 23.02.2011.

The Practice of Cultural History in Britain

LUDMILLA JORDANOVA

Introduction

It is widely acknowledged that cultural history is difficult to define. In the English language, the word *culture* presents some distinctive difficulties connected with the nature of classes and elites. So the history of that word, which is peculiarly complex, sits uneasily behind any attempt to speak about the characteristics of cultural history. What is also sitting there, equally uneasily, is the general history of the country in question. My task is to say something about cultural history *in* Britain: since historical practice is shaped by so many factors, such as resources, the structure and funding of higher education, attitudes to the past and national preoccupations, the history *of* Britain is necessarily relevant. However, cultural history produced *in* Britain or *by* British scholars is not necessarily *about* Britain. It is true that, as in most countries, our national history dominates both research and teaching. Nonetheless, some of our most influential cultural historians have not written about British history. My interest here concerns the ways in which historians working in Britain have practiced.

Immediately, however, it is necessary to issue a health warning. I argue that it is hard to identify national traditions in cultural history that are specifically *British*. This is partly because the field has been so little institutionalized. The key area, I suggest, is rather *social* history. My experience is that historians are eclectic, piecing together bits and pieces when it comes to sources, perspectives, approaches and theories. I find it hard to identify schools of history, in the way that the *Annales* were deemed to have produced *annalistes*. The closest perhaps is the impact of Quentin Skinner's approach to the history of political thought. It could be argued that culture has played its part in a style of history that is so closely associated with Cambridge. But on the whole when we use the phrase *cultural history* that is not what springs to mind. So what we have, I will suggest, is a great deal of cultural history, which is heterogeneous. It would not be useful to provide simple lists of people, projects and places, for example, hence I have approached the huge challenge in a different manner. First, I consider what the problems are with defining cultural history. Then I pursue further some of the themes that arose in the process and especially the relationships between social and cultural history. The final section adopts a different, autobiographical vantage point.

Defining Cultural History

It seems to me that there are three broad approaches we can take in defining cultural history. First, it is possible to say simply that just as political history is the history of politics, so cultural history is the history of culture and then expend effort on defining *culture*—a term that is remarkably resistant to being pinned down. Second, we could claim that cultural history is what those who call themselves cultural historians do: *culture* is not, according to this approach, defined so much as allowed to emerge through scholarly practices. Third, it may be worth thinking about the areas of history that cultural history stands in implied comparison or explicit opposition to, in which case it is largely negatively defined. Whatever approach is taken, however, cultural history privileges the capacity of human beings to generate ideas, ways of life, meanings, objects, images and sounds, texts and so on. Yet these terms immediately show one of the problems with trying to tie down *cultural history*—there are innumerable fields that specialize in such areas—film studies, history of dress and musicology, for instance. Many of them are not, at least in Britain, normally represented in departments of history. Hence a great deal of cultural history goes on outside history as a discipline, and is particularly prominent in departments that focus on the study of literature.

There is another way of thinking about the current state and recent history of cultural history in Britain, which is a version of the second approach I just mentioned. This took self-definition as the major criterion, and a similar criterion could be applied to institutions, organisations, degree schemes and so on, that call themselves and define their own identity in terms of *cultural history*. A major British example, the cultural history degree at Aberdeen, is discussed elsewhere. While it is hard to generalize given the large number of Universities and Colleges in Britain with their diverse disciplinary structures, I would say that cultural history is remarkably *un*institutionalised in formal, structured ways. There is a Social History Society, but no organization dedicated to cultural history. Nor, so far as I know, are there any dedicated funding streams for the field. There is no British journal that is concerned exclusively with cultural *history*;

although the word *culture* or *cultural* appears in quite a few journal titles, these are mostly interdisciplinary periodicals.

In Britain, if you are searching for work in *cultural history*, you might well find it in a geography or area studies journal, in publications that emanate from English literature or from period-specific situations—medieval studies, eighteenth-century studies and so on. Yet I would say that most undergraduates in history departments have a sense that there exists a field called *cultural history*, they generally know whether it appeals to them or not, and they can recognize examples of it that are put before them. All this suggests that cultural history in Britain is characterized more informally, even intuitively, than formally and organizationally.

At this point we might turn to my third approach. If there are few formal ways in which *cultural history* is presented, developed and reinforced, then perhaps the grasp of what it is comes from a contrast with other types of historical practice. Built into this contrast, has been, I think, a feeling that cultural history is innovative, even though many of those who wrote historical works, in, for example, the eighteenth century, were, precisely, writing cultural history. Students, then, sense differences between economic, political, diplomatic, demographic and social history on the one hand, and cultural history on the other. But they, like us, might be hard pressed to give a positive and precise account of its defining features. So, by default, defining cultural history becomes an exercise in contrasting it with other kinds of historical activity. It is probably easiest to make a contrast between cultural and political history. The latter has enjoyed a dominant position for a long time in Britain, and there are those who would argue that it still does. There is a stereotype of political history, that it is concerned with elites, government, and the formal exercise of power, according to which it privileges those at the top, especially men, and neglects those at the bottom of society, especially women. But there is actually nothing in the concepts *state*, *politics*, *authority* or *government*, for example, that is antithetical to *culture* or *cultural history*. The recent interest in political culture, particularly evident in work on the French Revolution, makes point neatly.

Social/Cultural

In Britain arguably the most interesting and complex example of definition by contrast is the relationship between social and cultural history. In one sense cultural history appears more innovative and conceptually sophisticated by comparison with social history. But to make matters more difficult, in another sense, cultural history can be presented as a natural outgrowth of social history. The impact of anthropology is an obvious theme in any discussions of the nature of cultural history in the last quarter of the twentieth century. Social history has been more shaped by other social sciences, such as sociology, political economy and economics. By and large the level of engagement with anthropology on the part of cultural historians has been relatively superficial and has consisted more in reading than in direct collaboration. Furthermore, one particular individual, the late Clifford Geertz, seems to have exercised a disproportionate amount of influence, through it should be said, a limited number of articles and essays. Practitioners who have been trained and seriously combine the two, such as Alan McFarlane, are rare. Macfarlane, in addition to his anthropological work, has written about social, local and demographic history as well as about witchcraft, a topic that is both manifestly *cultural* and well suited to anthropological treatment. Perhaps, the key term here is *belief*—fundamental for anthropology as it was practiced until recently, necessarily central to culture, and capable of referring to intellectual, emotional and spiritual commitments in a non-judgemental manner. Keith Thomas, whose *Religion and the Decline of Magic: Studies in Popular Beliefs in Sixteenth and Seventeenth Century England* was published in 1971, would at that time, I suspect, have considered himself to belong to the social rather than the cultural variety of history, although his work has always been concerned with what most people would call *cultural history*. A good example, his early pioneering article on *the double standard*, examines beliefs and assumptions as these are translated into social, political and economic practices.

My point is twofold. First, in the 1970s social historians were proclaiming the importance of the *social*, which included phenomena that could just as well be called *cultural*. Hence my claim, which I will elaborate, if briefly, in due course, that, in the British context, the relationships between social and cultural history are especially significant. Second, in so far as there was a social science that inspired this wide-ranging form of social history, it was more anthropology than sociology or any other social science. Historical sociology is a distinct field of *sociology* not of history and continues to be practised—strictly speaking there is no equivalent term for a field of *history*, social history is as close as it gets. There were members of the British academic community at that time, who were thinking about the relationships between sociology and history and Gareth Stedman Jones, is a good example. His writings have always been concerned with categories of thought as well as with social practices, yet I suspect he would not describe himself as a cultural historian. There were, I believe, some good reasons why anthropology appealed to historians far more than sociology. Put crudely, it was because anthropology was thought to legitimate belief systems other than, even alien to our own, and to offer ways of studying them as cultural systems that possessed integrity in their own right. Thus anthropology could be equally inspirational for the study of, say, popular protest that involved types of behaviour—dressing up and other forms of disguise—that at first sight seem bizarre to modern eyes, and to historians of magic, witchcraft, and astrology— domains about which most 20th century historians were deeply sceptical. Note it was cultural and social anthropology not physical anthropology that appealed to historians then. Other social sciences seemed to offer less immediate and attractive ways forward, even when, within history, the emphasis was on social phenomena so broadly defined as to include cultural ones. Anthropology was, by virtue of its subject matter, perceived as especially alluring, and that is itself a cultural judgement. My comments suggest a peculiar intimacy between the *social* and the *cultural* in the British context.

The post-war interest in the social was itself an oppositional move—it sought to topple political history from its perch at the top of the historical tree, and to do so for political reasons, although of course these two uses of the word *political* are quite distinct. Many on the left felt that high politics, the doings of elites, states and governments, neglected the experiences, voices and struggles of the majority, which deserved, even demanded attention. In opposing and attempting to displace what seemed like an old fashioned, and hierarchical form of history, they were trying to shift the power and authority within the profession to other kinds of scholarly activity. At that moment, which I locate in Britain in the 1960s and 1970s, it would hardly have been appropriate to call this new kind of exploration of the past, *cultural* history, since there is always an anxiety in Britain, that culture is posh—like the Royal Opera House, Covent Garden—and hence also insensitive to plebeian life. Culture and class are mutually implicated. Yet the *culture* of plebeian life is itself a major research field, inspired between the 1960s and 1990s by the remarkable work of E.P. Thompson and others.

In practice, it was precisely the culture, as well as the social and economic conditions of life of the masses that was actually being explored. Thompson's *Whigs and Hunters* of 1977 neatly makes the point. We should note, furthermore, that in the 1970s, social and economic history were still tightly linked. Now their relationship is fragile, economic history is a much smaller field than it was four decades ago, and a number of economic historians practise in departments of economics. In those heady times when two major journals, *Social History* (1976) and *History Workshop Journal* (1976) were founded, labour history was an important field, whereas now, at least in Britain, it seems to me to be distinctly marginal. Yet economic history and labour history can both be pursued with cultural matters at their heart and I believe that cultural historians should be concerned to support and defend them too. Given our concern with social and cultural hierarchies, there is still a feeling in the UK that *art* history, for example, out of which some of the most important and distinguished cultural history is currently coming, is a subject that has little to offer historians—the concern about elitism applies. And it applies, interestingly enough, both to the practitioners and the objects of study. Art history has attracted many students from privileged backgrounds and to some extent continues to do so. Art works themselves can be stereotypically presented as divorced from quotidian concerns and hence unable to speak to them. I am not, of course, endorsing these claims, merely pointing out that even with the recent enchantment with cultural history, there are still suspicions and anxieties about its boundaries, and the frameworks that shape it, as well as about its objects of analysis.

At the same time, there is a genuine sense in which social history spawned the *new* cultural history. I dislike these claims to novelty, since cultural history has been practised for centuries, and I feel it would be profitable for us now to acknowledge and explore its past and engage with specific examples of it. Recent work on the Enlightenment, for example by Mark Phillips, has been doing just this. Nonetheless, the point remains that, partly for career reasons, cultural history was presented as *new*, and that social history was a principal, although not exclusive source for the historiographical impulses that, in the English speaking worlds, we associate with figures such as Natalie Zemon Davis, Lynn Hunt, and Joan Scott, all of whom are American historians of France.

A Special Relationship?

This is the place to acknowledge a feature of British historiography that is inescapable, namely the close alliances and affinities between North American and UK historians. Naturally, these stem, at least in part, from the fact that both write in English, and also from shared philosophical, political and religious traditions, despite the manifest differences between the countries. But the fundamental issue here, surely, is power. History as it practised in the United States is powerful; it exercises its sway over many other parts of the world, and above all in Britain. How might we analyse this sway and compare it with the impact of *continental* traditions? I suspect that a shared commitment to empiricism plays a part. I suspect too that there are ideological affinities at work, manifest, for example, in the general impact of American feminism upon the United Kingdom in the late 60s and 70s, and specifically in the inspiration that British historians of women and gender found in American history writing in this period. There is also a resources question lurking here: resources and prestige are difficult to separate. There is, after all, a lot more money around in the North American academy than there is in Britain, and many prominent historians who were born, educated and trained in the UK now practice there: Simon Schama, John Brewer, Linda Colley, and David Cannadine, for example, all of whom have produced works, which, if in a variety of senses, qualify as *cultural history*. The conditions of work in the United States are markedly superior to those in the UK, while academics there arguably enjoy more respect and status than their British counterparts.

In that respect, North America is more like Continental Europe, at least to this English person's eyes. I well remember the extensive newspaper coverage in France that followed the death of Fernand Braudel (1902-1985), which seemed to me then, and still seems to me now, utterly unlike anything that could happen in the context in which I live and work. In these senses then, and despite the differences between the two areas, when we speak about cultural history in Great Britain, what is happening in North America is a central consideration, and it is even more central, I suggest, than in other domains of history, such as political history, where we have our own long and independent traditions of scholarship that have been shaped by the British political situation as, for example, a more or less continuous monarchy for centuries, and with a particular kind of parliamentary structure in which landed elites played a dominant role until relatively recently. The Anglo-American alliance may then be one significant respect in which our forms of cultural history differ from those on Continental Europe. I am certainly not saying that this is a good thing, I am only saying that an alliance manifestly exists.

Defining Europe

I should not have lumped European countries together and used the adjective *Continental* about them in the previous sentence, not least because it is then unclear how Scandinavia fits in. In areas such as the family and gender history there are considerable affinities between Scandinavia and Britain. This was a holding operation, and also a slightly ironic gesture in the direction of what has been happening in our philosophy departments, where there is now a field called *Continental philosophy* to distinguish it from English-speaking analytical traditions. Here again is definition by contrast, and in my view of a particularly intellectually questionable kind. So, before I pick up again the thread of the relationships between social and cultural history in Britain, let me say a word about the ways in which cultural history has been shaped by forces that are *not* American. This raises interesting questions about colonial, imperial, subaltern influences as well as *continental* ones. For example, Anna Green, the author of *Cultural History*, is working in an Australian context, where there is a strong and vibrant historical community, which has a prominent role in public debate. In colonial and post-colonial contexts, culture, however defined, is central: both these contexts and the ways in which historians are approaching them are helping to shape cultural history, especially in Britain where empire has been so central to national identity.

The wave of so-called *new cultural history* in Britain definitely increased interest in the *Annales* school—evident, for example, in Peter Burke's book, *The French Historical Revolution* of 1990. Burke himself is recognized as one of the most successful and influential of Britain's cultural historians, albeit one who is unusually aware of the richness of European and Latin American historiography, past and present. Yet I find it difficult to think of a single British (cultural) historian who could be called a fully-fledged *Annaliste*. Two other strands of French historiography are worth mentioning for their impact in Britain: work on *mentalités* and approaches to books, reading and culture associated with Roger Chartier. *L'histoire des mentalités* has travelled, naturally enough, through English speaking historians who themselves work on France, and it is striking that in general, historians *of* France have been exceptionally influential in the UK and North America. For example, Colin Jones, who has published extensively on eighteenth-century France and the Revolutionary period, including on medicine, is the current President of the Royal Historical Society. His work is resolutely *cultural*, even if it would not itself be described as *Annaliste*, exploring *l'histoire des mentalités* or conducted in the manner of Chartier. My point is that many, many historians in Britain would be either aware of or have read directly the writings of Philippe Ariès, to take probably the best known writer on *mentalités*, even if they do not directly emulate him. Without a doubt he has shaped the ways the history of childhood and the history of death are studied in the UK, sometimes directly and sometimes by historians opposing him. Since he integrated toys and paintings into his work on the discovery of childhood, and all manner of visual and material culture into his work on death, any possible definition of cultural history would include him, even as many British historians are critical of him. Thus, the idea that styles of scholarship are defined by contrast and opposition works within as well as between fields. *French* cultural approaches are well known in the British Isles, they are in some ways influential, but not principally in the sense of attracting direct followers. A few *big* names attract a disproportionate amount of attention.

On the whole, however, intellectual traditions in other European countries, such as *Begriffsgeschichte*, are little known or appreciated in the UK. Of course there are some exceptions, most notably the virtual obsession with Jürgen Habermas among many of those working on the long eighteenth century. Other influences on British cultural history, such as that of the sociologist Norbert Elias, presumably owe a great deal to residence in the country. The same can be said for the legacy of the Warburg Institute, which moved to London in 1934, although there is a complex argument to be made here about the relationships between the history of ideas/intellectual history and cultural history, since on one reading they necessarily overlap considerably, whilst on another they have become quite distinct scholarly communities.

Cultural historians in Britain, then, are selectively aware of European trends, but languages are a significant barrier in a country where doctoral students, for example, frequently work solely in their native tongue, which would be impossible in many parts of Europe. Those working *on* other countries engage with their historiographies, but, apart from France, the cultural-historical methods and approaches of European countries are rather little known in the UK. We tend to define Europe as France. Individuals with a global reputation, such as Carlo Ginzburg, are an exception, but reading his books does not constitute engagement with Italian intellectual traditions.

Cultural and Social History

I want to return to the relationships between social and cultural history, bearing in mind that in practice, social and cultural history are *both* entwined, *and* in some circumstances, distinct, mutually defining. In the British case, social history was the innovative and politically engaged historical field of the 1960s and 1970s and it was allied with economic history, and indeed with other social sciences, as well as approaches such as oral history, social*ist* history, women's history, history from below and so on. It was at this time that the Social History Society was founded (1976), and started publishing the journal called *Social History*. In 2004, however, the journal was refounded as *Cultural and Social History*. Later issues of the new journal carry a statement at the front:

> "Recent epistemological challenges have shaken the core assumptions of many historians. 'Culture' is now seen as a product of social practice, and therefore at the heart of society itself. *Cultural and Social History*, the official peer-reviewed journal of the Social History Society (SHS), aims to ad-

dress disciplinary shifts between social and cultural historians. The journal emphasizes the ways the 'social' and 'culture' are inextricable and enable a deeper understanding of each other."

There is no evidence I can discern that the contents of the journal have altered markedly following the change of name. Perhaps what this change signals then, is less a shift in the content or manner of historical activity and more a recognition of the need to be seen to be open to the outcomes of *recent epistemological challenges*. This phrase is perhaps shorthand for what is sometimes presented as the impact of post-modernism, critical theory and theoretical perspectives in general. Hence, in this context, *cultural history* stands less for specific subject matter than for a particular orientation towards the practice of history. The second sentence also invites comment. Now? Surely the whole tenor of anthropology is precisely that *culture is a product of social practice*, and hence its impact, which dates back to the 1960s at least, was already leading historians in just this direction when the Social History Society was initially founded. Thus what has changed, I am suggesting, is less a novel interest in *culture* as such, than a recognition that *cultural history* stands more securely for an array of values, such as epistemological sophistication, than social history does. What stems from this recognition is exactly a wish, on the part of at least some sections of the historical community, to be identified with these values, for which *cultural history* stands as a summary, a tag, a convenient shorthand. *Social history* was a highly diverse field with respect to values and epistemological sophistication, which reinforces the sense that *cultural* primarily has rhetorical charge.

This is not to assert that *cultural history* is an empty phrase; it is merely to recognize that it has a range of meanings and that it is persuasive in a historically specific way. One of the things it is used to signal, for example, is using a wider range of sources, including visual and material, and less frequently, musical ones. Another is a desire to work in more explicitly conceptualized way. A further one may be the expression of a kinship with other disciplines. A great deal of what passes for interdisciplinary history is also, I would say, cultural history. There is indeed an enormous amount of *cultural history* going on in Britain at the moment, some of it in history departments, but much of it in English, French, geography and so on: it is manifestly *interdisciplinary*. There is some cross-fertilisation and shared endeavour, but nothing consistent. What Britain lacks, by contrast, is formally institutionalised cultural history. It also lacks some specific traditions that have been important elsewhere, such as folklore studies. I cannot account for this situation, only report it. One implication of what I have described is that it is virtually impossible to gage what "questions and topics are particularly in demand or have already been dealt with to a large extent." When it comes to the future, what will happen is anyone's guess.

Cultural *studies* in Britain tends to occupy a place in our academic life that is rather far removed from history, as is evident from the work of Stuart Hall. This is not just because it is more concerned with contemporary phenomena, after all, contemporary *history* is a field that is flourishing at the moment. Rather the distance is about types of training on the one hand and of theoretical frameworks on the other. I see cultural history within history departments as integrated, and hence enjoying close links with, indeed being simply an accepted part of present-day practice, without particularly needing banners proclaiming itself as a distinct field. What I also see, however, is that mainstream history has not really come to terms with *theory*—central to cultural studies—and that it has little to do with the social sciences. On my account, then, cultural history—which is strikingly polymorphous—is well placed in Britain, without being especially delineated as a distinct form of history. I am not sure that it would benefit from being more clearly defined and set apart from other forms of history, although I do think that historians would benefit from the discipline as a whole being considerably more active in building alliances with other fields which practise, in some sense, *cultural history:* my own particular interest is in the potential of art history to productively inform historical practice.

I certainly see myself as a cultural historian, although that is not the only label I would use. Sometimes I would call myself an art historian, a historian of science and/or medicine, a historian of gender or simply state that I am *a historian*. I also do work that comes under the category of *medical humanities*, a discipline that *does* have a certain institutional profile largely because of funding from the Wellcome Trust, but which nonetheless remains under-determined in terms of approaches, framework and content. In one sense medical humanities is all about *culture*, and includes cultural history/history of medicine within its remit, so perhaps that is a further potential disciplinary identity that I could use. In any individual's life, there are strategic and emotional decisions to be made about which labels to adopt, which journals to publish in, organisations to join, jobs to apply for, and the fact that I have such a choice tells us a lot about the kinds of fragmentation that exist within and around the discipline of history. I have suggested that the phenomenon of fragmentation reveals processes of professionalization and institutionalization, political and economic forces as well as what, for want of a better word, we could call *fashion*. One way of understanding how all this works is experientially, so I now provide a different kind of account of cultural history in Britain—an autobiographical one.

Ludmilla Jordanova

An Experiential Account

I was born in 1949, and took history at school only up to the age of 16. The history we learned was predominantly political, with a little social and economic. And it was British. I came back to history as a second-year science undergraduate, in 1969, when I took a course in history and philosophy of science. In that context, ideas, discoveries and theories occupied the centre stage, and the contexts in which *science* was conducted, still less used and disseminated, hardly explored at all. That changed to a degree when I specialized in the subject in my third year and was taught by the late Roy Porter. At that point, I think he would have described himself as a social historian, although he has come to be associated with cultural history. The third-year work was more contextual, but I picked up any historical knowledge I needed, for example, of the French revolution, piecemeal and not systematically as an undergraduate studying history would.

By the time I got my first degree in 1971, I had encountered work on magic and science, had some grasp of the importance of astrology, knew about writers such as Frances Yates, Arthur Lovejoy and Marjorie Hope Nicolson. In other words I had been trained in many of the key areas of cultural history, including *the history of knowledge*, without the label. When I started doctoral research in the same year, the very first departmental seminar was given by the anthropologist Mary Douglas, whose impact upon both historians and philosophers of science was vast. In that world, historians and philosophers worked together, if not always harmoniously, and questions about concepts and ways of understanding mental operations were fundamental. Furthermore we were concerned with what was then called, *science and society*. All of these features can, in retrospect, be seen as contributing to what would come to be called *the new cultural history*, including an interest in the nature and conditions of knowledge. Hence Michel Foucault was widely read by historians and philosophers of science well before he became so fashionable in literature, cultural studies and so on. Further trends, such as science and literature, reinforced what I suppose we could call a *cultural turn*.

I observe, first, that these cultural approaches were and are significantly interdisciplinary, and second, that they did not necessarily appear as a zone deliberately labeled *cultural history*. By the time I left Cambridge in 1978 having done a doctorate and held a research fellowship for three years and taught in history, social and political science and education as well as history and philosophy of science, and researched wax anatomical models and opera as well as a range of written sources, I guess I was doing a kind of cultural history that I have been more deliberately developing ever since, including by taking a degree in art history. For me this was about developing a path that *felt* right rather than consciously reflecting upon *cultural history* as a category. This changed however when, early in 1993, I was invited to apply for a post at York that was explicitly designed to develop further cultural history there—they already had a small one-year master's programme. I spent my three years there reflecting and helping to organize events on *cultural history*, but am not sure that we came to any new conclusions about it.

My next job was in a department of *world art studies and museology*, followed by a post running an interdisciplinary research centre. I currently teach in a history department, where there are many cultural historians, especially among the early modernists. Nonetheless the primary classification within the department is by period rather than historiographical style. One of my colleagues, the distinguished cultural historian Anne Goldgar, teaches courses that make explicit that they are *cultural history*—for example, Themes in Early Modern Cultural History, a second-year undergraduate option—while the rest of us deploy ideas and approaches that can be read that way. For example, I have taught an MA module called "The Construction of Modern Heroism, 1725-1930". The word "construction" clearly signals a particular historiographical orientation, that could be described as *cultural*, while the dates signal an interest in *longue durée* phenomena, which could be described as *mentalités*. Yet I do not especially present the course either publicly or in my head as *cultural history*. I cannot see that anything in particular would be gained by it, yet, as I have shown, my entire approach to my work has been shaped by thinking about culture and how to study such a protean and elusive concept, and by a seminal figure I have not so far mentioned, Raymond Williams, whose *Keywords: A Vocabulary of Culture and Society* (1976) as well as his books such as *The Country and the City* (1973) have been major influences, as have art-history scholars, such as Michael Baxandall and Marcia Pointon.

So one question that arises from my account is when and where has it been advantageous or necessary to signal the presence of *cultural history*? I have suggested that, given the array of approaches and disciplines that are currently practising what is on any definition recognizable as *cultural history*, there can be no simple answer. At the same time, I can see that for marketing purposes, for example, clear boundaries and signals can be helpful. At the level of research, however, surely it is vital simply to be flexible and open.

I shall conclude, however, on two rather different notes. In his 1983 book on *Gender,* Ivan Illich memorably says that this phenomenon is more about what occurs between the ears than between the legs. I appreciate this thought; perhaps cultural history is the activity that places what happens between the ears at centre stage, and develops its practices and principal analytical modes accordingly. Some might say that the concept of *representation* would play a leading role, but I suggest that *mediation* is even more important. Cultural history conceptualizes, examines and gives priority to mediations. My second thought is that if this is correct, then all history must be cultural history, since our discipline, like others, such as art history and literature, gives priority to human doings, which always entail mental operations of some kind. However, the ways in which historians practise is shaped by many forces. Even if we have the centrality of mediation in common across Europe, we still have our socially constructed baggage. It is difficult to identify the national elements among the rich mix of preconceptions, assumptions, generational effects, political and religious commitments and individual idiosyncracies that shape the ways in which communities of historians view the past. In so far as it is possible to generalize, cultural history in Britain is thriving, and perhaps there is something significant in the fact that it does so in a rather higgledy-piggledy fashion.

Literature

ARIES, PHILLIPPE, Centuries of Childhood: a Social History of Family Life, New York 1962 (first published in French in 1960).
ID., The Hour of Our Death, New York 1981 (first published in French in 1977).
BARRELL, JOHN, The Dark Side of the Landscape: the Rural Poor in English Painting, Cambridge 1980.
BAXANDALL, MICHAEL, Painting and Experience in Fifteenth Century Italy: A Primer in the Social History of Pictorial Style, Oxford 1972.
ID., Patterns of Intention: on the Historical Explanation of Pictures, New Haven 1985.
BREWER, JOHN, The Pleasures of the Imagination: English Culture in the Eighteenth Century, London, 1997.
BURKE, PETER, The French Historical Revolution: the Annales School, 1929-89, Cambridge 1990.
CANNADINE, DAVID, Ornamentalism: how the British saw their Empire, London 2001.
CHARTIER, ROGER, The Cultural Uses of Print in Early Modern France, Princeton 1987.
COLLEY, LINDA, BRITONS: Forging the Nation, 1707-1837, New Haven 1992.
DAVIS, NATALIE ZEMON, Society and Culture in Early Modern France: Eight Essays, London, 1975.

DOUGLAS, MARY, Purity and Danger: an Analysis of Concepts of Pollution and Taboo, London 1966.
ELIAS, NORBERT, The Civilizing Process: The History of Manners, Vol. 1, Oxford 1978 (first published in German in 1968).
FOUCAULT, MICHEL, The Archaeology of Knowledge, London 1972 (first published in French in 1969).
ID., The Birth of the Clinic: an Archaeology of Medical Perception, London 1973 (first published in French in 1963).
GEERTZ, CLIFFORD, The Interpretation of Cultures: Selected Essays, New York 1973.
GINZBURG, CARLO, The Cheese and the Worms: the Cosmos of a Sixteenth-century Miller, London 1980 (first published in Italian in 1976).
GOLDGAR, ANNE, Tulipmania: Money, Honor, and Knowledge in the Dutch Golden Age, Chicago and London, 2007.
GREEN, ANNA, Cultural History, Basingstoke 2008.
HABERMAS, JÜRGEN, The Structural Transformation of the Public Sphere: an Inquiry into a Category of Bourgeois Society, Cambridge, 1989 (first published in German in 1962).
HALL, STUART, Television as a Medium and its Relation to Culture, Birmingham 1975.
HUNT, LYNN, Politics, Culture, and Class in the French Revolution, Berkeley/London 1984.
ILLICH, IVAN, Gender, London 1983.
JONES, COLIN, Madame de Pompadour: Images of a Mistress, London 2002.
LOVEJOY, ARTHUR, The Great Chain of Being: a Study of the History of an Idea, Cambridge, Mass. 1936.
MACFARLANE, ALAN, The Family Life of Ralph Josselin, a Seventeenth-Century Clergyman; an Essay in Historical Anthropology, Cambridge 1970.
ID., Witchcraft in Tudor and Stuart England: a Regional and Comparative Study, London 1970.
ID., Marriage and Love in England: Modes of Reproduction, Oxford 1986.
NICOLSON, MARJORIE HOPE, Mountain Gloom and Mountain Glory: the development of the Aesthetics of the Infinite, Ithaca, N.Y. 1959.
PHILLIPS, MARK, Society and Sentiment: Genres of Historical Writing in Britain, 1740-1820, Princeton, N.J. 2000.
POINTON, MARCIA, Hanging the Head: Portraiture and Social Formation in Eighteenth-century England, New Haven/London 1993.
PORTER, ROY, English Society in the Eighteenth Century, Harmondsworth 1982.
SCHAMA, SIMON, Citizens: A Chronicle of the French Revolution, London 1989.

SCOTT, JOAN, Gender and the Politics of History, New York 1988.
SKINNER, QUENTIN, The Foundations of Modern Political Thought, Cambridge 1978 (2 volumes).
STEDMAN JONES, GARETH, From Historical Sociology to Theoretical History, in: British Journal of Sociology 27 (1976), p. 295-305.
THOMAS, KEITH, The Double Standard, in: Journal of the History of Ideas 20 (1959), p. 195-216.
ID., Religion and the Decline of Magic: Studies in Popular Beliefs in Sixteenth and Seventeenth Century England, London 1971.
THOMPSON, E.P., The Making of the English Working Class, London 1963.
ID., Whigs and Hunters: the Origin of the Black Act, London 1975.
ID., Customs in Common, London 1991.
WILLIAMS, RAYMOND, Keywords: A Vocabulary of Culture and Society, London 1976 (a revised edition appeared in 1983).
YATES, FRANCES, The Art of Memory, London 1966.
ID., The Rosicrucian Enlightenment, London 1972.

The Cultural History MA at the University of Aberdeen, 1986-2011: a personal reflection

NICK FISHER

The undergraduate programme in cultural history at the University of Aberdeen began almost twenty-five years ago, but is now being discontinued. The last cultural history students will graduate next year. It is of course hard to be cheerful when writing about the last days of a programme to which so many people contributed so much care and effort, but my abiding memory will always be of the enormous enjoyment that many of us got from teaching cultural history in the early days, in the growth part of the curve, and at its peak. We all learned so much that we would otherwise not have been able to.

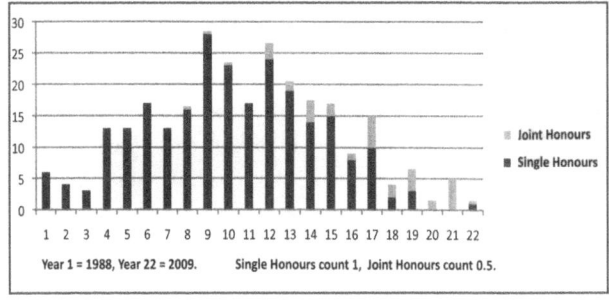

Table 1: Aberdeen Cultural History Graduates 1988-2009

My younger colleagues who have kept the flame burning in the period of decline assure me that this is still very much the case: the teaching is enormously rewarding. From the start, cultural history was a liberation from conventional disciplinary limits. Moreover, it served as a much-needed morale booster in the face of the university-wide depression caused by the Thatcher government's cuts to university funding in the 1980s, which had a severe effect on Aberdeen.

We need a word about the context, and about how the most conservative and geographically isolated of the ancient Scottish universities came to start such a unique experiment. Aberdeen University, founded in 1495, was for most of the twentieth century an ordinary Scottish university. This means among other things that the students entered about a year younger than their English counterparts, and that they were admitted not to departments but rather to faculties (Arts, Divinity, Medicine, Science, Law), which has implications for my story: it is much easier for Scottish students than English to change their intended direction once they have sampled one or two years of university study. Moreover, the broader four-year Scottish honours degree is different from a three-year English degree. And when after the Second World War the other Scottish universities, St Andrews, Glasgow, and Edinburgh were forced by the conditions attached to government funding to become more aware of international comparisons and competition, Aberdeen self-consciously remained the most traditionally Scottish of the universities. It was also rather small, with 2500 students in 1960.

The 1960s saw a period of huge expansion in British education, with the foundation of many new universities. In search of the economic benefits of a more educated population, student numbers were intended to more than double in the fifteen years from 1962, facilitated by generous student grants to all who qualified for university entrance. In Scotland the number of universities was increased from four to eight. Of the older universities, Aberdeen was particularly singled out for growth. Glasgow and Edinburgh were thought by the administrators of the Scottish Education Department to be big enough already, while the little city of St Andrews was considered unable to cope with a large increase in student numbers. The target numbers for Aberdeen were raised and raised again, from the actual 2500 in 1960 to targets of 4500 for 1967, of 8180 for 1976, and finally of 10.500 for 1981. These planned expansions were intended roughly to parallel the physical and economic growth of the City of Aberdeen as a result of the discovery of North Sea oil. With the encouragement, indeed the insistence, of the University Grants Committee, the distributor of British government funds to universities, the University of Aberdeen set about building the classrooms and student residences, and hiring the staff, that would be required for all these new students. Unfortunately, nobody told the students that they were expected in Aberdeen, and there were no efficient mechanisms for directing student choice. When I was appointed in 1976, the student population was around 5500, not the intended 8180. As a result, when the economic crisis for universities came in 1981, Aberdeen was found to be over-provided with both buildings and staff; and it had too many small and thus supposedly inefficient departments, such as my own, History and Philosophy of Science, with its staff of 3. The cut in Aberdeen's government grant announced that summer was 19%, compared with a national average of 11%. The University's response was to announce 169 academic staff redundancies, compulsory if necessary, including all the inefficient little departments.

A vigorous academic defence was led by mass meetings of the lecturers' union, the Aberdeen Association of University Teachers (AAUT). The University meanwhile offered quite generous compensation packages for early retirement, and by April it was clear that enough academics had accepted these packages, or had left for other universities less badly affected, so that the required savings in staff costs had been achieved, and the threat of further sackings and closures was formally lifted. But it has to be said that the radicalisation and the militancy of the staff that arose during that year ensured that their attitudes towards the University, including feelings of loyalty and trust, were never the same again.

The immediate outlook for the future of teaching and learning at the University was now rather bleak. After all the work that had gone in to reducing staff costs, it was clear that it would be some time before the flow of new young lecturers could start again. How then could innovation in teaching, at little or no cost, be encouraged? One individual who gave this much thought was Dr. Judith Hook of the History Department. She was a scholar of 17th century English art, and of the more general history—indeed the cultural history—of Renaissance Italy. Judith's work culminated in the publication of her biography of Lorenzo de' Medici in 1984. She had been particularly active in the struggles of the AAUT, when she and I had been close comrades in arms. She was forever dreaming up new schemes, often of doubtful practicality. In early 1984 she had heard that the new British television channel, Channel 4, was seeking suggestions for new programmes, possibly some of them academic. She sat at my kitchen table discussing a proposal for an intellectual history series. In Britain we talk about plans being made on the back of an envelope; if one is talking about politics or about budgetary planning, it is rather rude and dismissive to say this. But some important plans start on the backs of envelopes, and here is the beginning of Aberdeen's cultural history.

 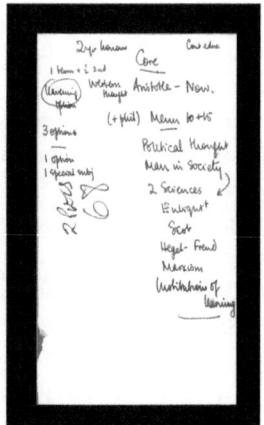

Table 2

I can't really make much sense of it after 26 years—and this is not remotely what happened. Channel 4 would certainly not have thought much of it. (Channel 4 has found its niche as the British home of *Big Brother*, and intellectual history would be entirely alien to it.) Fortunately Judith also pursued these ideas within the University, and towards the end of academic year 1983-84 organised a meeting with members of the History Department and others such as myself who had an interest in interdisciplinary teaching. That summer Judith went to Florence as usual for her research, and in August she suddenly died there of a brain haemorrhage.

Partly in memory of Judith, her colleagues in the History Department sought to carry her exploration further. The immediate occasion for the resumption of discussions was a visit by the cultural historian Roy Porter to give a lecture to the Department in March 1985. In conversation afterwards, he was most encouraging of our efforts at interdisciplinary teaching. A number of us took these forward over the summer and autumn. In the summer two significant decisions were made: to spread the invitation to talk as widely as possible by word of mouth, and to invite Joan Pittock Wesson of the English Department, who had organised a successful series of interdisciplinary seminars in the 1970s, to become convenor of the group. By the autumn *intellectual history* had become *cultural history*, as both a more inclusive approach and more widely interdisciplinary—not to mention more modern—and detailed planning for an honours course in cultural history had begun. When the course proposal was submitted to the Arts Faculty Planning Committee in December, it was turned down on the grounds that a time of financial stringency was no time to be experimenting with new ways of teaching; this was of course the exact opposite of our argument that it was precisely because of the financial constraints that one had to come up with new ways of doing things.

So we appealed to the full Arts Faculty meeting against this initial refusal, and we won the vote, which allowed us to proceed. Apart from the intellectual arguments for the proposed cultural history course, and the emotional arguments in memory of Judith Hook, there were three other main reasons for this turnaround. The practical argument was that we had so many possible contributors that no one of us would be overburdened by the additional teaching. Translated into political terms, this same argument about numbers meant that the group and its many friends throughout the Faculty could attract enough votes to win. And the clinching political fact was that after the radical struggles of the early 1980s, nobody wanted to be told what they should do or what they should think by figures of authority such as deans and their planning committees.

Let me outline the normal structure of an arts honours degree that we were threatening to subvert. An Aberdeen arts student would typically take three courses in year 1, two in year 2, and then in years 3 and 4 (*junior and senior honours*) would specialise in either those same two disciplines (*joint honours*), or only one of them (*single honours*). The overall menu was not an entirely free choice: there were rules governing permitted combinations of disciplines, and there were particular prerequisites for certain courses. And until the early 1970s there had been a general prerequisite that all arts students had to take at least one course in philosophy, once a characteristic of all Scottish arts degrees. The degree structure for science students was comparable, except that single honours was the norm. Overall, the expectation was that candidates for an honours degree, whether single or joint, would be prepared for their honours classes by two years of prior study in their discipline(s).

What we cultural historians were proposing was an Honours degree which assumed no earlier preparation, and would thus begin from zero in Year 3. This was entirely anomalous. It was proposed that we took *any* student with the standard number of passes in earlier courses, including students from the Science Faculty (or elsewhere). We would teach them intensively a basic course in the cultural history of north-west Europe from the Enlightenment and the French Revolution, through the romanticism and nationalism of the 19th century, up to the onset of the First World War, all over 24 weeks. This would be preparatory to more specialist courses in the senior honours year.

As students were considering their futures towards the end of academic year 1985-86, posters were circulated inviting any students interested in the new cultural history degree to contact the Convenor or any member of the core group.

(It should be emphasised that altogether many more than the ten staff members named on the poster were involved.) In October 1986 our first intake was six students.

They took a single course which had 4-6 lectures a week and one or two seminars. One of the seminars would discuss the week's *key text*, an insistence from members of the English department. The first text was Francis Bacon's *New Atlantis* as part of the 17th century background to the Enlightenment. Later in the year the concept of *text* broadened to include several non-literary works; Haydn's *Creation* as an Enlightenment text was one; the Great Exhibition of 1851 in London was another (the latter has been my chief personal research interest ever since). In keeping with the interdisciplinary nature of the course, two or sometimes even three members of staff participated in the seminars, and all for six students! This generosity could not last for very long, although many years later there were still a few seminars with staff from two different departments. The emphasis throughout was on cultural interconnexions, easily enough traced in the European Enlightenment, but also to be found throughout the 19th century.

Another feature of the cultural history teaching was that it involved more than the regular teaching staff. The University Archivist, Colin McLaren, gave a series of lectures on the cultural history of libraries. Other recruits included a second librarian whose PhD dissertation had been on the history of the book trade, the curator of the University's anthropological museum, the University's public relations officer who had previously worked for Scottish Opera, and a careers adviser who had an interest in the notion of the wilderness. People such as these welcomed the opportunity to teach their special interests that they would not normally have had. All at different times added to the richness and diversity of the cultural history course. (It is perhaps no coincidence that several of our students went on to work in libraries or museums.)

It should be said that in the tradition of British empiricism, the Aberdeen student's conception of cultural history was not theory-based, but was allowed to grow by slow empirical example. Such theory as we taught came later, and built on this empirical base. One result of this was an almost universal feeling among the students, maybe half-way through the introductory junior honours year, of being lost in a forest of disconnected information. "What is this cultural history?" they would ask. This feeling of dislocation would eventually pass, as group consciousness and solidarity reached some kind of an answer, allowing the students to make the connexions. Even among the small numbers of our initial intakes, esprit de corps, group solidarity, was always a striking feature.

The Cultural History MA at the University of Aberdeen, 1986-2011

In senior honours, our initial six students found the same generosity of staff teaching time which would be unthinkable today: eight optional courses for six students:

M.A. WITH HONOURS IN CULTURAL HISTORY: Senior Honours 1987-8		
Special Options:		
		Students
Death and the Family	Andrew Wear	2
Darwin and Victorian Thought	Robin Gilmour	2
Ideas of Language	David Cram	1
Russia and America	Paul Dukes	1
Structuralism and after	Michael Spiller	2
Commerce and Art	David Irwin	1
Childhood	Joan Pittock Wesson	2
The History of Sexuality	Mike Hepworth and David Oldman	1
Reading lists should be obtained from tutors before the end of this term.		

Table 3

And at the end of their fourth year, they took all their final exams over a few days, as was then the practice:

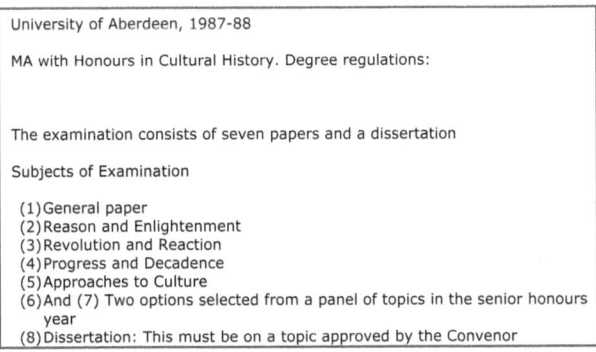

University of Aberdeen, 1987-88

MA with Honours in Cultural History. Degree regulations:

The examination consists of seven papers and a dissertation

Subjects of Examination

(1) General paper
(2) Reason and Enlightenment
(3) Revolution and Reaction
(4) Progress and Decadence
(5) Approaches to Culture
(6) And (7) Two options selected from a panel of topics in the senior honours year
(8) Dissertation: This must be on a topic approved by the Convenor

Table 4

That first year, two of our six students achieved first class honours degrees.
I should briefly mention another activity that helped to forge a sense of common identity among the staff, and to put Aberdeen's cultural history on the map. Four successful international conferences were held in the summers of 1987 to 1990.
For a while it looked as if our enjoyment of the teaching was going to have diminishing, perhaps terminally diminishing, returns. Our class of six was fol-

lowed by four, and then by three. In a naked attempt at recruitment we proposed a second-year *feeder* course from 1988, but this was turned down—this time with no hope of appeal. But suddenly in 1989 recruitment took off, presumably due to favourable recommendations among the students: we had thirteen, thirteen, seventeen. By our ninth year of operation, we had twenty-nine graduates.

What sort of students did we get? Those with the initiative and determination to change from their original direction. Later, in the 90s, as the University made more and more effort to recruit *mature students* (a technical term meaning those more than 23 years old when they enter) we got a disproportionate number of those. Mature students, who often turn to university to change the direction of a life they have come to see as unsatisfying, tend to opt for courses that offer cultural enrichment rather than the financial riches held out by vocational courses. At least one of our adult students used cultural history to rebuild his life more profoundly. On 6 July 1988 the Piper Alpha oil platform off Aberdeen exploded killing 167 workers; there were 59 survivors. One of these, Bob Ballantyne, entered the University as a mature student and chose to graduate in cultural history. Some time later, when all of our courses had been modularised (that is, they had become self-contained and graded at the end of each course, so that one could take individual cultural history courses without signing up for the whole degree), we also got much more than our share of visiting Europeans and Americans, attracted by unusual courses they could not get at home. And over the years there was roughly a two to one ratio of women to men among cultural history graduates.

A major change which accompanied our success in the 1990s was the decline of our pool of teachers. It almost seemed as if staff numbers were inversely proportional to our success in attracting students. The fall-off in contributors might have been due to increasing teaching duties in a *home* department, or transfer elsewhere in Britain, or the non-renewal of a temporary contract, or retirement, or death—all of which affected individuals among our staff. Or someone who had given a few lectures over the years would go on research leave, and on return would be unwilling to pick up the responsibility again. Or a contributor who had at the beginning given ten or twelve lectures a year was now down to two or three. By the late 1990s, more than half the teaching was done by four or five core staff, and wider contributions had become more the exception than the norm.

But there were other changes in the 1990s which may have contributed to this situation. In 1992, due to our growing numbers of students, Cultural History was for the first time granted the status of an independent academic department, and the Convenor given a formal part-time appointment as Head of Department. During the following year, the first appointment of a full-time Lecturer in Cultural History was made: this was a cultural anthropologist, who planned and introduced a successful second-year feeder course, as well as a popular senior honours option. The new department was housed in a renovated ancient building away from the main campus.

After two years this arrangement was subjected to an *Internal Teaching Review*, an inquisition based on the government's official *Teaching Quality Assessment*, and like the latter requiring a mountain of paper describing every course in the smallest detail. The proceedings of the review were notable for the extremely strong support for our teaching given by our students, and also by our external examiners from past years such as Roy Porter and Peter Burke. The result of the inquisition was that—for various reasons which I need not go in to—the experiment of departmental status for cultural history was judged not to be a success. The group was to be moved back on campus to lessen any tendency of the students to consider themselves special and apart, and the administration of the group was to be under the supervision of another established department. Philosophy was chosen, chiefly in order to avoid the big guns of History and English, both of which tended to be hostile to cultural history. Powerful individuals in those two departments regarded cultural history not only as inferior as a discipline, but also as a seducer of their intended students. On the other hand, the Teaching Review recommended that full time appointments to cultural history should be extended. In early 1995 I was appointed Director, and my colleague Bill Scott, historian of the French Revolution, was made full-time Senior Lecturer, in addition to our anthropologist Lecturer. We were also given a third of the time of a Teaching Fellow, Leigh Clayton (a Lecturer in all but name, who did not have a Lecturer's research commitment), and were further supported by Peter McCaffery, a retired sociologist who was paid by the hour. Partly as a result of its success, the cultural history group was becoming very different from the wide circle of enthusiastic volunteers who had initiated it.

Cultural history flourished at this time, under the most sympathetic dean we ever encountered. Now that we had secure staffing, we were able from 1996 to introduce an additional second-year course, *The Culture of the human and natural environment*, which complemented the recruiting effects of our introduction to anthropology.

At the same time, the compulsory core of courses was maintained, and indeed extended to a compulsory course on the culture of the 20th century to be taken in fourth year. So unlike in all the other programmes in the Arts Faculty, our students were allowed a free choice only in their two optional courses. Nobody seemed to mind this lack of choice—except perhaps members of other departments, who objected that cultural history seemed always to be special case, a constant anomaly.

1995/6 Compulsory courses:	
CU 3002	Reason, Enlightenment, Revolution (9)
CU 3003	Approaches to Culture 1 (3)
CU 3502	Romanticism, Progress and Decadence (9)
CU 3503	Approaches to Culture 2 (3)
CU 4012	Modern Times: Perspectives on the Twentieth Century (6)
CU 4506	Cultural History Dissertation (6)
Plus one optional course from each semester:	
CU 4002	Structuralism and After (6)
CU 4003	Art and Commerce (6)
CU 4004	Race and Politics (6)
CU 4005	Women in History (6)
CU 4006	Patterns of Power and Politics in Modern French History (6)
CU 4502	Childhood (6)
CU 4503	Culture of the Renaissance and Reformation (6)
CU 4504	Music and Musical Life in the Twentieth Century (6)
CU 4505	Religion and Rejection of Religion in Western Europe (6)

Table 5

I have already said that at this period of our greatest numbers of students at all three levels, the bulk of the teaching was done by four or five of us, of whom three were full time. We were desperately overworked, with ratios of students to staff which would not have been tolerated in infant school, but a now unsympathetic dean was deaf to pleas for more staff. It has been a feature of British universities since the financial crises of the 1980s and a political call for public accountability that a supposedly accurate price is put on everything from paper clips to staff salaries to tractors for the playing fields. When I was director of the programme in 1998, the figures of income and expenditure showed that cultural history's student numbers were bringing in about £200.000, but our costs were less than £100.000; we were thus subsidising the rest of the Arts Faculty. I argued strongly for the appointment of two new staff members to relieve the teaching overload, but was told that these figures were merely notional. Four years later, equally notional figures were used the other way to justify the dismantling of the programme. "Cultural History is losing money," said the new dean, without providing any evidence. Now the figures were considered not notional, but the basis for real cuts.

One other result of the success of our two second-year courses was that these were now made prerequisites for entry into cultural history honours, thus making it like all other disciplines in the Faculty, and removing an anomaly which would upset any tidy-minded dean. This meant that we could no longer freely take in refugees from English or History or wherever who had become unhappy with their original intentions. Recruitment to the honours years did suffer, although not radically so at first.

One very obvious problem with cultural history teaching being in the hands of just a few teachers was that it became vulnerable to any change in personnel. My contract was not renewed in 1999, and my colleague Bill Scott retired a year later. We were replaced by new appointments from outside, but this could be tricky. To go back a few years, before I was made Director the post had been advertised externally, but it was found that the outside candidates were not sufficiently in tune with the existing group. Later, when replacements for myself and Bill Scott came to be appointed, their expertise naturally differed from ours, and so the core courses had to change. Leigh Clayton, our teaching fellow, who was now essentially full time in Cultural History, was particularly helpful in keeping the 19th- and 20th-century core courses going, but the Enlightenment course, which since the very start in 1986 had been the bedrock of our programme, was replaced in 2001 by a less focused course with a much longer timespan, *Continuity and change, 1500-1800*.

The real bombshell came in 2002, when as I have already said the Dean of Arts claimed that Cultural History was making a loss, and dissolved the group. Our anthropologist who had been my successor as Director moved to the new Anthropology Department. Leigh Clayton's contract was not renewed. There is a shameful suspicion that this was because after so many years teaching on fixed-term contracts, it was a legal requirement that at the next renewal the University had to give her a permanent contract. Rainer Brömer, who had been hired as a one-year replacement and kept on for a second year, was also "let go", to use the euphemism. The remaining staff joined the History Department, with my successor as historian of science, Ben Marsden, as convenor of the cultural history programme. With these changes, and especially the sackings, the core of the programme fell apart. The 19th- and 20th-century courses were immediately abandoned. The second-year courses did not long survive, and the prerequisites for cultural history honours became an unheard-of combination of history and religious studies and anthropology courses.

The effects on student recruitment and morale were obvious. The changes were announced before the end of summer 2002. Many of the existing junior honours students simply disappeared, and did not return for their senior honours year.

A University-wide reorganization followed a year later. Every seven years or so Aberdeen University is subjected to a major structural change, intended to transform it into the hottest university outside London, Oxford, and Cambridge. Somehow this never quite seems to work as it should. The big idea in 2003 was the abolition of faculties and departments, and the establishment of colleges and schools. History and Art History and Divinity and Philosophy became a single school, resulting in a final loss of autonomy for what little remained of cultural history. Despite his heroic efforts to keep the distinctive degree going, Ben Marsden's position as convenor of the cultural history programme was abolished, and, as another example, the approval of dissertation topics for cultural history students was passed to the historian responsible for the history dissertations. He was described to me by one colleague as clearly an enemy of cultural history.

As there came to be less and less that was distinctive about cultural history courses, so students combined them more and more with other disciplines as joint honours. Early on, we had been able to resist attempts to bring us in to joint honours combinations by using the argument that the core programme could not be broken into small parts suitable for combination, and in any case Cultural History was *the* archetypal joint honours course, since it encompassed so many diverse disciplines. As a result the great majority of the cultural history graduates over the first fifteen years, during the up curve, did single honours, whereas almost all of the recent graduates have done joint.

From the other side, the side of the need for homogenization, of the avoidance of anomaly, comes the argument from historians that "We're all cultural historians now." I suppose a few members of our history departments are using approaches that were once the province of the cultural historian. But they are no more true teachers of cultural history than American teachers of English literature who were so excited by what they called "the new historicism", otherwise known as old cultural history.

And now the end is in sight at Aberdeen. But how good it was while it lasted! And yet all is not quite lost. A phoenix rises from the ashes. Due to the energy of my colleagues David Smith, Ben Marsden, Ralph O'Connor, and others, an international conference to celebrate 21 years of cultural history at Aberdeen was held in July 2007. Out of that grew the International Society for Cultural History, with its own successful conferences at Ghent and Brisbane (and now Turku). And the international network so established has led indirectly to this conference in Mainz. I gather also from David that there is now the possibility of an international journal of cultural history. And back in Aberdeen he runs a successful continuing cultural history seminar series.

This has been a very personal and inevitably partial account of our experience in Aberdeen, where we were able to build a cultural history programme from nothing, initially at very little cost. Different parts of that experience will resonate with different people. Some of it will not be applicable outside Scotland at all. But I hope that what I have said will be of interest and of some use to you all.

Perspectives of the Cultural History in Latvia: The 20th century and beyond

MĀRTIŅŠ MINTAURS

In the course of the 20th century history-writing has been frequently discussed in public debate on related political and ideological issues as well as within the profession itself representing a wide spectrum of concepts and methodological approaches across the field.[1] Thus, when dealing with the writing of cultural history regarded as a specific part of historiography, one has to be aware and take into account a few indispensable aspects.

First of all, it is a given that the very notions of both *culture* and *history* have been changing recurrently[2] since the turn of the 20th century thus allowing talk of several *turns* in writing cultural history.[3] Another aspect to mention is that also cultural history has been placed at a point where different theoretical concepts had been intersecting with the local situation in the social, political and academic domain of particular societies.[4] Moreover, considering the variety of themes and research topics linked with the label of *cultural history* it is, perhaps, even more exposed to identity-making practice[5] and related issues having a certain feedback effect upon historiography.

The subject of this paper is the writing of cultural history in Latvia during the 20th century with a particular focus on its conceptual framework applied by the authors investigating socio-cultural aspects of the past. Despite the fact that cultural history of present-day Latvia has been an *ad hoc* subject since the late

---

1 IGGERS, 1997, p. 8-16.
2 SCHORN-SCHÜTTE, 2001, p. 489-515.
3 See: ULBRICHT, 2003.
4 DANIEL, 2006, p. 195-219.
5 KASCHUBA, 2001, p. 19-42.

19th century onwards, one could hardly find a single work reflecting the structure or contents of such studies nor the concepts applied in publications.[6]

Therefore, the intention here is to provide a historiography survey of the field while the limited space here only permits the outlining of the main trends and the mentioning of major actors of the field. For this reason we consider it useful to focus mainly on the works published in Latvia due to the direct impact they had on history-writing in Latvia compared to the studies issued abroad during the period of Soviet occupation from 1944 to 1991, when the access to such publications was very limited.

There are four distinctive stages in the historiography of Latvia in the 20th century[7] speaking both for the conceptual and institutional level, of which we should provide a brief characterization before turning to a more detailed insight into development of cultural history-writing. In fact, as it has already been noted by historian Andrejs Plakans, the shift from one stage to another "more often than not took the form of *replacement* [emph.i.o.] rather than *transition* [emph.i.o.] and contained far more discontinuity than continuity".[8]

(1) The Baltic-German tradition of history-writing activities in the present-day Latvia and Estonia dates back to the late 17th and early 18th century, marking the end of chronicle-writing practice of the mediaeval period. This tradition was closely linked to the awareness of specific conditions of the Baltic Provinces like Kurland (a Duchy *de iure* subjected to the Polish-Lithuanian Commonwealth, 1561-1795, then Russia), Livland and Estland both being the provinces of Sweden (1621-1721) and the Russian Empire (1721-1918) subsequently.

(2) The second tradition, one might call the Latvian national historiography, emerged in the Republic of Latvia during the inter-war period (1918-1940), positioning itself as a clear opposite to the Baltic-German in many aspects, including the issues of cultural history.

(3) The Soviet-Latvian historiography, intended to replace both the Baltic-German and the Latvian national tradition, was set in the second half of the 1940s along with the re-establishment of the Soviet political control over the Baltic states shared some characteristics of history-writing in the Soviet

---

6 The comprehensive article by Helēna Šimkuva should be mentioned here although dealing primary with the attitude towards the cultural heritage of the Baltic German community in Latvia describing briefly the concepts used in writing cultural history, see: ŠIMKUVA, 2001, p. 405-426.
7 See for details: ZELČE, 2000, p. 40-42.
8 PLAKANS, 1999, p. 293.

Union in general. It was enduring *pro forma* up to the year 1991 while starting to collapse as early as the late 1980s.

(4) The historiography of Latvia during the Post-Soviet period (approximately twenty years from regaining independence in 1991 or, if still considering the terms of formal political periodization, conditionally up to the year 2004), when the Republic of Latvia became a member state of the European Union.

In the following, an attempt has been made to provide a provisional insight into developments of cultural history-writing at each stage of the Latvian historiography mentioned above, giving some reflections on the institutional level of the field as well as on themes and concepts shared by distinct authors.

I

The contents of the Baltic-German historiography have been previously analyzed in an anthology[9] as well as in numerous case studies, while the local traditions of writing cultural history is a subject less reflected on so far. This is probably due to the fact that the amount of publications in a way corresponding to cultural history is impressive considering the lack of standard works in this area.

In order to comprehend the situation during which the first attempts to write regional cultural history had emerged, one should look at the last two decades of the 19th century. The Baltic German historiography was strongly connected with a specific identity of the community, finding itself placed under dual pressure from the Latvian resp. Estonian community as well as the Russian administration at this period of time.[10] Therefore the Baltic-German historians were mostly concerned with the agrarian history and history of law having a certain political context regarding the actual issues[11] wherewith becoming remarkably ethnocentric even in the eyes of their contemporaries.[12]

---

9 See: GARLEFF, 1986 and HEHN, 1986.
10 PISTOHLKORS, 1995.
11 PISTOHLKORS, 1986.
12 See: KEYSERLING, 1881 speaking of distinct interpretation of history among the Estonians, and compare to: GARLEFF, 1986, p. 270 about the general opinion in the Baltic German historiography around the outbreak of the World War I.

At the academic level history in the Baltic Provinces was represented at the University of Dorpat/Tartu (reopened in 1804)[13] yet political factors came into force here in the second half of the 19th century. With the unification policy becoming more intensive especially since 1883, a permanent tension between the Baltic-German community and the Imperial Government set in because the hitherto German-dominated local educational and administration system was gradually taken over by the Russian officials.[14]

At the turn of the 20th century the impact of historical school of jurisprudence upon the Baltic German historiography intended to confirm the *historical rights* of the Baltic Germans[15] seems quite obvious. By that time the historical school of jurisprudence developed a specific form of cultural history, particularly dealing with legal culture believed to represent the *national spirit* of community[16]. This should also be taken into account in order to understand why for most of the Baltic German authors the investigation of regional history had turned into a representation of their ethnic and cultural identity.[17]

However, there is no need to exaggerate the significance of political context attributed to the Baltic-German historiography, as these activities, though constantly supported by local nobility corporations both in terms of research management and financing, could also be inspired by scientific interests of historians and other investigators, aware of the value inherent to historical materials they were dealing with.

During the late 19th and early 20th century the development of historical studies in the Baltic Provinces was left to relay on associations like the *Kurländische Gesellschaft für Literatur und Kunst* (1815-1939) located in Mitau and the *Gesellschaft für Geschichte und Altertumskunde der Ostseeprovinzen Russlands* in Riga (1834-1939), as described above. These organizations became the only institutions to perform a systematic historical research in the region and also contributed to the investigation of the cultural history.[18]

Around the last decades of the 19th century the shift in historiography was evident: the collecting of textual and archaeological materials turned into the first systematic accounts of cultural history. At first, the activities carried out by

---

13 GARLEFF, 1978, p. 349.
14 THADEN, 1984, p. 221-226.
15 LAZDIŅŠ, 2006, p. 36.
16 SCHORN-SCHÜTTE, 2001, p. 498.
17 See: LENZ, 1986, p. 214-215 and compare to: HIRSCHHAUSEN, 2006, p. 345-349.
18 HACKMANN, 2001, p. 21-22.

Perspectives of the Cultural History in Latvia

local history museums[19] manifested a kind of pragmatic or even didactic understanding of this task resulting in two remarkable exhibitions devoted to cultural history of the Baltic Provinces Livland and Kurland, established in Riga (1883) and in Mitau (1886) respectively.[20] Nevertheless, this approach was still somewhere in between the passing tradition of antiquarianism and the possibility for a synthesis of historical materials with *cultural significance*.

When speaking about the origins of writing cultural history in the Baltic Provinces, the name of Hermann Freiherr von Bruiningk (1849-1927) needs to be mentioned. Bruiningk was known mostly for his various activities, such as holding the office of secretary of the nobility corporation *Livländische Ritterschaft*, president of the *Gesellschaft für Geschichte und Altertumskunde* and the organizer of historical source editions *Livländische Güterurkunden* (I-II, 1908-1923) at various times in his life, yet he should also be remembered for his ca. 160 publications devoted to cultural history themes.[21]

In 1882 von Bruinigk published an essay which was to become a corner stone for development of professional cultural history studies in the Baltic Provinces.[22] It was the first attempt to outline parameters for the local history of high-culture production in the sense common for the Victorian age,[23] including activities in crafts and fine arts, particularly in architecture, sculpture and design.

This approach was later sustained in the works of architect and art historian Wilhelm Neumann (1849-1919)[24] emphasizing the same apparently *impartial* issues as seen from a perspective of the Russian administration. However, the turn towards cultural history was explained by von Bruiningk himself in 1906 as a reaction to current political situation demanding additional steps to protect the Baltic German culture: *"Heute redet man nur noch von der Erhaltung unserer Kultur, und so hat die Geschichte selbst der Geschichtsforschung neue Aufgaben gestellt."*[25]

---

19 See: BUCHHOLTZ, 1887 and NEANDER, 1894.
20 NEUMANN, 1914, p. 286.
21 GARLEFF, 1978, p. 347-348.
22 BRUININGK, 1882.
23 BURKE, 2004, p. 32. Apropos, von Bruiningk's personal connection to the English culture mentioned by his contemporaries (HOLLANDER, 1933, p. 9) could also be of some importance here.
24 See, for instance: NEUMANN, 1913, p. 14-54.
25 Quoted after: HOLLANDER, 1933, p. 20.

One particular subject of cultural history von Bruiningk was most successful at was the history of Livonian Church; he became the only historian of the Baltic Provinces to be prized for his work devoted to late mediaeval practice of worships in Riga.[26] The book was recognized as a significant case study on an international level by a connoisseur Albert von Poncelet (Brussels) in 1905 because of its complex approach integrating an essay about the universal meaning of the Roman-Catholic liturgy and the thorough reconstruction of its use in the specific conditions of Livonia.[27]

However, the interest in the latest concepts of history-writing in Baltic German historiography at the beginning of the 20th century was altogether modest, as most of the authors preferred the academic tradition of historicism as represented by Leopold von Ranke (1795-1886) and Georg Waitz (1813-1886).[28] The evidence to the contrary seems to be everything but occasional, including a publication titled *Moderne Geschichtswisseschaft* appearing in the proceedings of the *Kurländische Gesellschaft für Literatur und Kunst* in 1909.[29] Written by Georg Wiedemann (1857-1927), a history teacher in a province gymnasium,[30] this article provided an introduction to ideas of Karl Lamprecht (1856-1915) as explained in his book published a year before that. This score is significant for the local historiography itself, as it is the first text pertaining to notable problems of the craft.

It would obviously be an overstatement to claim that this was how the Baltic-German historiography participated in the methodological discussion called the *Lamprechtstreit*[31], because the purpose of Wiedemann's publication was in fact to inform the local audience about the possibility for a new interpretation of history based less on political circumstances and individual characters of its actors, but pointing to the role of geographical factors and social psychology. According to the author quoting Lamprecht, this approach obviously has to include the history of ideas reflecting different aspects of human cultural activity typical for a certain period of time.

It is hard to estimate the relevance of this arrangement towards the new concept of history for the Baltic-German historiography, if any. In fact, the once notorious standard work in history of the Baltic Provinces compiled by another

---

26 BRUININGK, 1904, p. 45-272.
27 HOLLANDER, 1933, p. 21-22.
28 WITTRAM, 1936, p. 7.
29 WIEDEMANN, 1910, p. 10-20.
30 LENZ, 1970, p. 865.
31 DANIEL, 2006, p. 210-216.

prominent historian of the day, Leonid Arbusow, Jr. (1882-1951), was set very much in the previous positivistic tradition, while some brief characteristics of geographical and ethnographical milieu were present here as well.[32] One could also presume that the tradition of *Landesgeschichte* inherent to the Baltic-German historiography of the 19th and the 20th century in general still provided at least a theoretical perspective for a more complex view on the issues of cultural history, although not without certain ethnic and political bias.

The Baltic-German historiography continued after the World War I in the new-born nation-states, the Republic of Latvia and the Republic of Estonia. In the case of Latvia the Baltic-German historians again found themselves in a situation believing in the need to underline the *German factor* in the local history of political events and social life to cultural aspects; they recurrently opposed the views shared by representatives of the Latvian national historiography.[33] Yet the inter-war period proved to be too short to write a comprehensive study in cultural history.

After the displacement of the Baltic-German community to Western Europe in the course of the World War II and due to the *Iron Curtain* afterwards, this tradition of history-writing up to the 1970s had little chance of influencing the developments of historical science in Latvia apart from exclusions such as the history of art and exact sciences[34] but on the empiric level alone, while any theoretical concepts of non-Soviet origin incurred critique.

II

The second stage of the history-writing process in Latvia during the 20th century is related to the inter-war period and the establishment of the Latvian national historiography. The Republic of Latvia founded in 1918 set up its cultural policy according to concepts of political nationalism, which was common for every newly created nation state in the Central and Eastern Europe in their own particular way.[35]

---

32 ARBUSOW, 1918, p. 288-313.
33 HEHN, 1986, p. 377.
34 ŠIMKUVA, 2001, p. 414-415.
35 STRADIŅŠ, 1998, p. 47-48.

In September 1919, while the country was still engaged in the Independence War (1918-1920), the University of Latvia was founded in Riga including the Department of History at the Faculty of Philology. At the same time the Latvian National Archive was founded[36] gathering historical documents from the early 13th century onwards, today preserving one of the major collections in Europe.

While some of the Baltic-German academic professionals were initially represented at the University, ethno-political contradictions of the day[37] led to a split in the academic community in the course of time: one example was the case of Arbusow[38], who was blamed for a biased misinterpretation of the Latvian history and thus forced to leave the University in 1935.

Indeed, one could hardly speak of any continuity in the traditions founded by the Baltic-German authors regarding the contents of national historiography: instead of the previous trend towards the somewhat regional approach of the *Landesgeschichte,* a different concept of *Volksgeschichte* stating the history of Latvians became the main priority for of all kinds of historical investigations.[39]

The interest among the Latvian intellectuals concerned with the issues of nation-building activities around 1900 in their native history was until then mostly evident in the field of recurrent ethnographical studies of folklore and material culture objects.[40] Now, as the national state was founded, the first contemplations to write history for the future surfaced in the early 1920s. Especially the efforts of historian Augusts Tentelis (1876-1942), later holding key positions at the University and other institutions relevant for the craft,[41] should be mentioned among others, for he was the first to formulate essential concepts of how Latvian historians ought to create a new interpretation of history.

In 1923 Tentelis published a declaration considering "the nearest tasks for Latvian historians"[42] requesting a comprehensive approach of history while placing an emphasis on themes and subjects connected in particular to the Latvians and their historical impact seen in the European context. In other words, the new-born history of Latvia should not merely represent *national science* for

---

36 PLAKANS, 1999, p. 293. Today: Latvian Natonal History Archive.
37 See: KAUSE, 1995, p. 113-120.
38 As presented in detail by Prof. Ilgvars Misāns in his study *Leonid Arbusow d. J. und die lettische Geschichtsschreibung* (2007), a manuscript.
39 PLAKANS, 1999, p. 303.
40 PRIEDĪTE, 1999, p. 4-17. Compare to: WOHLFART, 2006, p. 215-261.
41 For A. Tentelis' professional and administrative activities see: ŠNĒ, 2009, p. 53-71.
42 TENTELIS, 1926, p. 38-44. The text was published three years after presentation in a scholar workshop.

some political or ideological reason, but rather because every kind of historical explanation requires a certain subjectivity -stemming from the national (i.e. ethnic) identity or professional disposition of the author.[43]

It should also be noted that Tentelis was quite critical towards the state of affairs in national historiography taking shape in front of his own eyes, pointing at what he called "a dilettantish romanticism" of attempts to reconstruct the structure and forms of social life attributed to prehistoric society,[44] in fact, a subject of bitter methodological discussions among Latvian historians and ethnologists soon after. Tentelis also found it necessary to pay tribute to the Baltic-German historians for their activities in the field of the *Landesgeschichte* while admitting that "oversight" of the native inhabitants has been a typical feature elsewhere, related to ethnic and class prejudices of the ruling elite.[45]

The claim to "rediscover the true Latvian history" was to remain a wishful and yet current issue throughout the twenty years of independence as showed by statements of Arveds Švābe (1888-1959), the most prominent Latvian historian of the inter-war period. In fact, it was as late as in 1940 when Švābe was still reminding Latvian historians of their duty to achieve this new paradigm in (and for) the history of Latvia in order to provide a comprehensive picture for the coming generations: "[...] for it is the basic theses in present-day historiography that researching history must rely on the investigation of the natives and their land [...] and this certainly has to be observed also for the history of Latvia".[46]

The development of Latvian national historiography in the inter-war period was also influenced by the transformation of the political system after *coup d'état* in May 15, 1934 from a liberal democracy to the dictatorship of Kārlis Ulmanis (1877-1942) lasting till June of 1940. In 1936 the Institute for the History of Latvia was established under the guidance of Tentelis as a state-promoted organizational centre for history studies on an academic level. Besides, the Chair for History of Latvia was established at the University led by Arveds Švābe. The official aim for the Institute, also reflecting the expectations of authoritarian regime regarding history-writing practice, was "to research the history [...] according to the spirit of nationalism and truth".[47]

---

43 ID., p. 41.
44 ID., p. 38, 43.
45 ID., p. 39.
46 ŠVĀBE, 1940, p. 53.
47 ZEIDS, 1939, p. 8.

It's effect on history-writing obviously becoming ethnocentric, looked quaint when in 1939 Tentelis explained that it has never been the true intention of the Latvian conception of history to replace the old (i.e. the Baltic-German historiography) for its own sake, just to change the old biased perspectives.[48] However, it did not take long for Švābe to explanation contrary opinion of the same aims including *inter alia* "the work of *gradual verification i.e. deconstruction* of historiography created by the Baltic [German] nobility and burghers in order to construct a new history of the nation".[49] As noted before, this task was later successfully taken over by the Soviet historiography.

On the other hand, when becoming an important element in the ideology of Ulmanis' authoritarian regime,[50] historiography also profited from this protectionism leading to institutional changes as well as the possibility to obtain remarkable funding now available from the state.[51] For example, it has been stated, with some naivety, that the Institute provided a chance to activate history *research* per se while historians at the University were mainly engaged in history *teaching*.[52] It was also during this time that the first academic periodicals devoted to history appeared in Latvian. Along with the publication series, which started already in the 1920s by the University of Latvia and the Latvian National Archive,[53] there were two more academic journals issued up to the year 1940 being the quarterly *Journal* of the Institute published since 1937 (resumed in 1991) and another periodical magazine concerned with history named *Antiquities and Arts* (*Senatne un Māksla*) issued by the Ministry of Education since 1936.

Although there was a certain progress regarding the institutionalization of history studies and crafts in general, constraints were nonetheless placed on the contents of history. At an official level the spirit of nationalism mentioned above was explained as the duty of historians to demonstrate a continuity of the Latvian nation as if it had prevailed since the 13th century[54] in order to maintain legitimacy of the present authoritarian Latvian state in general and its political system in particular. As the matter of fact, no institutions existed with the purpose to take care of the issues of cultural history in particular, although one could

---

48 TENTELIS, 1939, p. 20.
49 ŠVĀBE, 1940, p. 58.
50 HEHN, 1986, p. 388.
51 FELDMANIS, 1995, p. 133-138.
52 ŠTERNS, 1981, p. 3-9.
53 See: PLAKANS, 1999, p. 295-296.
54 ŠVĀBE, 1940, p. 112-113.

indeed speak of a kind of *Kulturkampf* being carried out during the 1930s as to *Latvianize* the current social and cultural milieu of Latvia.[55]

However, Andrejs Plakans has argued for a different assessment of the tendency towards writing an exclusively national history at that time. He also observed that the methodological consequences pointed at similar calls for "history from the bottom up" in Western historiography since the 1960s, advancing into studies of particular social groups carried out by the authors themselves belonging to these communities, e.g. in the case of history of women or the Native Americans.[56] If it is not regarded as an example of "reading history backwards"[57], this statement indeed has a certain point; yet one should also keep in mind that the Latvian national historiography obviously tended to emphasize every possible contrast between the Latvian and the Baltic-German culture taken for granted, to say the least.[58]

Latvian nationalism was the leading paradigm for cultural history-writing as seen from the works devoted to the Duchy of Kurland, a favorite research topic of that time. A conclusive analyses recently performed by Imants Lancmanis[59] asserts that it was yet another way for the authoritarian regime to gain a kind of historical substantiation by using associations with the idealized image of Duke Jacob Kettler (1610-1682) compared to the one of Ulmanis as the new *pater patriae*. Curiously enough, the fact that it was a state ruled by the Baltic-German nobility and that the heir apparent of the mediaeval Livonia was far less popular in traditional history interpretations of the inter-war period, actually played no considerable role here.

Another aspect of interest inherent to the Latvian historiography of the inter-war period was that the historical school of jurisprudence remained in its place, but had a different vector: for now efforts were made to substantiate the *historical equity* for the Latvians. Besides, the prevalence of so-called *inner history* over other aspects of past human investigation[60] also speaks for a typical feature inherited along with this concept.[61]

---

55 BLEIERE, 2006, p. 153-155.
56 PLAKANS, 1999, p. 304.
57 DAVIES, 1997, p. 1000.
58 ŠIMKUVA, 2001, p. 409.
59 LANCMANIS, 2005, p. 89-95.
60 ŠVĀBE, 1940, p. 63.
61 SCHORN-SCHÜTTE, 2001, p. 498.

Arveds Švābe, with the history of law being a centerpiece of his professional interests, was just the person to maintain this continuity of concepts[62] based on condition that law and legal culture in a given society are phenomena arising from the special "community of social life" shared by a particular nation.[63] This conception, obviously adopted from Numa Fustel de Coulanges (1830-1889), was used in Švābe's work *The Latvian Legal History* approaching the development of legal institutions as a part of social history including historical mentality of the native population from the Viking Age to the second half of the 19th century.[64]

This leads us to the key question of this paper, as legal history was actually one of the core elements in the historiography of Latvia in the inter-war period. As for the conceptual frame of cultural history, we start with a general explanation of the term available in the first national encyclopedia of Latvia issued during the inter-war period and edited by Švābe, including two different aspects in its definition.[65]

On the one hand, a close connection was noted between the domain of cultural history, believed to differ from the routine studies of political and military events of the past, as well as of sociology and ethnology, the latter including research of both material culture items and folklore materials representing the *mental culture* of the nation. In this way, the concept of cultural history in question here actually reflected the ideas of Lamprecht[66] although the author was not quoted directly in the text pointing at Kurt Breysig's (1866-1940) "attempt to find the laws for the development of culture" instead.[67]

On the other hand, the definition of the subject was constructed to compound the Neo-Kantian perspective and concepts of the *Geisteswissenschaften* alike, explaining that

> "[...] cultural history, though investigating individual facts representing certain epochs and regions, is not a discipline of its own: it is just a constituent part of historical science in general, dealing with the specific contents of religion, philosophy, economics, law and other spheres of human activities".[68]

---

62 LAZDIŅŠ, 2006, p. 22-23.
63 ŠVĀBE, 1940, p. 76.
64 ŠVĀBE, 1934-1935, col. 22115-22116.
65 Kultūras vēsture, 1933-1934, col. 18882.
66 SCHORN-SCHÜTTE, 2001, p. 501.
67 Kultūras vēsture, 1933-1934, col. 18882.
68 ID.

At this point it is possible to assert that a general connection to the German tradition in the philosophy of history remained the most evident in Latvia during the inter-war period, as seen from the works quoted in contemporary publications. A particular interest in the epistemology theory of Wilhelm Windelband (1848-1915) and Heinrich Rickert (1863-1936) was shared by philosopher Teodors Celms (1893-1989), actually concerned with the Husserlian phenomenology and cultural critic.[69] In relation to history Celms emphasized Rickert's concept of *theorethische Wertbeziehung* concluding that "it is not the task of a historian to judge the events of the past, rather to establish their significance in accordance to some cultural value of an overall importance - be it science, art, morality etc."[70]

This was an opinion similar to the principles of history-writing proposed by Augusts Tentelis[71] speaking of the necessity to understand the author of a historical text describing a world of his own (although not using the word *mentality* directly[72]) thus allowing the historian to reveal facts related to cultural history to an extent greater than before.

The problem whether an objective estimation according to cultural history events was possible or not was picked up by Švābe in his conceptual essay devoted to tasks of the Latvian historians.[73] However, his answer was a strict refusal, looking upon cultural history as precisely distinguished by its immanent subjectivity. To confirm this statement, Švābe turned to the thesis produced by Johan Huizinga (1872-1945) about history as a science of a somewhat spiritual form inherent to a certain culture.[74] Therefore, history on the whole and especially cultural history in particular can only be understood by representatives of the culture in question which in turn makes explanatory contradictions inevitable considering the variety of appraisal criteria and the force of irrational factors.

Another way of negotiating the specific objectives of cultural history and the possible directions documentation was represented by historian Robert Vipper (1859-1954), who in 1924 decided to emigrate from the Soviet Union to Latvia,

---

69   For the biography and works of T. Celms see: KŪLE, 2002, p. 9-33.
70   CELMS, 1939, p. 109.
71   TENTELIS, 1926, p. 42.
72   Compare to a remark of Plakans saying that the Latvian inter-war period historiography seemed to know "nothing of Marc Bloch, Lucien Febvre, and the *Annales* School [...]", see: PLAKANS, 1999, p. 304.
73   ŠVĀBE, 1940, p. 89-90.
74   Quoting the German version of J. Huizinga's work: *Wege der Kulturgeschichte* (1930), ID., p.90.

where he stayed for the next sixteen years. As a professor at the University of Latvia from 1927 to 1938, Vipper lectured on the modern history and was also interested in the issues concerning philosophy and methodology of history. His book *The Great Problems of History* published in 1940 provided a brief survey of theories from Vico (1668-1744) to the discussions of the early 20th century.

Following the Neo-Kantian distinction between the exact and humanitarian sciences, Vipper pointed out the subjectivity of all history explanations[75] while concentrating on the German Historical School of Economics and in particular on Werner Sombart's (1863-1941) concept of *erklärende Wissenschaft,* which he believed constituted a new paradigm of historical methodology.[76] However, according to his definition, this approach turned out to be merely a description of *cultural development* without any distinct borders.

In his theoretical contemplations Vipper used to agree with Oswald Spengler (1880-1936) to maintain the idea about cultural history as a complex subject.[77] Vipper also noted that his perspective was different from that of Spengler while Vipper himself was less interested in, as he stated, the aesthetical and philosophical issues of history attributed to Spengler's approach rather than in the events responding to "the social way of life, political changes and wars as well as the destiny shared by theories of a religious, moral, social and political origin".[78]

In 1936 Vipper published a preposition for new periodization of the "social and cultural evolution" in Europe as follows: 1) The Age of Barbarism from the 6th to the 10th century; 2) The Age of Ecclesiastical Culture from the 10th to the end of the 13th century; 3) The Age of Urban Culture from the 13th century to the 1560s; 4) The Age of Aristocratic and Monarchical Culture from the 1560s to 1789; 5) The Age of Bourgeois or Democratic Culture from 1789 to the 20th century included.[79]

This system was clearly inspired by Spengler's ideas as seen from Vipper's perspective, speaking of a period covering three or four centuries and characterized by a particular complex of ideas and the associated *Weltanschauung* as the core of this periodization.[80] Although the very notion of culture was not explicated by Vipper in any particular detail, it is evident from the context that it

---

75 VIPERS, 1940, p. 29.
76 ID., p. 137.
77 ID., p. 117.
78 VIPERS, 1940, p. 120.
79 VIPERS, 1936, p. 9-10.
80 ID., p. 9.

was the history of ideas and social institutions to constitute the evolution process mentioned above. Once again, nearly every aspect of human history was to be included, e.g. agriculture and industry, science and art, administration, finances as well as the foundations of customs, family and social structure of society.[81]

When dealing with the theoretical issues of cultural history another Russian emigrant, Vasilii Sinaisky (1876-1949), a professor of civil law at the University of Latvia from 1922 to 1944,[82] should be mentioned regarding his theory about the origins of culture and law. Interpretation of culture as "the manifestation of religious spirit" offered by Sinaisky[83] resembles the ideas of Pavel Florensky (1882-1937), yet it could be more fascinating to look at some of Sinaisky's thoughts on the role of writing in ancient cultures, e.g. hieroglyphs, expressing either a technical or secular and sacral meaning in ancient religious rites, jurisprudence, philosophy and architecture,[84] actually responding to far more recent conceptions to that point.[85]

On the other hand, the studies of V. Sinaisky could be compared to those of Švābe, considering their common intention to link the history of law and the history of culture in general. Here also the sociology of culture as developed by Alfred Weber (1868-1958) might be regarded as another aspect shaping the context of their works according to a similar understanding of culture being created by particular society.[86] A more distinct parallel between Švābe and Sinaisky was the perception of culture and civilization as two opposite concepts shared by both authors.

Considering the definition quoted above, culture for Sinaisky was a representation of the universal world order and regularity. Thus culture consists of values and meanings elaborated by man in his communication with the world created by God, while civilization is to be only a form for the substance of culture subordinated to the latter in its ontological status. The spirit of particular culture, in turn, is conditioned to *the spirit of the age*, a *Zeitgeist* indeed, to work as the moving power for human creativity.[87] Therefore, in order to understand a certain culture in a way sufficient for a meaningful investigation, one has to turn towards the historical context for the period of time in question.

---

81 ID., p. 11.
82 See: PACHMUSS, 1988, p. 45-50.
83 SINAISKIS, 1937, p. 79.
84 SINAISKY, 1939, p. 9-27.
85 See: ASSMANN, 2007, p. 48-65 and p. 87-129.
86 SCHORN-SCHÜTTE, 2001, p. 503-504.
87 SINAISKIS, 1937, p. 77-80.

Arveds Švābe was altogether less original regarding the contents of culture and civilization than to follow the current trend in depicting civilization as the cosmopolitan element of human life, also related to the universal standards and ways of social perception contrary to that of culture with a strong national foundation expressed in common mentality, origin, language, and also usually a common destiny. Thus civilization is for the most part represented by urban environment opposed to rural milieu as the cradle of national culture.[88]

The works of Arveds Švābe are of particular interest in the context of this paper considering the role he had in the establishment of cultural history discipline within the Latvian national historiography. According to his autobiography, Švābe started his studies in 1912 at the private A. L. Shan'avsky University in Moscow, at first in biology, then in history as he became interested in Latvian ethnology and culture.[89] In 1921 Švābe published a book *The History of Latvian Culture* attempting to reconstruct the cultural and social life of the Latvians starting with the prehistoric age and the subsequent period of mediaeval Livonia. This project was never concluded in the form the author intended, yet it was the beginning for A. Švābe to come forward with a theory of cultural history.

In this regard, Švābe's book was marked by two basic statements typical for the understanding of tasks and methods of cultural history-writing in Latvia since then. Firstly there was a thematic explanation of political origin stating that the main task of the book will be the illustration of the struggle of the Latvians to retain and develop their culture under disadvantageous circumstances. Secondly, the methodological part of the issue explained the meaning of cultural history: a complex of investigations related to the material, social, and spiritual culture of the nation. This complex included a number of particular subjects concerning also the sexual, religious, scientific and aesthetic aspects of social life.[90]

The didactic part of this concept concerning objectives of the Latvian culture history was later adjusted according to the common spirit of the authoritarian regime, explained in the prescribed definition of main tasks, to study the cultural influences coming from abroad, to extract the national specific of Latvian culture and to investigate the reception, absorption and fusion of different cultural elements and, last but not least, to evaluate positive and negative consequences

---

88 ŠVĀBE, 1940, p. 92.
89 During studies A. Švābe acquainted himself to the works of Wilhelm Wundt (1831-1920), John Fraser (1834-1904), Lucien Levi-Brule (1857-1939), and Emile Durkheim (1858-1917), see: ŠVĀBE, 1947, p. 217-219.
90 ŠVĀBE, 1921, p. 1.

of any kind of exterior impact historically present in the Latvian culture.[91] Since this approach was manifested not only in the works of Švābe alone, it was rather a trend described by Šimkuva as the monologist tradition[92] characteristic for cultural history-writing practice in Latvia.

In 1939 the structural issues composing the cultural history were subsequently further explicated in a program drafted by Švābe for the forthcoming study about the history of Latvian culture, this time prepared by the State Council of Culture, intended to coordinate and control professional institutions engaged in all kinds of activities regarding the *cultural life* under guidance of the authoritarian regime. The program outlined seven paragraphs consisting of several subjects, to mention just the major topics: (1) history of settlements i.e. historical demography including topography and types of settlements; (2) economic history; (3) social history; (4) history of municipalities and domestic policy; (5) history of the Church and its denominations; (6) history of spiritual culture including the history of ideas; (7) history of the material culture in the ethnographic sense of the term.[93]

This concept of cultural history was in fact one of a *total history* propagated by Lamprecht at the turn of the 20th century and intended to cover nearly every single item of human activities apart from military events and diplomacy altogether characteristic for the inter-war period in general.[94]

Although Švābe decided to narrow down this concept afterwards, two kinds of subject definitions were still proposed. The first, for an operation on a larger scale, was described above, while the second interpretation of cultural history followed a somewhat "older and limited understanding", which Švābe preferred most, still derived from the *Geisteswissenschaften* of the 19th century and speaking of "the manifestations of the national spirit in folklore, literature, art, religion, customs and in the material appearances of social life".[95]

A methodological problem emerged in regard to cultural history as *national science*. The importance of folklore, notably the Latvian folk songs for it and the possibility to use them as a historical source was discussed in two different approaches in the 1920s-1930s from a socio-cultural or historical perspective. Švābe's book *History of the Latvian Culture* caused a discussion and received

---

91 ŠVĀBE, 1940, p. 91.
92 ŠIMKUVA, 2001, p. 411.
93 STRAUTIŅŠ, 1939, p. 87-88.
94 See: ULBRICHT, 2003, p. 58.
95 ŠVĀBE, 1940, p. 88.

critical reviews.[96] Švābe considered the folk songs to be sociologic material to study the structure of society and social relationships preserved in some, as he believed, documentary relicts of the legal culture.[97]

Linguist and ethnologist Pēteris Šmits (1869-1938) agreed with Švābe that all written mediaeval sources are biased by nature because they are composed by non-Latvian authors and should therefore be pitted against the Latvian folk songs[98] as being closer to the initial ethnic culture when compared to folk tales and legends sharing motifs of a more international character.[99] This opinion was supported by another ethnologist Kārlis Straubergs (1890-1962) recognizing the folk songs to be a historical source of extraordinary value.[100]

However, the main problem with the Latvian folk songs being treated as a kind of historical source arises from the impossibility to determine an exact chronology for them even in the terms of centuries. Arveds Švābe was also aware of this obstacle as well as the threat to perceive "such disseminate fragments from the past [...] as the relicts of a cultural system that actually never existed in this form constructed by ethnologists thereafter",[101] as his critics noticed. For example, Augusts Tentelis was among the first to point out the problematic chronology of folklore, concluding that folk songs should not be treated as historical facts but rather as material for ethnic psychology studies.[102]

Logical arguments against the somewhat romantic and biased belief in the exclusive historical value of folk songs were also mooted in 1925 by Jānis Bērziņš (1883-1940), a historian and director of the Latvian National Archive, who noted the fact that this *source* was actually constructed in its textual form, with some exceptions, in the second half of the 19th century only and had been exposed as such to the political requirements of the Latvian national movement.[103]

---

96 BALODIS, 1938, p. 378.
97 ŠVĀBE, 1921, p. 6.
98 ŠMITS, 1937, p. 321-338. Compare to: ŠVĀBE, 1940, p. 88.
99 ŠMITS, 1936, p. 243.
100 STRAUBERGS, 1938, p. 564-565.
101 ŠVĀBE, 1940, p. 89.
102 TENTELIS, 1926, p. 43.
103 BĒRZIŅŠ, 2003, p. 48.

Moreover, Bērziņš performed a strict examination of folk songs according to the prescribed principles for critique of sources divided into relicts (*Überreste*) and narrative texts (*Tradition*)[104], coming to the conclusion[105] that the Latvian folk songs include elements of both types, yet having neither theoretical grounds nor factual evidence to be considered more objective than the traditional written sources historians ought to deal with.

The socio-cultural approach to the use of folklore materials as historical sources represented by Švābe, Šmits and Straubergs in the 1930s was determined very much by the concept of social ethnography developed by Wilhelm Heinrich [von] Riehl (1823-1887) in the middle of the 19th century, especially in regard to its "associative and intuitive" methodology.[106] Yet this approach could seem perhaps a little less out-dated when considering a similar trend in the German *Volkskunde* of the early 1920s attempting to identify the nation's forms of life in the past along with their whys and wherefores.[107]

Thus the Latvian national school of historiography of the inter-war period shows two particular trends regarding cultural history: one of searching for new themes and subjects to investigate and the other concerned with the adaptation of different concepts taken from Western Europe, especially following the German tradition of the *Geistes-* and *Kulturwissenschaften*. As rare as it was, cultural history nevertheless shaped an actual trend in the development of the national historiography, while at the same time leaving us guessing what could have been the outcome of these initial attempts if the course of political events had taken another path.

The tradition of the inter-war period Latvian national historiography developed and slightly rectified itself in exile after 1944. As for the cultural history, it was presented in a book published by essayist and literature critic Andrejs Johansons (1922-1983) in Stockholm and devoted to the cultural history of Latvia in the 18th century.[108] This merely descriptive book offers a cluster of factual evidence yet still not catching the latest epistemology issues and it has remained the sole attempt to create a systematic survey of the local cultural history.

---

104 See: BRANDT, 2003, p. 61 for terminology.
105 BĒRZIŅŠ, 2003, p. 59-64.
106 KASCHUBA, 2006, p. 42-54.
107 ID., p. 61.
108 See: JOHANSONS, 1976, p. 7-68.

III

World War II and subsequent years of Soviet occupation (1940-1941/1944-1991) profoundly changed the circumstances for history-writing in Latvia. After the displacement of the Baltic-Germans in 1939-1940, the next surge of emigration followed in 1944; this time majority of the Latvian intellectuals left country to avoid expected oppressions of the returning Soviet regime. Although most of the pre-war historians continued professional activities in exile at a surprising extent, they were mainly concerned with the history of politics and economics, in some particular cases turning also to accounts that fell somewhere into the wide field of social history.[109]

In the course of Latvia's Russification after the World War II the historical science had to undergo substantial changes in both institutional and personal issues. The Latvian Institute of History was reorganized in 1946 and integrated in the new system of the Academy of Sciences of the Latvian SSR, created according to Soviet standards; in fact, the word *Latvia* was carefully removed from its title. Until 1959, according to common practice in the USSR, it was called the Institute of History and Material Culture, the latter part standing for ethnography as a component of historical research, while later on the title became shorter: the Institute of History of the Academy of Sciences.

The history studies remained *pro forma* a significant component in terms of higher education as well as research of the past. In the years known as the Soviet period an increasing amount of historians had institutional bases in both the Latvian State University and the Academy of Sciences while at the same time lacking the opportunity of a diversified reconstruction of the past, for priority was given to political and economic issues of the recent history.

The works published on the Soviet Latvian historiography reveal to have no references to the very notion of cultural history at all while including sections devoted to ethnography and publications describing educational and cultural activities in the second half of the 19th century.[110] The situation was quite similar in the early 1980s to mention, in fact, a new field of historiography being established concerning the "Investigation of Development of the Latvian Socialist Culture"[111] dealing with works on the Soviet cultural policy in Latvia after the World War II. Thus the situation in Latvia during the Soviet period could be

---

109 ANDERSONS, 1981, p. 57-76.
110 See: BIRON/DOROSHENKO, 1970, p. 151-169 and p. 221-225 respectively.
111 VĪKSNA, 1983, p. 192-208.

compared to that in the German Democratic Republic[112], where the works either devoted to the history of ideas or the history of culture had to be stopped on the level of *official historiography* actually being the only possible one.

The Soviet political regime also set new conditions for historians to retain a monopoly during the whole period in question and resulting in (1) a rigorous ideological control over the profession, (2) the obligatory use of historical materialism as the basic concept, and (3) accepting priority for subjects of political and economic history. Besides, research of the cultural aspects of history was to follow the custom of not *overestimating* the Western impact on the Baltic Region now being a part of the Soviet Union.[113] The new state of affairs in historiography started with radical critics of previous conceptions, for instance, against the impact of Neo-Kantian tradition for the reason that such concepts are contradictory to the causal explanation of history in the sense of the Marxist theory as interpreted by the Soviet ideology.[114]

The second political demand to history-writing affected personalities, as most of the historians of the inter-war period was considered to be anti-Soviet by nature and therefore unwelcome even if they no longer resided in Latvia. In fact, Robert Vipper, who spent the last years of his life (1941-1954) as a Soviet academic in Moscow, was the only person allowed to represent previous tradition in historiography explicitly, although he was also criticized for his "idealistic conceptions".[115] Obviously, it was difficult for the Soviet officials to accuse him of being a *Latvian bourgeois nationalist*, a cliché often used to mark *persona non grata* for the regime, which was the case for both Arveds Švābe and Augusts Tentelis.

Another problem typical for historians of the Soviet period was an overall limited influence from abroad, yet with some exclusion in regard to member states of the Warsaw Pact.[116] This restriction was indeed ideological, deriving from the fact that particularly the so-called Baltic Republics were considered unreliable in terms of loyalty to Soviet Union because of the national independence being dept alive in the social memory of the local population.[117]

---

112 SCHORN-SCHÜTTE, 2001, p. 504.
113 IVANOVS, 2005, p. 256-270.
114 ZUTIS, 1947, p. 60 quoting two articles by TENTELIS and ŠVĀBE in this regard.
115 LŪSIS, 1982, p. 227.
116 For example, the book by TOPOLSKI available in Latvia during the Soviet period (TOPOLSKI 1976).
117 BENNICH-BJÖRKMANN, 2007, p. 54.

Nevertheless, there is no need to speak of a kind of *isolation* from the outside world of history-writing, for there were also remarkable attempts to catch the spirit of the age by authors such as Vasilii Doroshenko (1924-1992), a historian of economics noted on international level for researching the issues of trade and agriculture in the early modern age Livonia. His monograph *The Estate and the Market* published in 1973 in Russian should be mentioned[118] dealing with economy of the Jesuit Collegiums situated near Riga at the turn of the 17th century. Here the quantitative data of production and trade was used to represent the ground level of history while the main task for Doroshenko was to demonstrate how the cultural context formed economic activities of the age dependent on the mentality shared by members of the Jesuit community as social actors.

In the Soviet period the writing of cultural history in Latvia drifted almost completely to the domain of ethnography and art history (including the history of literature), and was perceived as merely a marginal research object, consequently leading to provincialism. This was noted by historian Alnis Svelpis (1928-1990) in the interdisciplinary conference of historians, sociologists, philosophers and linguists named *Cultural Traditions and Cultural Milieu* held at the Academy of Sciences in the spring of 1988.[119] Yet another problem arising from this was the lack of theoretical foundations comparable to the experience of the West in the second half of the 20th century[120], which could be used to take up the writing of cultural history in the proper sense of the word. This can also be illustrated by the fact that, until the late 1980s, there were no attempts in Latvia to adopt the semiotic theory of culture[121] developed by Yuri Lotman (1922-1993) which was well-known at that time.

The ideological frame of the Soviet historiography, emphasizing the class war relationships as the dominant driving force in society, caused a dual attitude towards cultural history: the material part of historical heritage, i.e. the cultural monuments like buildings and works of art, were still regarded as objects worth evaluating and studying contrary to the historical context of these objects.[122]

---

118 DOROSHENKO, 1973, p. 123-140.
119 Kultūras tradīcija, 1989, p. 133.
120 ID., p. 137 to quote the paper of Prof. Rihards Kūlis presented at the conference.
121 ŠUVAJEVS, 1995, p. 43-45.
122 LANCMANIS, 2000, p. 183.

However, there were also some advantages in the study of art history as indicated by the book of Imants Lancmanis about Liepāja, first published in 1983[123] and hardly ever influenced by demands of the Soviet ideology. Instead, it presented a wide spectrum of events and actions reaching far more than just a historical account of architectural and sculptural items preserved in the town. Here again the approach was to reconstruct the correlation between the epoch as a social frame and the actions of individuals and groups in the course of history creating its contents and sometimes changing the borders of the parameters.

This means that in both cases of Doroshenko and Lancmanis one could point to some influence by Fernand Braudel's (1902-1985) ideas representing the second generation of the *Annales* School because of a similar intention to reconstruct the interplay between the *static elements* and the *dynamics* of history as represented on different *levels of events* taking place in certain space and time. Moreover, Braudel's interpretation of history with the accentuation of economic processes was also more suitable for Soviet historians trained in accordance to the Marxist methodology, especially in regard to bonding material conditions or *civilization* with particular human activities usually marked as the manifestation of *culture*.[124]

There were also some other patterns regarding the history of science as well as the history of book-publication in Latvia, which should be considered when speaking of the investigation of the cultural history in the Soviet period. As noted before, there was a limited possibility to publish texts on cultural history issues attributed to the *legacy* (sic!) of the Baltic German community from the 1970s onwards.[125]

This direction was especially promoted by academic Jānis Stradiņš developing the history of exact sciences in Latvia since the late 1950s while touching also the issues of cultural history.[126] Although, following the classic tradition of biographical essays about individual scientists or institutions more or less related to a particular historical context,[127] Stradiņš' publications represented

---

123 Here the reference is provided to an extended version of the book published recently in German, see: LANCMANIS, 2007.
124 IGGERS, 1997, p. 51-64.
125 ŠIMKUVA, 2001, p. 414-418.
126 STRADIŅŠ, 1982, p. 282-296.
127 DANIEL, 2006, p. 361.

the most prominent and, perhaps, also the most popular way of writing cultural history in the Soviet Latvia.[128]

On the other hand, somewhat less popular but certainly not less important was the research direction one might include into the trend in the West labeled the history or reading.[129] Here a detailed investigations taking decades were undertaken by librarian and bibliographer Aleksejs Apīnis (1926-2004), resulting in his three monographs on the history of the Latvian book publication and its impact upon the social and cultural processes in Latvia from the early 16th to the late 19th century[130] as well as in the research devoted to manuscript literature of the Latvian pietists (*Herrnhuter*) in the 18th and 19th century.[131]

Aside from the overall positivistic and descriptive disposition of these works related *inter alia* to their trail-blazing role in the research field, there was a publication in 1991[132] worth mentioning in regard to the methodological principles Apīnis relied on to deal with the culture of reading in Latvia. These principles reflect the influence of concepts common for the history of ideas while the periodization of Mediaeval, Renaissance, Baroque and Enlightenment culture actually reminds of the *typology of culture* practiced since the second half of the 19th century, here denoted by the author as the "universal stages of the spiritual life"[133] of a given society.

However, Apīnis also used the concept of culture divided into sectors of institutionalized or systematized activities of high-culture and those attributed to "the primordial forces of folk-culture" presuming that the history of reading will provide a new perspective on the interplay of these aspects.[134] On the whole, this essay can be regarded as an envoy for the possible directions yet to emerge in cultural history research in the future.

---

128 This research project was completed recently with a work titled *The Beginnings of Science and Higher Education in Latvia*, see: STRADIŅŠ, 2009, p. 557-570.

129 BURKE, 2004, p. 60-61.

130 See: APĪNIS, 1977, p. 15-333 and APĪNIS, 1991, p. 195-214.

131 APĪNIS, 1987, p. 199-217.

132 Reprinted in and hence quoted after: APĪNIS, 2000, p. 7-27.

133 ID., p. 8.

134 ID., p. 23.

IV

In conclusion, some words should be said about the most recent developments in the historiography of cultural history of Latvia. Although the twenty years spent after the restoration of the independent state are somehow comparable to the inter-war period observed above, it is nevertheless a very recent history indeed. The post-Soviet era has marked a new stage in the historiography of Latvia affecting many aspects.

Although there still is no single institution particularly engaged in cultural history research, the Latvian State Historical Archives has turned into a centre of historical investigations, to mention the quarterly periodical *Latvijas Arhīvi/ Archives of Latvia* issued since 1994 and the document edition series named *Sources of History* published since 1999.[135]

Another editorial project related to cultural history starting the Academy of Sciences on an intentional level in the 1970s was finished recently in 2007 when the four volumes representing Johann Christoph Brotze's (1742-1823) collection albums named *Zeichnungen und deren Beschreibungen* were published including subjects of social and cultural history of the late 18th and early 19th century as the descriptions and images of building constructions, ethnographic items and customs of social estates as well as historical landscape of the age in general.[136]

New institutions such as the Academy of Culture founded in 1990 and engaged mainly in the cultural theory issues[137] have been created. In fact, this has been an actual trend in Latvia since the 1990s because historiography here did not experience the established discussion taking place in 1960s-1980s in the West between authors supporting the Anglo-American trend of *Cultural Studies* and that of cultural history or the *Kulturwissenschaften* attributed to the German tradition.[138]

While the collapse of the Soviet political and ideological control system provided an opportunity for advancing investigations considering any possible subject of cultural history, the actual situation of regained national independence is once more proving to have priority over political history. This resulted in statements being inherited from the 1930s, such as that "the history of Latvia is

---

135 See: http://www.arhivi.lv/index.php?&302, 20.07.2010.
136 BROTZE, 1992-2007.
137 http://www.lka.edu.lv/modules.php?op=modload&name=News&file=index&topic =71, 20.07.2010.
138 ASSMANN, 2006, p. 16-25.

first and foremost the history of Latvian nation"[139] including also cultural history of the Latvians as one of its subdivisions.[140]

However, at the same time a different trend has become evident, attempting to change the very perspective applied to the cultural history of Latvia. This new approach is more related to that shared in historical anthropology bringing out the particulars rather than the imagined inner coherence of culture present at every society or social group.[141] This confirms the opinion that the "Latvian culture is, in fact, the result of the interaction of different cultures historically bound to the territory of present-day Latvia"[142]; standing therefore for a *multicultural reality,* one should observe the cultural history of Latvia in its very basic principles. In fact, the synthesis of different perspectives typical of an age in their particular historical context could be illustrated by the book about coexistence and confrontation among the inhabitants of Riga in the late 19th and early 20th century.[143]

Since the early 1990s there was a trend to acquire theoretical concepts of the *Annales* School[144] as well as cultural history, to mention Ute Daniel's article *Kultur und Gesellschaft. Überlegungen zum Gegenstandsbereich der Sozialgeschichte* (1993) published in Latvian to start a discussion of the issue.[145] However, the concepts related to gender history[146] and the social anthropology[147] have been most influential; to be mentioned here is the monograph by Vita Zelče concerned with the Latvian newspapers as media for building an intellectual frame for the public space of the emerging Latvian nation in the 19th century[148], reflecting the impact of social sciences also evident in the latest historiography of Latvia.

---

139 BĒRZIŅŠ, 2000, p. 9.
140 ID., p. 43.
141 ULBRICHT, 2003, p. 78.
142 ŠIMKUVA, 2001, p. 406.
143 See: OBERLÄNDER/WOHLFART, 2004, p. 11-31.
144 In 1993 François Ewald's interviews with representatives of the *Annales* School was published in Latvian, see: ŠUVAJEVS, 1993, p. 9-121.
145 DANIELA, 1993, p. 115-132. Reference to the original publication at: SCHORN-SCHÜTTE, 2001, p. 512.
146 This trend was introduced by an anthology on various aspects of feminism, see: NOVIKOVA, 2001, p. 203-230.
147 ĶĪLIS, 1998, p. 98-138.
148 ZELČE, 2009, p. 484-487.

Finally, a particular perspective for cultural history research could be noticed relating to the field of oral history also promoted since the 1990s by the Institution of Sociology and Philosophy at the Academy of Sciences with the project of *National Oral History: The Resource for the Analyze of Cultural, Social and Identity-Building Processes*.[149] Yet once again, a parallel to the former German Democratic Republic could be observed there in regard to the concept of experience in the oral history becoming so popular,[150] perhaps, as an imaginary way to compensate the compulsory loss of social memory during the years of the Soviet political rule.

Thus some aspects of the new cultural history are evident in the recent historiography of Latvia in a sense of understanding culture not as a complex of institutional bodies or *objects*, which was criticized in the late 1980s,[151] but rather in terms of culture as the frame of different activities shaping the context for historical explanations.[152] Considering there are notable works reflecting the impact of interdisciplinary approach along with new source materials published, it is also quite evident now that the cultural history of Latvia in the proper sense of the word is yet to be expected.

Literature

ANDERSONS, EDGARS, Latviešu vēsturnieku darbs, in: Archīvs XXI (1981), p. 57-76.
APĪNIS, ALEKSEJS, Latviešu grāmatniecība no pirmsākumiem līdz 19. gadsimta beigām, Rīga 1977.
ID., Neprasot atļauju. Latviešu rokraksta literatūra 18. un 19. gadsimtā, Rīga 1987.
ID., Grāmata un latviešu sabiedrība līdz 19. gadsimta vidum, Rīga 1991.
ID., Soļi senākās latviešu grāmatniecības un kultūras takās, Rīga 2000.
ARBUSOW, LEONID JUN., Grundriss der Geschichte Liv-, Est- und Kurlands, Riga 1918.
ASSMANN, ALEIDA, Einführung in die Kulturwissenschaft. Grundbegriffe, Themen, Fragestellungen, Berlin 2006.

---

149 See also a site related to this project: http://www.dzivesstasts.lv/en/default.htm, 20.07.2010.
150 ULBRICHT, 2003, p. 63.
151 See note 125.
152 SCHORN-SCHÜTTE, 2001, p. 511.

ASSMANN, JAN, Das kulturelle Gedächtnis. Schrift, Erinnerung und politische Identität in frühen Hochkulturen, 6th ed., München 2007.

BALODIS, FRANCIS, Vēsture un vēstures palīgdisciplīnas, in: Zinātne tēvzemei divdesmit gados 1918-1938, ed. by LUDIS ADAMOVIČS, Rīga 1938, p. 373-387.

BENNICH-BJÖRKMANN, LI, Between Resistance and Opposition: Developments after Stalinism, in: Latvia and the Eastern Europe in the 1960s-1980s. Materials of an International Conference 10 October 2006, Riga (Symposium of the Commission of the Historians of Latvia, 20), ed. by ANDRIS CAUNE et. al., Riga 2007, p. 45-72.

BĒRZIŅŠ, JĀNIS, Par mūsu tautas dziesmu kā vēstures avotu izlietošanu, in: Latvieši. XX gadsimta 20. un 30. gadu autoru rakstu krājums, ed. by MUNTIS AUNS/HELĒNA GRĪNBERGA, Rīga 2003, p. 47-65.

BĒRZIŅŠ, VALDIS (ed.), 20. gadsimta Latvijas vēsture I, Rīga 2000.

BIRON, ANATOLII/DOROSHENKO, VASILII, Istoriografia Sovetskoi Latvii, Riga 1970.

BLEIERE, DAINA et. al., History of Latvia: The 20th Century, Riga 2006.

BRANDT, AHASVER VON, Werkzeug des Historikers. Eine Einführung in die historischen Hilfswissenschaften, 16th ed., Stuttgart 2003.

BROTZE, JOHANN CHRISTOPH, Zeichnungen und deren Beschreibungen, Band I-IV, Riga 1992-2007.

BRUININGK, HERMANN VON, Kunst und Gewerbe in Livland, in: Rigasche Almanach für 1883, Riga 1882, p. 49-76.

ID., Messe und kanonisches Stundengebet nach dem Brauche der Rigaschen Kirche im späteren Mittelalter, Riga 1904.

BUCHHOLTZ, ALEXANDER, Ein baltisches culturhistorisches Museum, in: Sitzungsberichte der Gesellschaft für Geschichte und Altertumskunde der Ostseeprovinzen Russlands aus dem Jahre 1886, Riga 1887, p. 122-140.

BURKE, PETER, What is Cultural History? Cambridge 2004.

CELMS, TEODORS, Patiesība un šķitums. Filozofisku, psiholoģisku un socioloģisku rakstu krājums, Rīga 1939.

DANIEL, UTE, Kompendium Kulturgeschichte. Theorien, Praxis, Schlüsselwörter, 5th ed., Frankfurt a. Main 2006.

DANIELA, UTE, Kultūra vai sabiedrība: No sociālās vēstures pie kultūrvēstures, in: Latvijas Vēstures Institūta Žurnāls 4 (1993), p. 115-135.

DAVIES, NORMAN, Europe. A History, London et. al 1997.

DOROSHENKO, VASILII, Myza i rynok: hoziaistvo Rizhskoi iezuitskoi kollegii na rubezhe XVI i XVII vekov, Riga 1973.

FELDMANIS, INESIS, Die lettische Historiographie, in: Zwischen Konfrontation und Kompromiss. Oldenburger Symposium "Interethnische Beziehungen in Ostmitteleuropa als historiographisches Problem der 1930er/1940er Jahre", ed. by MICHAEL GARLEFF, München 1995, p. 133-138.

GARLEFF, MICHAEL, Aspekte der deutschbaltischen Geschichtsschreibung in der 2. Hälfte des 19. Jahrhunderts, in: Journal of Baltic Studies 4 (1978), p. 339-353.

ID., Geschichtsschreibung der Neuzeit in der baltischen Provinzen 1870-1918, in: Geschichte der deutschbaltischen Geschichtsschreibung, ed. by GEORG VON RAUCH, Köln/Wien 1986, p. 233-272.

HACKMANN, JÖRG, Vereinswesen und Museen in den baltischen Provinzen, in: Das Dommuseum in Riga. Ein Haus für Wissenschaft und Kunst, ed. by MARGIT ROMANG/ILONA CELMIŅA, Marburg 2001, p. 20-24.

HEHN, JÜRGEN VON, Die deutschbaltische Geschichtsschreibung 1918-1939/45 in Lettland, in: Geschichte der deutschbaltischen Geschichtsschreibung, ed. by GEORG VON RAUCH, Köln/Wien 1986, p. 371-398.

HIRSCHHAUSEN, ULRIKE VON, Die Grenzen der Gemeinsamkeit. Deutsche, Letten, Russen und Juden in Riga 1860-1914 (Kritische Studien zur Geschichtswissenschaft, 172), München 2006.

HOLLANDER, BERNHARD, Dr.phil.h.c. Hermann von Bruiningk (1849-1927), in: Mitteilungen aus der livländischen Geschichte, Band XXIV, Riga 1933, p. 6-39.

IGGERS, GEORG, Historiography in the Twentieth Century: From Scientific Objectivity to the Postmodern Challenge, Hanover/London 1997.

IVANOVS, ALEKSANDRS, Sovietization of Latvian Historiography 1944-1959: Overview, in: The Hidden and Forbidden History of Latvia under Soviet and Nazi Occupations 1944-1991 (Symposium of the Commission of the Historians of Latvia, 14), ed. by VALTERS NOLLENDORFS et. al., Riga 2005, p. 256-270.

JOHANSONS, ANDREJS, Latvijas kultūras vēsture 1710-1800, Stockholm 1976.

KASCHUBA, WOLFGANG, Geschichtspolitik und Identitätspolitik. Nationale und ethnische Diskurse im Kulturvergleich, in: Inszenierung des Nationalen. Geschichte, Kultur und die Politik der Identitäten am Ende des 20. Jahrhunderts (Alltag & Kultur, 7), ed. by BEATE BINDER et. al., Köln 2001, p. 19-42.

ID., Einführung in die Europäische Ethnologie, 3rd ed., München 2006.

KAUSE, HELMUT, Letten und Deutsche in der Republik Lettland, in: Tausend Jahre Nachbarschaft. Die Völker des baltischen Raumes und die Deutschen, ed. by WILFRIED SCHLAU, München 1995, p. 112-122.

KEYSERLING, GRAF LEO, Eine Bitte an unsere Historiker, in: Baltische Monatsschrift 28 (1881), p. 355-360.
ĶĪLIS, ROBERTS (ed.), Atmiņa un vēsture no antropoloģijas līdz psiholoģijai, Rīga 1998.
KŪLE, MAIJA, Phenomenology and Culture, Riga 2002.
Kultūras tradīcija – kultūrvide, in: Karogs 4 (April 1989), p. 128-140.
Kultūras vēsture, in: Latviešu konversācijas vārdnīca, 10. sējums, Rīga 1933-1934, col. 18882-18883.
LANCMANIS, IMANTS, "Kurzemes hercogienes Dorotejas vēstules" lasot, in: Latvijas Arhīvi 1 (2000), p. 183-185.
ID., Das Herzogtum Kurland-Semgallen. Ephemerer Bestandteil der Republik Lettland, in: Deutschland, Russland und das Baltikum. Beiträge zu einer Geschichte wechselvoller Beziehungen, ed. by FLORAIN ANTON/LEONID LUKS, Köln et. al. 2005, p. 87-108.
ID., Libau. Eine baltische Hafenstadt zwischen Barock und Klassizismus, Köln et. al. 2007.
LAZDIŅŠ, JĀNIS, Vēsturiskā tiesību skola un Latvija, in: Latvijas Universitātes Raksti 703 (2006), p. 21-43.
LENZ, WILHELM, Deutschbaltisches biographisches Lexikon 1710-1960, Köln 1970.
ID., "Alt-Livland" in der deutschbaltischen Geschichtsschreibung 1870 bis 1918, in: Geschichte der deutschbaltischen Geschichtsschreibung, ed. by GEORG VON RAUCH, Köln/Wien 1986, p. 203-232.
LŪSIS, KĀRLIS, Roberts Vipers (1859-1954), in: Apcerējumi par sabiedriskās un filozofiskās domas attīstību Latvijā, ed. by VALENTĪNS ŠTEINBERGS, Rīga 1982, p. 222-229.
NEANDER, THEODOR, Einiges über Provinzialmuseen, Zentralisierung und Localpatriotismus, in: Sitzungsberichte der Kurländischer Gesellschaft für Literatur und Kunst aus dem Jahre 1893, Mitau 1894, p. 7-14.
NEUMANN, WIHELM, Aus alter Zeit: Kunst- und kulturgeschichtliche Miszellen aus Liv-, Est- und Kurland, Riga 1913.
ID., Denkmalschutz und Denkmalpflege in den baltischen Provinzen Liv-, Est- und Kurland, in: Baltische Studien zur Archäologie und Geschichte, Berlin 1914, p. 285.-295.
NOVIKOVA, IRINA et. al. (eds.), Mūsdienu feministiskās teorijas, Rīga 2001.
OBERLÄNDER, ERWIN/WOHLFART, KRISTINE (eds.), Riga: Porträt einer Vielvölkerstadt am Rande des Zarenreiches 1857-1914 = Katram bija sava Rīga. Daudznacionālas pilsētas portrets no 1857. līdz 1914. gadam, Paderborn/Riga 2004.

PACHMUSS, TEMIRA, Russian Literature in the Baltic between the World Wars, Columbus 1988.

PISTOHLKORS, GERT VON, Geschichtsschreibung und Politik: Die Agrar- und Verfassungsproblematik in der deutschbaltischen Historiographie und Publizistik 1800-1918, in: Geschichte der deutschbaltischen Geschichtsschreibung, ed. by GEORG VON RAUCH, Köln/Wien 1986, p. 273-338.

ID., Deutsche, Esten, Letten, Russen: interethnische Beziehungen unter ständischen Vorziehen 1710 bis 1918, in: Tausend Jahre Nachbarschaft. Die Völker des baltischen Raumes und die Deutschen, ed. by WILFRIED SCHLAU, München 1995, p. 80-95.

PLAKANS, ANDREJS, Looking Backward: The Eighteenth and Nineteenth Centuries in Inter-War Latvian Historiography, in: Journal of Baltic Studies 4 (1999), p. 293-306.

PRIEDĪTE, AIJA, Establishment of a Discourse about National Identity in Latvia in the Late 19th Century and the Early 20th Century, in: Humanities and Social Sciences. Latvia 4 (1999), p. 4-17.

SCHORN-SCHÜTTE, LUISE, Ideen-, Geistes- und Kulturgeschichte, in: Geschichte. Ein Grundkurs, ed. by HANS-JÜRGEN GOERTZ, 2nd ed., Reinbek bei Hamburg 2001, p. 489-515.

SINAISKIS, VASILIJS, Dzīve un cilvēks, Rīga 1937.

SINAISKY, VASILII, Kul'tura i jazyk, Riga 1939.

STRADIŅŠ, JĀNIS, Etīdes par Latvijas zinātņu pagātni, Rīga 1982.

ID., Development of Latvia's Cultural Situation in the 20th Century, in: Cultural Policy in Latvia. National Report, Riga 1998, p. 42-51.

ID., Zinātnes un augstskolu sākotne Latvijā, Rīga 2009.

STRAUBERGS, KĀRLIS, Tautas dziesmu nozīme vēsturē, in: Latvijas Vēstures Institūta Žurnāls 4 (1938), p. 563-568.

STRAUTIŅŠ, PĒTERIS (ed.), Valsts kultūras padomes I sesija, Rīga 1939.

ŠIMKUVA, HELĒNA, Cultural and Historical Heritage of Baltic Germans in Latvia – Research Results and Prospects, in: The Baltic States at Historical Crossroads, ed. by TĀLAVS JUNDZIS, Riga 2001, p. 405-426.

ŠMITS, PĒTERIS, Tautas tradīcijas, in: Latvieši I, ed. by FRANCIS BALODIS et. al., 2nd ed., Rīga 1936, p. 241-244.

ID., Vēstures liecības pasakās, in: Vēstures atziņas un tēlojumi, ed. by FRANCIS BALODIS, Rīga 1937, p. 321-338.

ŠNĒ, ANDRIS, Augusts Tentelis – Professor and Rector of the University of Latvia, in: Profesors Dr. honoris causa Augusts Tentelis. Dzīve un darbs, ed. by MĀRĪTE SAVIČA, Rīga 2009, p. 53-71.

ŠTERNS, INDRIĶIS, Vēstures zinātne Latvijas Universitātē 1919-1940, in: Akadēmiskā Dzīve 23 (1981), p. 3-9.

ŠUVAJEVS, IGORS (ed.), Parīzes intervijas, Rīga 1993.

ID., Cita vēsture, in: Latvijas Zinātņu Akadēmijas Vēstis 2/3 (1995), p. 37-48.

ŠVĀBE, ARVEDS, Latvju kultūras vēsture, Rīga 1921.

ID., Latvju tiesību vēsture, in: Latviešu konversācijas vārdnīca, 11. sējums, Rīga 1934-1935, col. 22113-22250.

ID., Latviešu vēstures uzdevumi, in: Straumes un avoti II, Rīga 1940, p. 5-112.

ID., Mana dzīve, in: Trimdas rakstnieki I, ed. by PĒTERIS ĒRMANIS, Kempten 1947, p. 163-240.

TENTELIS, AUGUSTS, Latvijas vēsturnieku tuvākie uzdevumi, in: Rīgas Latviešu biedrības Zinību komisijas rakstu krājums 18, Rīga 1926, p. 38-44.

ID., Latviešu vēsture jaunā skatījumā, in: Valsts kultūras padomes I sesija, ed. by PĒTERIS STRAUTIŅŠ, Rīga 1939, p. 19-27.

THADEN, EDUARD, Finnland and the Baltic Provinces: Elite Roles and Social and Economic Conditions and Structures, in: Journal of Baltic Studies 2/3 (1984), p. 216-227.

TOPOLSKI, JERZY, Methodology of History, Warszawa 1976.

ULBRICHT, OTTO, Neue Kulturgeschichte. Historische Anthropologie, in: Fischer Lexikon Geschichte, ed. by RICHARD VAN DÜLMEN, Frankfurt a. Main 2003, p. 56-71.

VĪKSNA, DZINTRA, Izuchenie istorii razvitia latyshskoi socialisticheskoi kul'tury, in: Istoricheskaja nauka Sovetskoi Latvii na sovremennom etape, ed. by ANATOLII BIRON, Riga 1983, p. 192-208.

VIPERS, ROBERTS, Eiropas kultūrvēsturiskie laikmeti, Rīga 1936.

ID., Vēstures lielās problēmas, Rīga 1940.

WIEDEMANN, GEORG, Moderne Geschichtswissenschaft, in: Sitzungsberichte der Kurländischer Gesellschaft für Literatur und Kunst aus dem Jahre 1909, Mitau 1910, p. 10-20.

WITTRAM, REINHARDT, Geschichtsbewusstsein und Geschichtsbetrachtung im baltischen Deutschtum, in: Sitzungsberichte der Gesellschaft für Geschichte und Altertumskunde zu Riga aus dem Jahre 1935, Riga 1936, p. 5-28.

WOHLFART, KRISTINE, Der Rigaer Letten-Verein und die lettische Nationalbewegung von 1868 bis 1905 (Materialen und Studien zur Ostmitteleuropa-Forschung, 14), Marburg 2006.

ZEIDS, TEODORS, Latviešu vēstures zinātnes attīstība 1918-1938, Rīga 1939.

ZELČE, VITA, Arhīvi, vēstures pētniecība un vēsturnieki, in: Latvijas Arhīvi 1 (2000), p. 40-42.

ID., Latviešu avīžniecība. Laikraksti savā laikmetā un sabiedrībā 1822-1865, Rīga 2009.

ZUTIS, JĀNIS, Latvijas vēstures pētīšanas jaunie uzdevumi, in: Latvijas PSR Zinātņu Akadēmijas Vēstis 1 (1947), p. 59-69.

http://www.arhivi.lv/index.php?&302, 20.07.2010
http://www.lka.edu.lv/modules.php?op=modload&name=News&file=index &topic=71, 20.07.2010
http://www.dzivesstasts.lv/en/default.htm, 20.07.2010

A would-be science?
A history of material culture in Poland before and after the year 1989

IGOR KĄKOLEWSKI

Cultural history as a research topic is being taken up by many historians or smaller research groups at Polish universities or academic institutions in present-day Poland. However, in the twentieth century and at the beginning of the twenty-first century there is a lack of any institution dealing with research into cultural history in accordance with its statutes—with one exception. This exception is the Institute for the History of Material Culture of the Polish Academy of Sciences (IHMC PAS), which was renamed in 1992 into the Institute of Archaeology and Ethnology of the PAS (IAE PAS). Contrary to its original and present name, its research team, which was and still is not only made up of archaeologists and ethnologists, but to a large part also of historians, has not only carried out a great deal of research into concrete problem questions of the history of material culture in the last fifty years, but is also developing the discourse on the theory and methodology of cultural history research itself.[1]

At the same time, the history of the IHMC PAS—which was founded at a time when Stalinism in Poland was reaching its climax—deserves attention for two reasons: On the one hand, it is an interesting example of the relationship between an academic institute and the totalitarian and later—the more liberal the regime became—authoritarian state; on the other hand it is an example of an attempt, controlled from above, to establish a new academic discipline which

---

1 Cf. comparing the topic of material culture and cultural studies, above all from the ethnological perspective in German: FEEST, 2003, p. 239-254; HAHN 2005; KÖNIG, 2003, p. 95-118.

would comply with the ideological requirements of the Communist leadership. In my paper I would like to examine the development phases of research on cultural history at the IHMC—today IAE—against the background of the great political changes which gave the post-war history of Poland its corresponding rhythm, including the watershed of 1989 which brought about the end of the communist People's Republic of Poland.

The history of the IHMC begins in the first post-war years when the communist power was establishing itself in Poland, and then in the period of the setting-up of the system of totalitarian suppression during the heyday of Stalinism, i.e. around the years 1949 to ca. 1953/54.[2] The new communist policy of so-called *methodological reconstruction* began in the academic sector at the end of the forties. This *reconstruction* at that time consisted in revising the bases of the humanities and social sciences in the sense of Stalinist vulgar Marxism, the core of which in turn represented the concept of the philosophy of *historical materialism*. The Polish Academy of Sciences, founded in the 1950s, facilitated the *methodological reconstruction*. Its task was to centralise Polish science. The rulers' intention was that the scientists in the institutes of the PAS, cut off from teaching work at the universities, would attract other scholars to follow then and organise science following the model of the Academy of Sciences of the Soviet Union. The Institute of History of the PAS came into being in 1953. The takeover of its management by a group of ardent *progressive* historians—as radical Marxists, who were linked with the structures of the Polish United Workers' Party (PUWP), were called at that time—was, however, thwarted. Shortly after, the IHMC PAS was brought into being which was intended to propagate the *new* specifically Marxist scientific branch—the history of material culture. At the same time, the IHMC was intended to become a platform for interdisciplinary research within the triangle: *Archaeology-Ethnography-History of Material Culture*. In concrete terms, its task was to link together research problems of so-called prehistoric and early medieval archaeology, classical archaeology, the history of the material culture of the Middle Ages and the Modern Period, as well as ethnography.

From 1949 on, at the latest, its development was accompanied by a wide methodological debate. Its key participant was Prof. Kazimierz Majewski—a Classical Archaeologist. Before the Second World War he had been a lecturer at the then Polish University of Lwów and at the same time supporter of Poland's Communist Party, during the Soviet occupation (1939-41 and again after 1944)

---

2 On the genesis as well as the organisational beginnings of the IHMC PAS cf. among others, RUTKOWSKI, 2007, p. 221f., as well as the report: Instytut, 1977, p. 448.

he was Head of the Chair of Ancient History at the now Ukrainian-Soviet University of Ľviv, after 1945 he became Professor at the University of Wrocław and finally, after 1954, first Director of the IHMC PAS.[3] In his programmatic article from 1954, he defined the history of material culture as a completely sovereign academic discipline—alongside legal and economic history—for research into the social-technical side of production, but also into so-called *distribution* in Marx's metalanguage, as well as consumption.

The key role in this was played by methodological-theoretical prerequisites of Karl Marx's *historic materialism*, in its variant richly decorated with Stalinist vulgar formulations which was regarded as the basis for the new discipline. In addition at this time it was usual and indeed necessary to include quotations from the Soviet dictator's supposed collected works in every more important publication. These ideological prerequisites can be summarised in the following way: The new Marxist history of material culture was intended to deal above all with the "social-technical, thus material side of the production process" and research into the "working implements and material products which had been created with the help of these tools, as well as people's attitude to these tools and to the forces of nature, which were utilised in production in their historical development".[4]

This definition is characteristic for two reasons. On the one hand, the Marxist philosophy of historical materialism, convinced, it is true of the integrity of the historical process and the need for its complex view, puts the main emphasis above all on research into the so-called *basis* of the historical process which is connected with the *manufacture of material cultural objects*. On the other hand, research into the so-called *superstructure*, thus the *intellectual culture*, was treated, if not with clear contempt, then it was at least accorded a *subordinate historical significance as a consequences of the transformation in material culture*.

In addition, the second main emphasis of Marxist history of material culture lay in research, above all into the *technical-social side of the production process*, to a smaller extent by comparison into the technical-social side of phenomena which were connected e.g. with trade or consumption. By the way, this quite simply reflected the fact that in the Communist ideology of that time the main importance was attached to industrialisation and the development of industrial production as the main factors of economic development and at the same time the significance of trade and consumption was belittled. Characteristic for the

---

3 RUTKOWSKI, 2007, p. 54.
4 MAJEWSKI, 1953/54, p. 7.

new branch of historical science in Poland was that it fell back on the Soviet model, thus the fact that an Institute for the History of Material Culture also operated in the Soviet Union.[5]

At the same time, in the same number of the main organ of the IHMC, the periodical *Kwartalnik Historii Kultury Materialnej* (Quarterly of the History of Material Culture)—apart from the ideologised manifesto by Kazimierz Majewski[6]—an *authoritative* text for the new field of research appeared which was only little hampered by the stylistics of the official ideology. It is an extensive study of the beginnings of the modern horse-drawn cart by Józef Matuszewski, who even before the Second World War, thanks to a scholarship at the French École des Chartres, was well acquainted with the latest French historiography.[7] He adopted the theories of Richard Lefebvre de Notes, an outstanding technical historian, and "showed succinctly, almost boldly the importance of research into material culture for studies of civilisation as such".[8] In his article, Matuszewski showed how the principle of the horse's harness, derived from the ancient yoke, meant that the horse, by pulling with its neck, was unable to utilise all its motor possibilities; however, Matuszewski did not agree with de Notes who claimed exaggeratedly that this had almost led to the downfall of the civilisation of Ancient Rome. At the same time, he referred to the role of the horse collar widely spread in the tenth century as an essential factor in the economic development of medieval and modern Europe.

> "[...] at the same time, the study by J. Matuszewski opens our eyes for the whole sphere of feedback, which had been in darkness up to now, lying between mental, social and material culture. As a result of these positive initiations, [...] the authors and editorial board [of the VGMK—I.K.] became more sensitive to the need that the works published here are intended to show a wider cultural context".[9]

---

5 ID., in particular p. 11f.
6 Cf. also later opinions by the founding father of this branch of historical studies in the People' Republic of Poland on the topic of the history of material culture: MAJEWSKI, 1957, p. 209-244; MAJEWSKI, 1960, p. 1-14; MAJEWSKI, 1973, p. 395-409; MAJEWSKI, 1976, p. 109-115; MAJEWSKI, 1978, p. 207-218.
7 RUTKOWSKI, 2007, p. 48.
8 Cf. a review and analysis of the article by MATUSZEWSKI in: SZTETTYŁO, 1993, p. 23.
9 ID., p. 23f.

It seems that it would be a mistake to credit the creation of the Polish Historical School of Material Culture solely to Marxist inspirations and a certain ideological fashion of the Stalinist period. The real pioneer of the history of material culture as a separate field of research in Poland was probably the Poznań economic historian, Jan Rutkowski, who had already been outstanding long before the Second World War. Together with the historian Jan Bujak in Lwów, he was co-founder in 1930 of the *Roczniki Dziejów Społecznych i Gospodarczych* (Annals of Social and Economic History) — the Polish equivalent to the renowned French *Annales*, a periodical that had been founded a year before by Marc Bloch and Lucien Febvre. In this connection, it should be observed that the pre-war Polish School of Economic History of Bujak and Rutkowski, although it certainly remained under the influences of the French *Annalistes* in the 1930s, was born out of their own experience and formulated a similar programme to a certain degree independently of the *Annales* school.

Shortly after the war, at the end of his life, in the period still before the importunate Stalinist indoctrination of Polish science, Jan Rutkowski wrote two extensive texts propagating the commencement of large-scale studies on the history of material culture.[10] In this connection, Rutkowski sketched out the history of the development of cultural history, beginning with Thomas Buckle and Jacob Burckhardt — the founding fathers of this branch of historical studies around the mid-19th century — and also illustrating *the subdivision of culture and its history into the history of material, social and intellectual culture, generally accepted at that time in European scholarship*. For this reason, his standpoint can be described as being *holistic*. He maintained that basically intellectual and material culture should not be separated from one another and that *real history as a science in reality was a history of culture*. At the same time, however, he stipulated the extent of the research on the history of material culture as a special field that differs with regard to the focus of interest and methods from economic or legal history. In his opinion, the history of material culture did not just integrate research into the narrowly understood history of technology and lifeless objects into itself, but also into widely understood *everyday culture* (the latter was *nota bene* — completely in accordance with the approaches of the *Annales* school — contrasted with the classical history of events). Rutkowski was of the opinion that the *history of material culture should include interdisciplinary research, such as ethnology, archaeology and history*. The complex of research

---

10 The second paper in the form of an incomplete methodological study only appeared in 1959, cf. RUTKOWSKI, 1959, p. 5-61; cf. a review and analysis of the concept by Jan Rutkowski in: TOPOLSKI, 1980, p. 461-467.

themes should concern such questions as, e.g. the history of tools, industrial and agricultural technology, the history of transport and communication, the history of consumption, the material and moral bases of everyday and intellectual life, including the technical and material aspects of the history of education, the fine arts and architecture.

However, in the People's Republic of Poland in the first half of the fifties, there was only little room to pursue such a research programme into the history of material culture which would not have been ideologically burdened by Stalinism. The *methodological reconstruction* led to a centralisation of science, whose tool, in the opinion of the Communist rulers, should be the institutes of the Polish Academy of Sciences. The most treasured possession of this process was certainly the Institute for the History of Material Culture which was intended to integrate the research work of archaeologists and ethnographers under the dominance of the representatives of the *new* Marxist discipline of the history of material culture. In addition, at the beginning of the 1950s a new subject was introduced at universities: the History of Material Culture which absorbed the previously separate subjects, Archaeology and Ethnography. This attack on the sovereignty of traditional academic disciplines led to a veiled rebellion shortly afterwards, in which archaeologists played first fiddle.[11]

This rebellion was reflected in the votes during the wide methodological debate at the head office of the First Faculty of Social Sciences of the PAS in 1955, thus at a time when, almost eighteen months after Stalin's death, the first still timid signs of a weakening of the regime became visible. During this debate, three typical points of view were represented.

The first point of view could be described as being radical. It presupposed that a history of material culture existed as a separate social science which researched into the social-technical aspects of *class societies*. This point of view was also presented in the form of a completely vulgarised thesis which said that *intellectual culture was above all a product of the ruling classes* and therefore above all an object of research by *bourgeois scholarship*. On the other hand *material culture had been a product of the exploited classes*, and for precisely this reason it should be the main subject matter of research of truly *Marxist scholars*.

The second point of view, which represented a compromise so to speak, let the history of material culture come into being as an ancillary discipline which served historical science. Its supporters were in favour of an enigmatically for-

---

11 This debate can be reconstructed on the basis of the three texts published in *Kwartalnik Historii Kultury Materialnej:* KULCZYCKI, 1955, p. 519-562; HOŁUBOWICZ, 1955, p. 563-585 and the report of the debate: Dyskusja, 1955, p. 586-620.

mulated *decentralisation* in academic policy in the further future, although at the same time they declared themselves in favour of a dominance of the history of material culture at archaeological institutes.

The third point of view, which can be described as being practical, assumed the possibility that a history of material culture did not exist as an autonomous discipline, but as a group of research topics. A large part of the prominent archaeologists, whose autonomy was endangered, spoke out in this spirit as did also experienced and openly thinking historians.

When considering this debate, it has to be pointed out that the majority of its participants, regardless of the viewpoint they represented, made use of the Marxist stylistics accepted at that time in their argumentation, often quite simply to avoid the accusation of divergent thinking or even of disloyalty towards the Communist Party. A correct deciphering of this Marxist-Stalinist slang, which would let us determine who represented which point of view, today represents a great challenge, above all for historians of the younger generation, which they can often not master. The participants in the 1955 debate gladly fell back on Soviet models in this connection. The supporters of the first viewpoint named above, who demanded the creation of a new Marxist history of material culture as a separate, *progressive* science, quoted the fact that the Academy of the History of Material Culture had already been founded in Petrograd in 1919, which was later transformed into the Institute for the History of Material Culture of the Soviet Academy of Sciences. Their opponents fell back on similar stylistics and similar arguments; however, they said that behind the nameplate of the Soviet IHMC in reality there was just hidden an institute of archaeology. In this connection, they claimed that ultimately the "liquidatory endeavours of the Trotzkyist vermin"[12] against archaeology as a sovereign discipline in the Soviet Union had been curbed at the beginning of the second half of the thirties, thus during Stalin's purges.

The dispute about the sovereignty of the history of material culture as a separate discipline ended in Poland with a compromise. On the one hand, it was abolished as a subject at universities, on the other hand, however, the organisational structures of the IHMC PAS were retained as an interdisciplinary platform for archaeologists, ethnographers and historians who specialised in the history of material culture. After the political breakthrough of 1956 and with the relative liberalisation of cultural and academic life in the People's Republic of Poland, the IHMC PAS continued to exist in an organisational structure little changed by comparison with the initial period, despite certain changes in the 1960s, among

---

12 DYSKUSJA, 1955, p. 608.

other things after the anti-Semitic hate campaign controlled by the Communist authorities in 1968, to which many scholars, also from the academic milieu, fell victim.[13]

The ideological ballast decreased during the so-called *thaw after 1956* which had a decisively positive influence on the quality of the research work initiated by the IHMC. The interesting thing in this connection is that, from the end of the fifties, the IHMC was the only institute in the Eastern bloc to bear the name Institute for the History of Material Culture. In its environment, the supporters of the viewpoint according to which the history of material culture represented a group of research topics, the research into which should lead to a better acquaintance with the whole of cultural history, now set the tone.[14] In this connection, inspiration was openly taken from Jan Rutkowski's earlier concepts. The projects inspired at the beginning of the 1950s led to the publication of important works from the fields of economic history, as well as prehistoric and classical history, in the following decades. The research work from the field of the history of material culture concentrated above all on two epochs—the Middle Ages and the Modern Age—falling back on the following topics, among others: The history of Polish industry and Polish crafts, the settlement of the Polish territories, agriculture. The focus in this connection was also on the examination of the conditions of the material existence of different social strata.

Generally speaking, a shift of research priorities was recorded in the sixties and seventies away from topics, such as the production technology of crafts, agriculture and industry, to topics, such as the culture of everyday life, the history of communication and travel, as well as widely understood consumption.[15] This was certainly a reflection of the changes in the People's Republic of Poland, where industrialisation had been carried through in the fifties and early sixties, and thus in the sixties and seventies society's notice began to concentrate on consumption, the numerous deficits of which further strengthened researchers' attention. All the more so as the new government, which had seized power after the strikes on the Baltic coast in December 1970, made the *increase in society's level of consumption* into one of its most important propaganda slogans.

In addition, the shift in research priorities, above all to themes of the culture of everyday life, the history of communication and consumption, was due more

---

13 On the organisational changes in the structure of the IHMC PAS see among other things the report: DZIAŁALNOŚĆ, 1970, p. 727f.
14 Among others, the outstanding Polish medievalist Aleksander Gieysztor proposed such a perspective: GIEYSZTOR, 1958, p.143-154.
15 SZTETYŁŁO, 1993, p. 24f.

and more to the popularity of the works of the classical writers of the French *Annales* school, that had been translated into Polish, as well as Polish historians' active contacts with this milieu. After 1956, this active intellectual exchange was possible for younger Polish historians, mainly thanks to a wave of scholarships for France, financed, of course, by the French government. It can probably be asserted without exaggeration that, above all at the end of the fifties and in the sixties, French historiography, in particular the *Annales* school, represented the proverbial *window of the world* for Polish historiography. By the way, the fact that IHMC archaeologists conducted excavations on medieval sites, e.g. in the Côte d'Or and in Aveyron,[16] can give evidence of the importance of the contacts with the École Practique des Hautes Études (IV section).

All this was reflected in the methodological debates in IHMC circles. Particular attention was paid in the discussion at the end of the sixties and beginning of the seventies to the first volume of the *Civilisation materiélle et capitalisme* by Fernand Braudel published in 1967. The *pragmatists*, who defended the viewpoint of the integrity of material culture with culture as such, now made use of the *Annalistes'* concepts, which in turn called the autonomy of the history of material culture as a separate discipline into question. Let us here quote a voice from the methodological discussion at the IHMC in 1971:

"The attempts by contemporary French historiography here are interesting. In the circle of the well-known periodical '*Annales ESC*', a series of monographs on selected questions of material culture has appeared which as a rule take up the involvement of human beings in the shaping of this culture; on the other hand, they avoid presenting the history of objects, e.g. the history of resources, tools, etc., without associating them with the respective social group. Following this series of monographs, a methodologically innovative work by Prof. F. Braudel, *Civilisation materielle et capitalisme* appeared. In its introductory section, the characteristics of the material culture of the age of capitalism are recorded micro-analytically, and people are shown in their everyday life. Consumption is to the forefront which, in the author's opinion, necessitates the development of production, both technically and economically. The whole structure of modern civilisation (its fixed and variable elements) finds expression in the social and political life of this epoch."[17]

---

16 Cf. among other things the report: DZIAŁALNOŚĆ, 1970, p. 732.
17 PIETRZAK-PAWŁOWSKA, 1971, p. 106.

The new perspective fascinated and thus also shaped the scholars who defended the autonomy of the history of material culture as a separate academic discipline from a more traditional Marxist perspective. Their definition was expanded by the postulate of research works about widely understood consumption.[18] Research on the history of fashion were often also postulated in the wide context of mental and economic transformations.[19]

The growing influence of the historiography of the *Annales* school and in general the opening of Polish historiography in the seventies and eighties to worldwide research work on cultural history, which became apparent, for example, in research into widely understood structures of everyday life, into élitist culture versus popular culture, or into the newly defined history of material culture, finds its confirmation in many interesting monographs and syntheses outside the circle around the IHMC. On the other hand, in the IHMC milieu, the new direction of research, that became established in western Europe, the United States and Canada in the second half of the twentieth century under the name industrial archaeology or also *postmedieval archaeology*[20], also convinced them of the correctness of the endeavour to discover cultural contents in material objects. At the same time, old supporters of the Marxist defined history of material culture now began to newly discover the *symbolic level of [material] things*, maintaining:

> "We live among things and use them [...] in accordance with their intended purpose, but do not usually notice their symbolic side. However, precisely this side is a source of information for culture. They include significantly richer contents than words are capable of doing. Therefore, human beings have never limited themselves to words and use things in the exchange of ideas. Both the oil-lamp and the hammer and sickle [in symbolism, thus intellectual culture—I.K.] were newly discovered when their practical applicability had lost its significance with regard to civilisation."[21]

Despite the complete renunciation of ideological miasmas and the adoption of world-wide modern trends in cultural history research by IHMC PAS, and also despite its own creative contributions to this research work, after the watershed in 1989 and the restoration of full Polish sovereignty, this institution fell victim

---

18 PAZDUR, 1971, p. 85-105.
19 DYSKUSJA, 1971, p. 111 and 115.
20 PAZDUR, 1977, p. 457-469.
21 ID., S. 468; see also interesting comments: PAZDUR, 1973, p. 411-43.

to a kind of revenge. A revenge—that like every vengeance—was actually irrational in itself. This revenge consisted in the fact that at the turn of the years 1991 and 1992, the IHMC was renamed Institute of Archaeology and Ethnology and the term *History of Material Culture* was completely deleted, although at this institute—after the archaeologists—precisely historians, who dealt with exactly this field, represented the second largest group in numbers.[22] Oddly enough, in 1991, the Russian IHMC in St. Petersburg was reactivated that had been transformed into the Institute of Archaeology in 1959.

Fortunately, the change in the institute's name did not result in the dismissal of the still energetic and creative scholars dealing with the history of material culture. At present they represent the probably most numerous group of historians in Poland who deal with widely understood cultural historical research, who have an institutional framework, and—what is important in this connection—subject their research to profound methodological reflection.[23] They demand a resumption of the discussion of the theory of the history of material culture and point to the evolution of cultural history in the last 150 years, above all under the influence of structural, historical and cultural anthropology. Thus one becomes aware in what way the *anthropological-cultural perspective* vanquished the *positivistic-substantial research perspective*, that had been elaborated in the second half of the 19th century and still dominated in the first half of the twentieth, which in its view of reality presupposed its subdivision into the intellectual and material sphere, or—in another variant—a subdivision into an intellectual, social and material culture.

In this was, the *anthropological and structural perspective* begins to dominate in research into the history of material culture This assumes that the "analysis of cultural phenomena may not just be based on factually compiled and separately considered elements [...]. The fundamental characteristics of the objects examined are, namely, not so much dependent on the characteristics of their substratum, 'as on the method of the composition of the elements (the internal structure) and their place in a wider context (external structure)'".[24]

---

22 PAZDUR, 1977, p. 468.
23 A good example for this from the early nineties is the resumption of the discussion about the concept of the structures of everyday life and in general Braudel's concept of the history of material culture—for this cf. BOGUCKA, 1996, p. 247-253; KARPIŃSKI, 1996, p. 303-304; KOWECKA, 1996, p. 255-261; SOWINA, 1994, p. 153-158; SZAROTA, 1994, p. 239-245; SZTETYŁŁO, 1994, p. 181-182; TOPOLSKI, 1994, p. 461-467; WRZOSEK, 1994, p. 167-172.
24 TABACZYŃSKI, 1993, p. 15.

Therefore the change in perspective for research into the history of material objects from the positivistic-substantial to the anthropological-structural one led to these objects being seen as *correlates of the cultural heritage*. In 1993, Stanisław Tabaczyński, a Polish archaeologist and medievalist from the generation of those who began their careers at the IHMC in the fifties, stressed in his reflection on the contemporary state of the history of material culture that material objects as such do not depict the content of culture, "which is above all a 'reality of ideas', [however,] they do hold valuable information on the culture, they perpetuate temporal and spatial dimensions of cultural phenomena".[25]

New theoretical approaches are being elaborated in parallel to modern research into concrete ways of looking at problems in the history of material culture. Research into the newly defined *everyday life* brings particularly interesting results, e.g. with regard to the Early Modern Period and the extensive archive sources, such as lists of real property and similar documents which show *the history of human beings among things and vice versa*: *the history of things among human beings*. This in turn allows us to show the changeability, but also conversely the constancy of the processes of civilisation over a longer period of time.

> "In this view, the history of material culture comes directly into contact with ethnology, it is based on the achievements of medieval and modern archaeology, e.g. on industrial archaeology. In this sense—one researcher of the middle generation from the IHMC, Andrzej Pośpiech, observes—academic archive studies of written sources, manuscript archive materials [...] could be described as word archaeology. It discovers namely—just like an archaeologist through his excavations—archaeological monuments, sources of information about the conditions of life in the past, often unknown, fascinating through their exoticism and the colourful splendour of the detail".[26]

If one looks from this perspective—Pośpiech adds—"the history of material culture and mentality are one and the same thing".[27]

At the same time, material culture historians are accompanied more and more by *postmodernist awareness* that our "pictures of the past are our constructions, and not just simply the past as such. In truth namely, by speaking about the past we are conducting a dialogue with one another about our culture [and at

---

25 ID., p. 16; cf. TOPOLSKI, 1993, p. 421-425.
26 POŚPIECH, 1997, p. 218.
27 ID., S. 219; cf. also POŚPIECH, 1996, p. 263-270.

the same time] about their past".[28] This awareness accompanies me today, too, while I present the history of Polish research into the history of material culture in rough outline.

Literature

BOGUCKA, MARIA, Życie codzienne – spory wokół profilu badań i definicji, in: Kwartalnik Historii Kultury Materialnej 44 (1996), p. 247-253.
Dyskusja na posiedzeniu plenarnym Wydziału I Nauk Społecznych Polskiej Akademii Nauk w dniu 2 lutego 1955 roku nad zagadnieniami teoretycznymi historii kultury materialnej, in: Kwartalnik Historii Kultury Materialnej 3 (1955), p. 586-620.
Dyskusja, in: Kwartalnik Historii Kultury Materialnej 19 (1971), p. 107-128.
Działalność Instytutu Historii Kultury Materialnej PAN w 1969 r., in: Kwartalnik Historii Kultury Materialnej 18 (1970), p. 727-740.
FEEST, CHRISTIAN F., Materielle Kultur, in: Ethnologie. Einführung und Überblick, ed. by BETTINA BEER/HANS FISCHER (Ethnologische Paperbacks), Berlin 2003, p. 239-254.
GIEYSZTOR, ALEKSANDER, A propos de l'histoire des conditions matérielles de la vie humaine, in: Kwartalnik Historii Kultury Materialnej 6 (1958), fascicule suplement, Ergon, vol. 1, p. 143-154.
HAHN, HANS PETER, Materielle Kultur. Eine Einführung. (Ethnologische Paperbacks), Berlin 2005.
HOŁUBOWICZ, WŁODZIMIERZ, Uwagi o historii kultury materialnej jako nauce, in: Kwartalnik Historii Kultury Materialnej 3 (1955), p. 563-585.
Instytut Historii Kultury Materialnej Polskiej Akademii Nauk 1953-1977, in: Kwartalnik Historii Kultury Materialnej 25 (1977), p. 447-454.
KARPIŃSKI, ANDRZEJ, Everyday life – a new research trend in the history of culture, in: Kwartalnik Historii Kultury Materialnej 44 (1996), p. 303-304.
KÖNIG, GUDRUN M., Auf dem Rücken der Dinge. Materielle Kultur und Kulturwissenschaft, in: Unterwelten der Kultur. Themen und Theorien der volkskundlichen Kulturwissenschaft, ed. by KASPAR MAASE/BERND JÜRGEN WARNEKEN, Köln 2003, p. 95-118.

---

28 OSTOJA-ZAGÓRSKI, 1997, p. 217; cf. also OSTOJA-ZAGÓRSKI, 1994, p. 177-179 and finally the comments by this author on the topic of archaeology and humanities, OSTOJA-ZAGÓRSKI, 2002, p. 277-286.

KOWECKA, ELŻBIETA, Źródła do życia codziennego w XIX w. i metody ich badań, in: Kwartalnik Historii Kultury Materialnej 44 (1996), p. 255-261.

KULCZYCKI, JERZY, Założenia teoretyczne historii kultury materialnej, in: Kwartalnik Historii Kultury Materialnej 3 (1955), p. 519-562.

MAJEWSKI, KAZIMIERZ, Historia kultury materialnej, in: Kwartalnik Historii Kultury Materialnej 1/2 (1953/54), p. 3-26.

ID., Najnowsze badania nad historią antycznej kultury materialnej, in: Kwartalnik Historii Kultury Materialnej 5 (1957), p. 209-244.

ID., Uwagi o zakresie historii kultury materialnej i systematyce ergologicznej, in: Kwartalnik Historii Kultury Materialnej, 8 (1960), p. 1-14.

ID., Nowe uwagi do badań historii kultury materialnej antyku, in: Kwartalnik Historii Kultury Materialnej 21 (1973), p. 395-409.

ID., Dalsze uwagi o badaniu historii rzeczy, in: Kwartalnik Historii Kultury Materialnej 24 (1976), p. 109-115.

ID., Rozważań nad historią antycznej kultury materialnej ciąg dalszy, in: Kwartalnik Historii Kultury Materialnej 26 (1978), p. 207-218.

OSTOJA-ZAGÓRSKI, JANUSZ, W kwestii znaczeniowych treści kultury materialnej, in: Kwartalnik Historii Kultury Materialnej, 42 (1994), p. 177-179.

ID., [voice in the discussion:] Archeologia, etnologia, historia kultury materialnej—perspektywy badań, in: Kwartalnik Historii Kultury Materialnej 45 (1997), p. 215-217.

ID., Archeologia wobec humanistycznych koncepcji badań nad kulturą, in: Kwartalnik Historii Kultury Materialnej, 50 (2002), p. 277-286.

PAZDUR, JAN, Historia kultury materialnej Polski. Doświadczenia i propozycje, in: Kwartalnik Historii Kultury Materialnej, 19 (1971), p. 85-99.

ID., Technika jako przedmiot badań historii kultury materialnej, in: Kwartalnik Historii Kultury Materialnej 21 (1973), p. 411-433.

ID., Rzeczy i środowisko materialne oraz ich historia, in: Kwartalnik Historii Kultury Materialnej 25 (1977), p. 457-469.

PIETRZAK-PAWŁOWSKA, IRENA, [voice in the discussion:] Dyskusja, in: Kwartalnik Historii Kultury Materialnej 19 (1971), p. 106-108.

Pięćdziesiąt lat badań nad historią kultury materialnej, in: Kwartalnik Historii Kultury Materialnej 50 (2002).

POŚPIECH, ADAM, Prowincja szlachecka w Polsce XVII wieku. Ludzie—przedmioty—życie codzienne (zarys problematyki), 44 (1996), p. 263-270.

ID., [voice in the discussion:] Archeologia, etnologia, historia kultury materialnej—perspektywy badań, in: Kwartalnik Historii Kultury Materialnej 45 (1997), p. 217-220.

RUTKOWSKI, JAN, Historia kultury i próba systematyzacji jej zagadnień (do druku przygotował Janusz Deresiewicz), in: Kwartalnik Historii Kultury Materialnej 7 (1959), p. 5-61.

RUTKOWSKI, TADEUSZ PAWEŁ, Nauki historyczne w Polsce 1944-1970. Zagadnienia polityczne i organizacyjne, Warszawa 2007.

SOWINA URSZULA, 'Ferdynand Braudel a koncepcje historii kultury materialnej'. Dyskusja w Instytucie Archeologii i Etnologii PAN. Warszawa, 7 grudnia 1993 r., in: Kwartalnik Historii Kultury Materialnej 42 (1994), p. 153-158.

SZAROTA, TOMASZ, Życie codzienne — temat badawczy czy tylko popularyzacja? (Na marginesie serii wydawniczych Hachette i PIW-u), in: Kwartalnik Historii Kultury Materialnej 42 (1994), p. 239-245.

SZTETYŁŁO, JANUSZ, *Nec mergitur* — 40 lat 'Kwartalnika Historii Kultury Materialnej', in: Kwartalnik Historii Kultury Materialnej 41 (1993), p. 23-32.

ID., 'Kwartalnik Historii Kultury Materialnej' i Ferdynand Braudel, in: Kwartalnik Historii Kultury Materialnej 42 (1994), p. 181-182.

TABACZYŃSKI, STANISŁAW, Kultura i jej rzeczowe korelaty, in: Kwartalnik Historii Kultury Materialnej 41 (1993), p. 5-20.

TOPOLSKI, JERZY, Jana Rutkowskiego koncepcja historii kultury materialnej, in: Kwartalnik Historii Kultury Materialnej 28 (1980), S. 461-467.

ID., O składnikach i korelatach kultury, in: Kwartalnik Historii Kultury Materialnej 41 (1993), p. 421-425.

ID., Ferdynand Braudel a koncepcja historii kultury materialnej, in: Kwartalnik Historii Kultury Materialnej 42 (1994), p. 159-165.

WRZOSEK, WOJCIECH, Braudelowska idea kultury materialnej, in: Kwartalnik Historii Kultury Materialnej 42 (1994), p. 167-172.

Achievements and Contradictions in the Writing and Teaching of Cultural History in Hungary

ANDREA PETŐ

A book series bound in reddish brown leather can be found on the bookshelves not only of every historian but of every intellectual family in Hungary. From this statement it is obvious that this book series was a bestseller. Only after the books are removed from the shelf does it become clear whether they belong to the original series published between 1939 and 1942 or are reprints from 1990-91. This book series is the *Cultural History of Hungary* (*Magyar művelődéstörténet*) by Sándor Domanovszky in five volumes. The series, which was a collective effort of the leading historians of the period, promised a "different perspective" on history-writing, as indicated by Domanovszky himself in the introduction:

> "Focusing on the activity of the spirit which cannot be seen so sharply [...]. Instead of political life we would like to show the development of our culture to the reader [...]. Everything that fits into the social cohabitation and its frame belongs here. Besides the spiritual and cultural, what kind of material will also be covered in the volumes? The changing character of the toiled soil, the composition of the inhabitants by nationality, the economy, the various branches of intellectual life, and the way of life of different strata of the society [...]."[1]

---

1 DOMANOVSZKY 1990, Vol. 1. Introduction (all translations are mine unless otherwise indicated) p. 17.

The book was illustrated with 2500 pictures and after underlining the backwardness and isolation of Hungarian historiography, it gave a synthesis of historical research during the interwar period written by leading specialists in the subfields. The result as a synthesis was limited even in the eye of Domanovszky, who in the introduction explained that the reason why so many collaborators contributed to the volume was due to the lack of basic primary research. He also noted the differences in the approaches of the individual contributors, who, however, were all *experts* in their own respective fields, which made their contributions reliable. The motto of the introduction: "The work should offer what we can offer at the present state of our knowledge"[2] has serious epistemological consequences, which will be discussed later on in this article.

The success of the volume during World War II does not require much explanation, especially because it promised the familiar framework: "In this presentation the hero is replaced by the way of life, thinking, and creative activity of the mass of the nation."[3] But the success of the reprint after the *annus mirabilis* of 1989 does, I believe, require an explanation, and I will return to this point.

In 2010, Domanovszky does not even earn a Wikipedia entry on Hungarian historians, while the zeal to publish summary volumes on cultural history without first defining the nature of cultural history is still alive and well. I will examine the *urgent need* for summary volumes below.

After the collapse of communism the first summary work on cultural history was edited by the ethnographer László Kósa and published in 1997. It was also published and reprinted in 2003, and since 1999 it has been available in English as *Cultural History of Hungary* (*Magyar művelődéstörténet*).[4] The book is on the required reading list for several university courses in Hungary.[5]

The editor, Kósa, defined the purpose of the collection as follows:

> "The relationship between man and the natural world, the changes in and moulding of inanimate and animate nature, are the threads that run through our book from beginning to end: we analyse changes in the Hungarians' lifestyle and mentality, we examine their everyday experiences and their holidays through the ages, the surrounding material world, the ideologies that

---

2 ID.
3 ID.
4 KÓSA, 1999.
5 For an analysis of other encyclopedical publications after 1989 such as Pannon Chronicle and Hungarian Codex 1-5, see MONOK, 2006, p. 818-830.

have shaped their lives and circumstances, and the habits and institutions of human communication and co-existence."[6]

Parallel with this enterprise another important book series was begun: *The Encyclopedia of Hungarian Cultural History (Magyar Művelődéstörténeti Lexikon)*.[7] For more than a decade 400 authors collected entries for this mega enterprise. The first volume was published in 2003, and as of 2010 eight volumes have appeared. This enterprise faced several difficulties and it proceeds very slowly due to financial problems and—as I will argue later on in this paper—due to conceptual issues which were not solved by listing the entries in alphabetical order within the strict format of an encyclopedia.

The Encyclopedia defined its aim as "to share with readers the history of literature, the history of art, the history of music, medicine, military history, monetary history, the history of everyday life, the history of nutrition, religion, the history of schooling *etc.* [my emphasis A. P.]."[8]

It defined its scope as "the widest possible scope as defined by Hegel, not as history centered on events and politics. Hungarian as an adjective means Hungarian as the national framework of today's Hungary".[9] In the introduction to the *Encyclopedia of Hungarian Cultural History* the editor refers to this approach: "We know that by identifying Hungarian with present day Hungary we have not solved several interrelated questions; instead we have gone around."[10]

In this paper I present three different attempts to write the history of "culture" within a "Hungarian" national framework: one made during World War II, one seven years after the collapse of communism and one 17 years after the collapse of communism. I seek to reveal similarities and differences among these volumes in relation to their framing of the topic of cultural history. I do so by investigating three elements: imperial legacies, institutional developments and their relationship to interdisciplinarity.

---

6   Kósa, 1999, original translation on p. 7.
7   Introduction in Kőszeghy 2003, p. 8.
8   Id., p. 7
9   Kósa, 2003, I., p. 7.
10 Kőszeghy, 2003, p. 2.

1. The period before World War II

One element shared by the three series is immediately recognisable. All three volumes were produced in a national frame. Domanovszky even pointed out in his introduction that the only possible framework for historical analysis is the nation. The geographical focus has definitely switched from the imperial *Greater Hungary* (Kingdom of Hungary as a part of the Habsburg Empire), which was dominant during World War II, to Hungary within its present borders. Thus, those territories which historically belonged to the Kingdom of Hungary, are simply missing from the scope of current historical analyses.

What causes the amnesia and omission? During 50 years of communism the territories belonging to Hungary before the Trianon Peace Treaty of 1920 were taboo; they were doomed to oblivion. This is one of the reasons why the reprint of Domanovszky sold out so quickly in 1989. It promised knowledge about the *lost homeland* and filled a gap in historical knowledge caused by the quasi-national framework of communist history-writing.

The question is: Did it sufficiently change the scope of historical analysis to permit an evaluation of the dramatic changes that were related to the collapse of the Kingdom of Hungary? Cooper argued that "empires produced (a) strong empire-centered imagination".[11] People or citizens sought to make their way within the empire by means of collaboration and contestation, and this approach makes *the people*, the agents and the subjects invisible. In this paper I claim that the imperialist heritage poses a theoretical challenge to those who would write a new cultural history in Hungary.

But is there any change in the intellectual focus or, to rephrase the question, has the scope of writing cultural history changed at all?

Moving beyond the hopeless endeavour of defining cultural history, I examine instead the different influences and encounters that served to formulate the aims of the series. My aim is to answer the opening question: Why was Domanovszky's work a great success both during World War II and after the collapse of the communism?

The first issue to be examined is the issue of translation in a wider sense. The three volumes are all mentioned in this chapter under the heading of cultural history. However, they rather belong to the school of *Kulturgeschichte* — and to the subsection of *Universalgeschichte*, which includes everything but political and military history — than to new cultural history, and this partly explains the outstanding success of Domanovszky's work after 1989.

---

11 COOPER, 2005, p. 23.

The confusion over terminology began in the early 1860s when the specificity of Hungarian history was defined as a *cultural mission* (*kultúrmisszió*), which meant that for centuries the Hungarian nation had had to fight for its existence, leaving no time and space for *embourgeoisement*. Therefore the first generation of so-called cultural historians (*művelődéstörténészek*) tended to focus on political history under the heading of cultural history. The term in Hungarian (*művelődéstörténet*) means the history of education rather than the history of culture. For this reason, it can serve as a site for various intellectual approaches and political aspirations as far as the terminology is concerned. By the time the department of cultural history (*művelődéstörténet*) was founded there was a need for methodological and theoretical innovation in the field in line with European developments. Instead of establishing special subsections of history, the post World War I period brought in *spiritual history* (*szellemtörténet*). As the Bálint Hóman declared: "Spiritual history, or to use a synonym cultural history (*művelődéstörténet*), is conceptualised as the really right one."[12]

The Hungarian pioneers of cultural history (*kultúrtörténet*), Arnold Hauser and Karl Polanyi, had already emigrated from Hungary when the Domanovszky series was published in Budapest; their works remained unreferenced in these books. Domanovszky's work arose in the post-1919 period. For those who are unfamiliar with Hungarian history, it is worth noting that the year 1919, which marked the end of two revolutions in Hungary, saw the first exodus of leftist, critical intellectuals from Hungary to Vienna and Berlin, many of whom later moved to London and to the United States. The approach to culture of such historians as Polanyi or Hauser, who before 1918 belonged to the progressive circle *Huszadik Század* (Twentieth Century), was very different from that of Domanovszky, who headed the department of cultural history at Budapest University.

The other school of thought challenging the *spiritualised* version of cultural history, was economic history. Hungary's economic historians also considered their approach in universalistic terms as "the history of the nation", as was pointed out by Alajos Paikert (1866-1948), editor of *Gazdaságtörténeti Szemle* (*Review of Economic History, 1894-1906*), in his introductory comments to the first issue of the journal.

In his work, Domanovszky ignored sociological, psychological and economic analyses, which were regarded as suspiciously leftist in what was a conservative-rightist era. He followed the German type of *Geistesgeschichte* in his *Hungarian Cultural History*. Hungary lost its national dominance in the Carpathian

---

12 Quoted without a reference in VÁRKONYI, 1970, p. 147.

basin after 1920, but the official cultural politics of the interwar period retained a kind of neo-nationalism in the form of *cultural supremacy* (*kultúrfölény*) dangerously resembling *cultural mission* (*kultúrmisszió*). Historicising that imagined realm, writing about the lost territories was a subtle form of domination. The *strong empire-centered imagination* created culture as an imagined form of domination. This explains in part the success of the book then and also in 1989 when the ideological censorship promoting Soviet domination under the cover of *internationalism* collapsed. This led to the nostalgia for summary volumes published during the interwar Horthy era: the old encyclopedias became popular in the search for historical roots and as a means of reconstructing intellectual connections with the Horthy era that had been broken under communism. This revival of an imagined historical tradition forms the basis for new conservative history-writing in Hungary.

Domanovszky's summary work on Hungarian cultural history has been criticised for its lack of "coherence".

One of the first historians to criticise the endeavour during World War II was Bálint Hóman, a historian and a minister of culture (1932-42), who was sentenced to life imprisonment by the people's tribunals after World War II. He criticised the book series for "questioning coherence and continuity".[13] He also labeled cultural history as an "appendix to history".[14] History for Hóman was political history; *wie es gewesen war*. Moreover, for him the loss of national supremacy was just temporary, and as a powerful politician and intellectual he did his best to demonstrate this was so by supporting German war efforts. In his view concrete political and military action was needed, not "strong empire-centered imagination".

Hóman's criticism was paradoxically echoed by the doyen of Hungarian cultural studies, Kosáry, who was imprisoned by the communist regime after 1956. In 1983 he argued that Domanovszky's five-volume series "lacked any sign of internal coherence".[15] But this "coherence" was just different to one from that demanded by Hóman. For Hóman it was simply not the *right* history of culture, in view of its descriptive and positivist character and the fact that it was not "spiritual" enough.

---

13 HÓMAN, 1938, p. 33.
14 ID.
15 KOSÁRY, 1983, P. 16.

2. During communism

So is there any chance of achieving internal coherence in the case of cultural history? What do these constant demands for coherence tell us about the place of cultural history-writing in Hungary? How can or could cultural history move away from the "history of etceteras" as defined in the *Encyclopedia of Hungarian Cultural History*? Why is *new cultural history* missing from Hungarian historiography, even though micro-history, cultural anthropology and other new approaches are present in history-writing? In order to answer these questions, we need to briefly examine the institutional developments of cultural history-writing in Hungary.

It is no surprise that the department of cultural history led by Domanovszky and founded in 1898 was closed after the post-war communist takeover. The superiority of structures and class as explanatory categories left no space for the *Geistesgeschichte* or *cultural* history, which was also discredited politically because of its strong ideological ties to the interwar Horthy regime. Culture was defined only as a superstructure in relation to the economically determined social basis.

The Cold War quarantine of history-writing in Hungary, a development that could also be observed in other countries on the eastern side of the Iron Curtain, effectively prevented developments or experiments in history-writing. Historians that did not fit into the Marxist framework worked at the Institute of History or in various regional archives. Paradoxically, it was the Institute of History that was commissioned with writing what was supposed to be a Marxist summary history of Hungary in ten volumes, the so-called missing *synthesis* of Hungarian history.[16] At the beginning of the endeavour a debate started about how to define *culture*.

This debate signaled that, as the Kadar regime relinquished its hold on society, the unquestionable dominance of Marxist history-writing (including economic history as the main genre) was nearly over. Those who did not challenge the major ideological cornerstones of the Kadar regime, which by chance were all connected to the history of 20[Th] century (1919, 1945, and 1956), were permitted to experiment with certain new approaches to history-writing. Kosáry, for example, openly challenged the dominant Marxist idea of base and superstructure, the division between material and spiritual, and he advocated the concept

---

16 The first nine volumes have been published; the tenth on post-1945 history is yet to be published. These volumes are still used as the only available modern synthesis in education and research.

of "totalistic history".[17] Kosáry during the war and immediately after World War II was educated in France, and he was a follower of the *Annales* School. He believed in *long dureé*, the structures and patterns that shape and influence history, so if we know these we will know History. The *Annales* had a connection with Hungarian historians from 1966; conferences and workshops were organised. The major works by Chaunu and Braudel were translated into Hungarian within a few years of their publication in French. For these historians the focus of study was culture, as a single and unified element.

The first challenge to the Marxist historical cannon came when some historians tried to integrate the works of *Annales*, which, as I have already argued, fitted into the existing positivist framework. The debate, published in the main journals of the historical profession, *Századok*, in 1970 and in *Történelmi Szemle* in 1974, sketched the various approaches of Hungarian historians to the concept of culture. This debate had an enormous impact on the development of Hungarian history-writing: during the later years of the Kádár era, leading historians were given the chance to define the subject matter of history and the place of culture therein. Reading this debate today, one notices how the different concepts and trends of *Annales* and the German school of *Kulturgeschichte* were mentioned and used as analytical categories, even while the Marxist dogmas and taboos continued to be cleverly acknowledged. Braudel, Mandrou, Chaunu and their main works were mentioned along with early versions of discourse analysis, while, of course, the authors had to praise Lenin's concept of culture.[18]

Cultural history (*művelődéstörténet*) is defined as social history, as the history of mentality, and as an appendix to economic history. Niederhauser, employing a pragmatic approach, defined it as the material culture described by Domanovszky combined with the writing and editorial techniques of Huizinga and Burckhardt and supplemented with some interesting, catchy stories that have no real "scientific" value.[19]

Péter Hanák, one of the authors of the cultural history sections of the ten-volume History of Hungary and an active participant in the debate,[20] launched an attack on the traditional, positivist and vulgar Marxist frameworks, while also challenging the long-entrenched divisions of political, ethnic, social and

---

17 KOSÁRY, 1974, p. 440.
18 In some works the author, for example Braudel, is not mentioned. Instead, their works and ideas are presented as a way forward. MAKKAI, 1974, p. 432.
19 NIEDERHAUSER, 1974, p. 420.
20 HANÁK, 1974, p. 447-450.

economic history.[21] Having been influenced by Carl Schorske, he re-introduced cultural history (*kultúrtörténet*). He used culture as a set of symbols and as a constitutive element of people's understanding of the surrounding world. Hanák explained his growing interest in cultural studies as a response to the unsatisfactory explanatory models of the dominant political history: he looked for the singular and unrepeatable everyday practices of daily life.

The second institutional challenge occurred only in the early 1980s. In 1981, the Hungarian Academy of Sciences established the Committee on Cultural History (*Művelődéstörténet*), whose task was to coordinate research on the middle Ages, renaissance and baroque studies. Béla Köpeczi, a scholar of 18th century French literature, was appointed as the committee's chair. In 1982, Köpeczi became minister of culture, and thereafter the committee received all possible help (and intellectual shelter) from the communist authorities. His presence helped to institutionalise the committee's work within the Hungarian Academy of Sciences.

The time was ripe for the reconditioning of a department of cultural history. In 1981, the first head of the new Department of Cultural History at ELTE in Budapest, Béla G. Németh, defined the department's mission as the history of ideas, the history of institutions and the history of everyday life. For Németh "cultural history is a general historical science, which reaches out to all aspects of life through the tools of defining and underlining historicity".[22] After a long ban from teaching activity Péter Hanák was also hired as a professor in the department.

Summarising developments during communism, we can identify three tendencies that co-existed until 1989: the narrow application of the history of ideas; an inability to respond to the interdisciplinary challenge posed by new social scientific methods; and the intellectual legacy of Domanovszky, where cultural history was viewed as "general history". We may now be reluctant to remember 1989 as the *annus mirabilis*, but at the time there were several factors that made us hope for a paradigm shift in Hungarian history-writing: the end of direct ideological censorship (which, as we have seen, was already crumbling); the increasing importance of international exchanges; and the foundation of new higher educational institutions. Let us see whether and how these factors impacted the development of cultural history.

---

21 See more on this in PETŐ/SZAPOR, 2007, p. 160-166.
22 Németh quoted in DOBSZAY/FÓNAGY, 2003, p. 407. Original quote in NÉMETH, 1998, p. 39.

3. The post-1989 period with new attempts and failed interdisciplinarity

In the mid-1980s, together with the ideological opening, the methodologies of economic history, historical demography and sociology embraced by historians paid dividends in investigations into the roots of economic and social modernisation, including historical studies of gender history.[23] In 1987 the new generation of historians—mostly social historians, gathered to form the István Hajnal Circle—in opposition to the mainstream academics of the Hungarian Historical Association, founded in 1867. Their aim was to scrutinise the discourses of political history that had been used exclusively to write about history and to create their own professional and existential legitimacy. The arguments they put forward were very similar to the arguments cited by Domanovszky in his introduction to the five-volume series. Let us examine the consequences of social history becoming the dominant framework for a renewal of Hungarian history-writing after 1989 and as a force opposing the exclusive focus on political history and weakening what remained of the Marxist framework.

The Hajnal Circle sought to establish social history as an alternative to all other approaches to history-writing. However, this attempt led to marginalisation and localisation. One of the main intellectual and professional achievements of the group was the publication of a state-of-the-art volume entitled *Introduction to Social History* in 2003.[24] Tellingly, this introductory handbook, designed for use by university students, divides the various approaches to history-writing into old and new schools. Branches of history-writing such as urban history, religious history, economic history, historical demography, historical geography, political history and the history of culture (*művelődéstörténet*) were classified as *old* schools of writing history. Meanwhile, among the *new* schools, we find micro-history, historical anthropology, the linguistic turn, the history of mentality, psychohistory and gender. With this categorisation cultural history as a school of thought was subordinated to the German *Ideengeschichte* school. In the chapter on cultural history as "old history" the term itself was translated using such synonyms as cultural studies, the history of culture, *Kulturgeschichte,* and *Historische Kulturforschung*.[25] The confusion about the translation explains why there is a reluctance to take a position on the definition of cultural history and its relevance for Hungarian history-writing in the new millennium. The au-

---

23 PETŐ, 2003.
24 ZSOMBOR/KOVÁCS, 2003.
25 DOBSZAY/FÓNAGY, 2003, p. 387-413.

thors of the chapter on cultural history even formulated a critical counter argument against cultural history, one that strangely echoes the criticisms of Hóman and Kosáry. They characterised it as "unprofessional, driven by interests and extremes, lacking a methodological and theoretical zeal of its own, and excessively heterogeneous".[26]

Since heterogeneity was mentioned once again as a weakness, perhaps we should seek to explain the old-new attachment to *homogeneous* history-writing. Why did this attachment resurface after 1989?

The complex relationship of the historical profession to interdisciplinary approaches also influences the status of cultural history in Hungary. The social sciences and the humanities are still sharply divided along institutional lines. Cultural studies are mostly the domain of literary scholars, and this influences the chosen subject matter. For instance, the editor in chief of the *Encyclopedia of Hungarian Cultural History* is a literary scholar, and so the series focuses on the Middle Ages and the Early Modern period. Their emphasis upon micro studies and the publication of sources leaves no room for theorizing. This position is shared by the majority of Hungarian historians.

In this paper I claim that the discontinuity in the Hungarian historical canon has been falsely attributed to 1945.[27] The Hungarian historical canon was not even challenged by the modernist approaches after 1989 and it is resistant to modernist thinking, including the modernism that developed from the ideas of Polanyi and Hauser. My argument is that this is due to the *empire-centered imagination*, which has remained unchallenged ever since 1919. I also identify two additional factors: the emergence of social history as the dominant paradigm and the specificities of transatlantic connections.

Before World War II the new historical method of inquiry was the statistical method, (economic history) and this only strengthened the positivist base of history-writing. After 1945 statistical (economic) history formed a poisonous alliance with Marxist economic history-writing, which was regarded as the only explanatory framework for historical analysis. It is no accident that *Annales* was *allowed*, if not encouraged to establish a foothold in Hungary under communism. So in this sense Marxist historiography never challenged history's claim to objectivity as it was framed by Ranke. Indeed, the claim was strengthened by the (illusory) significance Marxist historians attached to *scientific* materialism, which produced ready-made explanations for all sorts of events and tendencies in the past. In the communist era, history not only acted to create and sustain

---

26 ID., p. 396.
27 PETŐ, 2011, p. 67-75.

national identity—as it had done ever since the emergence of the nation-states—but also served as a rationale for class struggle.[28]

During communism historians of the medieval and early modern period quietly joined the *Annales*-influenced European mainstream, publishing works on witches and female saints.[29] The other intellectual influence was the German ethnographical method. Before 1989, both major European historiographies established a presence behind the Iron Curtain means of academic exchanges and scholarships granted to young and senior researchers. This had intellectual consequences in 1989. These approaches to historiography, unlike the Anglo-Saxon schools, tended to look at everyday life and the life of small communities; the study of which remained untouched by culture as a symbolic system. Therefore it is no accident that social history emerged as a *new* field after 1989.

After 1989 both Germany and France, for different reasons, attributed secondary importance to history-writing in Central Europe. This contrasts with the increasing involvement of the United States in the region. German and French interest was revived with EU enlargement and the growing importance of the European Union as a potential site of resistance to American unilateralism. However, by the time the intellectual influence of the US academia increased in Hungary and in other Central European countries, the avant-garde cutting edge works in history were no longer produced in the field of Cultural History.

A paradigmatic change in history-writing was expected to occur with the emergence of a new generation of historians, trained in the second half of the 1980s. But these young historians did not identify themselves with Cultural History, which at Budapest University became a bastion of the *history of ideas*, especially after the departure of Péter Hanák. Instead they identified with other *new* branches such as historical anthropology or social history.

The removal of the ideological censorship of the communist party and the foundation of new universities opened up space for new sections within history departments, including social history and cultural anthropology. In Pécs (in 2000) and in Miskolc (1995) departments of cultural history were formed. These new departments produced large numbers of graduates until the introduction of the Bologna Process following Hungary's accession to the European Union. The Bologna Process, a reduction in state support for higher education, and a decrease in student numbers for demographic reasons, served to weaken the hegemony of the mammoth history departments whose institutional structure had remained unchanged since the 19th century.

---

28 GYÁNI, 1993, p. 893-915.
29 Just to list some early works: SZ. JÓNÁS, 1986; KLANICZAY et. al., 1989.

It is no accident that at the most inventive institution, the CEU, where American influences were the strongest, the History Department (headed by Péter Hanák from 1991) introduced courses on cultural history and hosted guest speakers from Greenblatt to Davis. Today the CEU offers MA and PhD courses in this field, but they are all in English.

The limited institutionalisation of cultural history is partly due to the lack of translated works in the broadest sense. Unlike the major works of the *Annales* tradition, which were translated into Hungarian in the 1970s or 1980s, few more recent theoretical works by foreign historians are available in Hungarian. Standard university textbooks such as *Introduction to Social History*, which summarise international developments in historiography, have only recently appeared. The authors, who might be considered founding members of cultural history, are categorised under *historical anthropology* in Hungary, which is very much a marginalised subject both intellectually and institutionally. A modernisation of the language of the historical profession is still awaited.

4. Conclusions

Alon Confino and Allan Megill pointed out how memory became the leading term in new cultural history at the end of 1990s.[30] Hungarian historiography was unprepared for this paradigm shift, owing to the imperial character of history-writing, a lack of openness to interdisciplinary perspectives, and the traditional structure of higher education. The positivist epistemological basis of history as a science has remained fundamentally unchanged in Hungary since 1989. Just as Hóman and Kosáry criticised the five volumes edited by Domanovszky, so we can make the important point that cultural history does not have a relevant intellectual repertoire and is resistant to interdisciplinarity.

These factors explain why cultural history, as it is written today in Hungary and presented in the third series analysed above, remains in the same paradigm: *Kulturgeschichte*. Of course, I do not want to set up hierarchies between the different approaches. My intention is to highlight the dangerous connections (*liaison dangereuse*) between uncritical versions of Marxist history-writing and positivist history-writing. Loomba argued that "Colonialism is not just something that happens from outside a country or a people, not just something that operates with the collusion of forces inside, but a version of it can be duplicated

---

30 CONFINO, 1997, p. 1386.

from within."[31] I argue that the relationship between the colonised and the coloniser, this strategic essentialism, is reflected in the rhetoric of history-writing, and we can trace this phenomenon by examining how new cultural history is written or rather *not* written in Hungary today. New cultural history that focuses on the individual as an agent of change is a doomed enterprise in this postcolonial framework.

Literature

CONFINO, ALLON, Collective Memory and Cultural History? Problems of Method, in: American Historical Review 102, 4 (1997), p. 1386-1403.
COOPER, FREDERICK, Colonialism in Question. Theory, Knowledge, History. Berkeley et al. 2005.
DOBSZAY, TAMÁS/FÓNAGY, ZOLTÁN, Művelődéstörténet, in: Bevezetés a társadalomtörténetbe, ed. by BÓDY ZSOMBOR/JÓZSEF Ö. KOVÁCS, Budapest 2003, p. 387-409.
DOMANOVSZKY, SÁNDOR, Magyar művelődéstörténet, I-V, Budapest 1990-1991.
GYÁNI, GÁBOR, Political Uses of Tradition in Post Communist East Central Europe, in: Social Research 60, 4 (1993), p. 893-915.
HANÁK, PÉTER, A kultúrtörténet problémái, in: Történelmi Szemle 3-4 (1974), p. 447- 450.
HÓMAN, BÁLINT, A történelem útja, in: Történetírás és forráskritika, Budapest 1938, p. 9-45.
KLANICZAY, GÁBOR et al. (eds.), Magyarországi boszorkányperek, Budapest 1989.
KÓSA, LÁSZLÓ (ed.), A Cultural History of Hungary: from the Beginnings to the Eighteenth Century, Budapest 1999 (Hungarian editions in 1998, 2003, 2005).
KOSÁRY, DOMOKOS, A művelődéstörténet helye a szintézisben, in: Történelmi Szemle 3-4 (1974), p. 438- 446.
ID., Művelődés a 18. századi Magyarországon, Budapest 1983.
KŐSZEGHY, PÉTER (ed.), Magyar Művelődéstörténeti Lexikon, Budapest 2003.
LOOMBA, ANIA, Colonialism. Postcolonialism, London 1998.
MAKKAI, LÁSZLÓ, Művelődéstörténet, mint értékrendszerek története, in: Történelmi Szemle 3-4 (1974), p. 429-437.

---

31 LOOMBA, 1998, p. 12.

MONOK, ISTVÁN, A művelődéstörténeti kutatásokról, in: Magyar Tudomány 7 (2006), p. 818-830.

NÉMETH, G. BÉLA, Művelődéstörténet, in: Művelődéstörténet. Tanulmányok és kronológia a magyar nép művelődésének, életmódjának és mentalitásának történetéből I–II, ed. by B. GELENCSÉR KATALIN, Budapest 1998, p. 39-43.

NIEDERHAUSER, EMIL, A kultúrtörténet kérdéséhez, in: Történelmi Szemle 3-4 (1974), p. 420-429.

PETŐ, ANDREA, Hungarian Women in Politics 1945-1951 (East European Monographs Series), New York 2003.

ID., New Differences? Competing Canonization of History of World War II, in: Überbringen—Überformen—Überblenden. Theorietransfer im 20. Jahrhundert, ed. by DIETLIND HÜCHTKER/ALFRUN KLIEMS, Köln et al. 2011, p. 67-75.

PETŐ, ANDREA/SZAPOR, JUDIT, The State of Women's and Gender History in Eastern Europe: The Case of Hungary, in: Journal of Women's History 19, 1 (2007) p. 160-166.

R. VÁRKONYI, ÁGNES, Művelődéstörténeti törekvések az európai és hazai polgári történetírásban in: Vita a művelődéstörténet kérdéséről, in: Századok 1 (1970), p. 136-148.

SZ. JÓNÁS, ILONA, Árpádházi Szent Erzsébet, Budapest 1986.

ZSOMBER, BÓDY/KOVÁCS JOSEF Ö., (eds.), Bevezetés a társadalom törté net be, Budapest 2003.

Beyond the Alpine Myth, Across the Linguistic Ditch
Cultural History in Switzerland

CHRISTOF DEJUNG

Switzerland knows very well how to sell her clichés. Travellers arriving at Zurich Airport are received by cowbells and pictures of sunny mountain pastures, while being transported with underground shuttle trains to passport control and customs. And the commercial website *swissmade.com* promotes its range of Swiss army knives, watches and wood carvings with the assertion that "following the stereotype, the Swiss all live in the Alps, tend to their cows and yodel when they are happy."[1]

Of course, the well-known image of Switzerland as a mountain state neglects large parts of reality. It does not take into account that over two thirds of the Swiss are not living in alpine villages, but in urban centres far away from the mountains. It also neglects the fact that Switzerland was one of the first countries on the European continent to become industrialised in the early 19th century and that it has today a highly productive machine and chemical industry, not to speak of her notorious banking system, all of them completely oriented to the world market. The image of Switzerland as a rural mountain state, however, became prevalent precisely in the 19th century, when the country underwent dramatic social changes with the advent of industrial production and the foundation of the federal state in 1848. The Alpine myth, on the one hand, naturalised national identity and served as an ideological tool to unify a country that was not only multilingual but also divided in various geographical, religious and

---
1 www.swissmade.com, 09.03.2010.

political minorities.[2] On the other hand, it was a symbol for pureness and down-to-earthness and hence a unique selling proposition to attract tourists from the European upper class in need of leisure and to promote industrial products such as watches or milk chocolate.[3]

The traditional cliché of Switzerland as a mountain state had its counterpart in a particular view on history. Switzerland was designed as a special case—a nation that had been a democracy for seven hundred years, had not taken part in the killings of the two World Wars and had not been entangled in the crimes of colonialism. Instead, Switzerland was described as a country that had always been neutral and true to its humanitarian mission. For a long time this notion was sustained by historical and cultural historical research, particularly in the late 19th and early 20th century. It has been challenged, however, by cultural historians since the late 1980s.

In the following, I will highlight three aspects. First, the tradition of cultural history in Switzerland after the late 19th century. Second, current research trends and an overview of some important institutions. Third, I will point out some remarkable differences in the impact of cultural historical paradigms in the French- and German-speaking parts of the country.

Traditions of cultural history in Switzerland since the late 19th century

Cultural history never was a clearly defined issue in Swiss academia. It was never institutionalised and never formed a proper school of thought with a distinct research agenda.[4] However, several scholars were interested in the role of cultural traits for the identity of the Swiss nation and in their significance for historical development in general. This tradition can be found particularly in the German-speaking part of the country since the late 19th century. In 1865/66, Otto Henne, state archivist of St. Gallen published his *Geschichte des Schweizervolkes und seiner Kultur von den ältesten Zeiten bis zur Gegenwart* (History of the Swiss people and its culture from ancient times to the present). Henne's opus aimed at explicitly boosting the identity of the Swiss nation. To this end, he emphasised that the Swiss were a special people due to their alpine provenance and that the Cau-

---

2 ZIMMER, 1998.
3 ROSSFELD, 2007.
4 See for an overview on cultural history in Switzerland the excellent review article of VALLOTTON/NATCHKOVA, 2008.

casian race could ultimately be traced back to the inhabitants of the Alps (which would make the Swiss the ancestors of what Henne called "the European race").[5] While Henne's work, despite its title, was much more interested in military and political matters than in culture itself, other works of this period explicitly followed a cultural historical research agenda. They can be roughly distinguished into three different approaches.[6] The first embraced scholars such as Karl Dändliker (1849-1910), the founder of the Swiss National Museum in Zurich, or the famous Jakob Burckhardt (1818-1897), who claimed that art and religion represented the mind of a particular historical epoch.[7] The second approach was formed by scholars from Fribourg, a stronghold of Swiss Catholicism, such as Kaspar Decurtins (1855-1916) or Gonzague de Reynold (1880-1970). They were critical of the liberal federal state, founded in 1848 against fierce opposition from the Catholic, and disapproved of democracy. In contrast, they claimed that it was Catholicism that guaranteed the continuity of federalism and the tradition of the *old Confederation* in the modern nation state. A result of their activities was the foundation of the *Zeitschrift für schweizerische Kirchengeschichte* (Journal for Swiss Church History) in 1907; after the 1980s, this journal had been influenced by the emerging histories of mentalities and of everyday life and was renamed into *Schweizerische Zeitschrift für Religions- und Kulturgeschichte* (Swiss Journal for the History of Religion and Culture) in 2004.[8] A third tradition came from folklore studies, which were especially influential at the University of Zurich with scholars such as Paul Geiger (1887-1952), Richard Weiss (1907-1962), Arnold Niederer (1914-1998) or Rudolf Schenda (1930-2000). In contrast to the approaches of Dändliker and Burckhardt, they were not interested in the intellectual or material culture of social elites but rather in the everyday culture of common people.[9]

In particular the folklore studies approach had an influence on what later became cultural history through the works of Rudolf Braun. Braun, who had published his studies on the transformations of everyday life of the population in a rural part of the canton of Zurich during industrialisation in the 1960s, had begun his academic career in folklore studies. Later on, he orientated himself more towards social and economic history and began to investigate topics such as the

---

5 HENNE, 1865, p. 3.
6 VALLATON/NATCHKOVA, 2008, p. 95-98.
7 DÄNDLIKER, 1884-1900; BURCKHARDT, 1860; BURCKHARDT, 1905.
8 VALLATON/NATCHKOVA, 2008, p. 96f.
9 ID., 2008, p. 97-99.

history of the body or the relationship of dancing with political power.[10] Also in Zurich, the economic historian Hansjörg Siegenthaler began to develop a theory of historical change that claimed economic crisis to be not the reason for cultural changes but rather the other way round: he assumed that the shifting of cultural paradigms led to collective uncertainty and as a consequence to economic crisis.[11]

Another important base for cultural history was Basel with scholars such as Markus Mattmüller, who investigated new approaches to the history of religion with a book on Leonhard Ragaz, or Martin Schaffner, who began to engage in the deployment of historical anthropology.[12] The Institute of History of the University of Basel was also one of the first in Switzerland to promote the method of oral history.[13] It was also in Basel, where František Graus (1921-1989) stimulated the use of cultural historical methods such as the history of mentalities for medieval history and influenced scholars such as Guy Marchal or Hans-Jörg Gilomen who later on became professors in Luzern and Zurich respectively.[14]

Whereas in the German-speaking part of Switzerland cultural history developed parallel to social history and actually was from the beginning an integral part of the social historical analysis, the situation was quite different in the French-speaking part of the country. There, the synthesis of cultural and social history was less common and began only in the 1980s. Before that, scholars who aimed to expand historical research beyond the established fields of political history engaged much more in intellectual history or the history of literature. Important historians of this tradition are Chady Guyot (1898-1974) from Neuchâtel or Marcel Raymond (1897-1981), Albert Béguin (1901-1957), Jean Rousset (1910-2002) or Jean Starobinski (1920) from Geneva.[15]

Current research trends

Since the 1990s, a new wave of cultural history established itself in Swiss academia. Influenced by poststructuralist theory, historians began to test new ap-

---

10 BRAUN, 1960; BRAUN, 1965; BRAUN, 2000; BRAUN/GUGERLI, 1993. For the academic impact of Braun see TANNER, 2010.
11 SIEGENTHALER, 1993.
12 MATTMÜLLER, 1957-1968; SCHAFFNER, 1992.
13 See for an overview on earlier works using oral sources for Swiss history SPUHLER et al., 1994.
14 GRAUS, 1974; MARCHAL, 2006.
15 VALLOTTON/NATCHKOVA, 2008, p. 104f.

proaches to the past. One of the first topics these new approaches were applied to was national identity. The traditional view of Switzerland as an innocent bystander of history had been challenged by historians since the 1970s. By borrowing particularly from the works of Eric Hobsbawm and Benedict Anderson, a younger generation of historians now pointed out that Swiss national identity was not something that was rooted in mediaeval times but was rather an invention of traditions emerging in the late 18th century. Particularly the two jubilees of the 1990s—the 700th anniversary of the Swiss confederation in 1991 and the 150th anniversary of the federal state in 1998—stimulated a multitude of studies on national identity.[16] National identity is of particular interest in Switzerland due to the multilingual nature of the country, its strong federalist structure and its subdivision in various geographical, religious and political minorities. How such a heterogeneous country could establish a stable national identity was a question that seemed worthwhile investigating.[17]

Other researchers tackled the question of citizenship and the exclusion of certain groups from the national community. They studied the rise of anti-Semitism and *xenophobia* in the late 19th century. This topic was not least initiated by the discussions of Switzerland's role in the Second World War and the rejection of Jewish refugees at the Swiss border during the wartime years.[18] Swiss gender history was stimulated by the question why Switzerland did not grant women the right to vote until 1971. How could it be that a country, which in the 19th century was among the avant-garde in republican thought, could become dead last in Europe in terms of progressive gender politics? This was a question several generations of gender historians tackled.[19]

Another field of research is the history of knowledge. In contrast to the approaches presented above, research in this field is less interested in the concept of the nation but rather in how the world view of historical actors came into being and how this constructive act interrelated to social power. Stimulated by the works of Michel Foucault and Bruno Latour, researchers investigated the history of the body, the history of sexuality and the history of science and technology.[20] One important institution in this field of research is the interdisciplinary centre for the history and philosophy of knowledge in Zurich.[21]

---

16 KREIS, 1991; MARCHAL/MATTIOLI, 1992; ALTERMATT et al., 1998.
17 ZIMMER, 2003.
18 MATTIOLI, 1998; KURY, 2003; STUDER et al. 2008.
19 JORIS/WITZIG, 1986; BLATTMANN/MEIER, 1998; MESMER, 2007; DEJUNG, 2010.
20 GUGERLI, 1996; TANNER, 1999; SARASIN, 2001; GROEBNER, 2004.
21 http://www.zgw.ethz.ch, 21.09.2010.

Several researchers have investigated environmental history and the social aspects of handling natural resources.[22] Studies of media and iconography were further fields of research. There are two National Centres of Competence in Research, sponsored by the Swiss National Science Foundation on these topics, one on the history of mediality and another on the power of iconic representation, both of which have a distinct interdisciplinary orientation and include researches from several universities.[23]

A most recent development is the application of postcolonial theories and transnational perspectives on Swiss history. Research in this area is concerned with the role of colonialism for the establishment of scientific disciplines such as physical anthropology or biology and with the significance of the colonial *other* for Swiss identity.[24] This is a field of particular interest, since Switzerland had no colonies of its own but was nevertheless culturally and economically deeply entangled with colonialism. One newly established institution to study these research topics is the interdisciplinary research centre Asia and Europe from the University of Zurich, which includes several historical projects.[25]

These developments of the last two decades were influenced by cultural theory. Discourse analysis, poststructuralist theories and methods of cultural anthropology became quite common in historical research. Although there is no school of cultural history in Switzerland—there is nothing like the *Annales* school or the subaltern study group within the country—, Swiss historians were very swift in the application of these theories as they adopted them from abroad. This process was facilitated by the fact that most Swiss historians are used to speak at least two foreign languages and that the Swiss National Science Foundation urges young scholars to spend some years abroad during their PHD studies or their postdoc years.

With respect to institutionalisation it has to be mentioned that there exists no particular society for cultural history in Switzerland. Yet, there are several informal research bodies and journals in which discussions of matters concerning cultural history take place. The most important medium is the journal *traverse—Zeitschrift für Geschichte* (Journal for History). It was founded in 1994 and has three issues per year. Every issue has a thematic focus, which often has a cultural historical orientation. Recent issues covered topics such as the history of emotions, domestic violence, the relations between humans and animals, the history of masculinity and the role of scientific images. The *traverse* publishes

---

22 WALTER, 1990; MATHIEU, 1998; PFISTER/SUMMERMATTER, 2004; WALTER, 2008.
23 http://www.mediality.ch, 21.09.2010; http://www.eikones.ch, 21.09.2010.
24 BRÄNDLE, 1995; WIRZ, 1998; HARRIES, 2007; PURTSCHERT, 2008.
25 http://www.asienundeuropa.uzh.ch, 09.03.2010.

papers in German, French, English, and sometimes even in Italian.[26] This multilingualism is characteristic of the Swiss scientific community, which is guided by the principle that all scholars should talk and write in their own language. This means, at least in theory, that every researcher should be able to understand at least two other languages, apart from his own.

As anywhere else, the impact of the linguistic turn and of poststructuralist theories divided scholars during the 1990s. In contrast to other countries, however, these debates were fought out rather behind closed doors and seldom in scientific journals or in the media.[27] Whereas—for instance—in Germany one could witness an enduring bickering between the advocates of the *historische Sozialwissenschaft* (historical social science) on the one hand, which advocated structuralist explanations for historical changes, and the advocates of the history of everyday-life and cultural history on the other hand, no such clash could be witnessed in Switzerland. One important reason for this lies in the size of the country. Switzerland is just not large enough to allow for distinct schools to be formed. Scholars stumble across each other at virtually every conference. Therefore, a strategy of concordance and conflict avoidance is crucial to professional survival. This avoids fruitless feuds between different schools and facilitates academic life. The downside of this scholarly armistice is that theoretical problems sometimes are not discussed with the rigidity they should merit.

Differences between French- and German-speaking historians

The scientific community of Switzerland can be distinguished in two linguistic sub-communities: the German and the French speaking community. Since the Italian part of Switzerland has only some 300,000 inhabitants and just a small University for architecture and communication studies, it plays no major role in academic life. On first impression, the communication between the French and the German speaking historians seems to work rather well. Several national publications, such as the *Swiss Journal of History*[28], the *traverse* or the Yearbooks

---

26 http://www.chronos-verlag.ch/php/traverse-new.php?lang=Deutsch, 09.03.2010.
27 One example of such a hidden dispute was an argument between Hansjörg Siegenthaler and Hans-Ulrich Jost about whether the foundation of the federal state in 1848 was caused by economic (Jost) or cultural motives (Siegenthaler).
28 The papers of this journal are online on: http://www.sgg-ssh.ch/de/szg/search.php, 09.03.2010.

of the *Society for Economic and Social History* include articles in French and German. The cooperation between historians from the two parts of the country is further evidenced by the fact that at the 2nd Swiss History Days in February 2010, one third of the 66 panels included presentations in both German and French. Half of the panels were held in German only and one sixth in French only.[29]

What can be said about the awareness of research in the other part of the country when we look at the scientific output of Swiss historians? This question was tackled by examining a sample of 143 articles, published between 1994 and 2006 in the *Swiss Journal of History*, the *traverse* and in the Yearbooks of the Swiss Society for Economic and Social History.[30] It shows that from the 102 articles written in German only 45 cite works published by scholars of the French-speaking part (table 1). Of the 41 articles written in French, 22 cite literature from the German-speaking part of the country. This means that only 26% of Swiss German historians cite works from their French-speaking fellows whereas 54% of francophone Swiss historians cite works from the other side of the linguistic ditch. These results seem to contradict the experience one often has when attending meetings or conferences with researchers from both linguistic areas; scholars from the German-speaking part are commonly much more willing, and also competent, to use the French language, than the other way round. Yet, the fact that historians from francophone Switzerland cite literature from the German speaking part of the country comes not least from the fact that many important studies and written sources on Swiss history are published in German and are therefore indispensable to cover the state of research.

	Number of Article	Literature of other Swiss linguistic areas cited	Explicit cultural historical orientation
Articles in German	102	25 (52%)	45 (44%)
Articles in French	41	22 (54%)	14 (34%)

Table 1: Analysis of articles published in German and French in three Swiss periodicals between 1994 and 2006

---

29 http://www.geschichtstage.ch, 10.03.2010.
30 The following issues were selected for the analysis: Swiss Journal of History: Vols. 44, 46, 48, 50, 52, 54, 56 (always the first issue of the year with the exception Vol. 56, where the second issue was analysed); traverse: Vols. 1, 3, 5, 7, 12, 13 (always the first issue of every year); Yearbooks of the Swiss Society for Economic and Social History those of 1996, 2002 and 2005.

What can the examination of these articles from the last 15 years tell us about the state of cultural history in Switzerland? The fact that historians in the French and German-speaking part of the country take note of each other does not necessarily mean that they have a common understanding of what cultural history is about. In fact, discussions at conferences indicate that scholars from the German- and French-speaking part of Switzerland sometimes follow quite different paradigms and are influenced by research traditions which are quite different. Indeed, the analysis indicates that cultural history has a different standing in the two regions and maybe is even done differently in the German and the French part of the country. Whereas 44% of the articles published in German have a distinct cultural historical orientation—*i.e.* they explicitly refer to the concept of culture and/or cite authorities such as Michel Foucault, Roland Barthes, Clifford Geertz, Norbert Elias or Joan Scott—this is the case with only 34% of those written in French.

	Number of articles	Literature of other Swiss linguistic areas cited	Explicit cultural historical orientation
Swiss Journal of History Articles in German Articles in French	14 8	8 (57%) 7 (88%)	4 (29%) 1 (13%)
Traverse Articles in German Articles in French	35 13	7 (20%) 4 (31%)	29 (83%) 10 (77%)
Yearbooks of Economic and Social History Articles in German Articles in French	43 20	11 (26%) 11 (55%)	22 (51%) 3 (15%)

Table 2: Detailed analysis of the three periodicals

The differences become even more significant when we compare the three periodicals (table 2). This comparison shows on the one hand that cultural history is not prevailing to the same degree in the various publications. Whereas in the journal *traverse* 83% of the German and 77% of the French papers have an explicit cultural historical orientation, only 29% and 13% do so in the *Swiss Journal of History*. This difference is not surprising in so far as the *traverse* was founded with the explicit aim to serve as a publication platform for cultural historians whereas the *Swiss Journal of History* has a much more general historical orientation. Striking, however, are the differences that become prevalent in the Yearbooks of the Swiss *Society for Economic and Social History*. Over half of the articles written in German commit themselves explicitly to cultural history whereas this is only the case with 15% of those in French. This confirms that cultural history definitely took hold in social history in the German-speaking part of the country, and to some extent also in economic history. In francophone Switzerland, social and economic historians are not—or not yet?—affected by the cultural turn and seem much more influenced by a historical materialist worldview.

Such differences in applying cultural theory for historical analysis might not be restricted to Switzerland. I would expect also some differences between various European countries in the way cultural history is incorporated. So maybe we should not only ask which topics cultural historians are investigating in different countries, but also *how* they are doing this. Such comparisons could give further insight into the significance of cultural history in Europe and could in addition also help to bring together the findings of traditional social, economic and political history with those of cultural history.[31]

Literature

ALTERMATT, URS et al. (eds.), Die Konstruktion einer Nation. Nation und Nationalisierung in der Schweiz, 18.-20. Jahrhundert, Zürich 1998.
BLATTMANN, LYNN/MEIER, IRÈNE (eds.), Männerbund und Bundesstaat. Über die politische Kultur der Schweiz, Zürich 1998.
BRÄNDLE, REA, Wildfremd, hautnah. Völkerschauen und Schauplätze Zürich 1880-1960. Bilder und Geschichten, Zürich 1995.
BRAUN, RUDOLF, Industrialisierung und Volksleben. Veränderungen der Lebensformen unter Einwirkung der verlagsindustriellen Heimarbeit in einem ländlichen Industriegebiet (Zürcher Oberland) vor 1800, Winterthur 1960.

---

31 Hans-Ulrich Wehler, one of the founding fathers of the influential Bielefeld school of Social history in Germany and a pronounce critic of cultural history is convinced that cultural history is not be able to convey a long-term historical synthesis like the modernisation theory that coined social history was. While one has not to follow Wehler with his condemnation of cultural theory, it is certainly true that a proper synthesis of social and economic history with the findings of cultural history has very seldom been done yet: WEHLER, 2005.

ID., Sozialer und kultureller Wandel in einem ländlichen Industriegebiet (Zürcher Oberland) unter Einwirkung des Maschinen- und Fabrikwesens im 19. und 20. Jahrhundert. Erlenbach-Zürich 1965.

ID., Von den Heimarbeitern zur europäischen Machtelite. Ausgewählte Aufsätze, Zürich 2000.

ID./GUGERLI, DAVID, Macht des Tanzes—Tanz der Mächtigen. Hoffeste und Herrschaftszeremoniell, 1550—1914, München 1993.

BURCKHARDT, JAKOB, Die Cultur der Renaissance in Italien. Ein Versuch, Basel 1860.

ID., Weltgeschichtliche Betrachtungen, Berlin 1905.

DÄNDLIKER, KARL, Geschichte der Schweiz, mit besonderer Rücksicht auf die Entwicklung des Verfassungs- und Kulturlebens von den ältesten Zeiten bis zur Gegenwart, Zürich 1884-1900.

DEJUNG, CHRISTOF, "Switzerland must be a Special Democracy". Sociopolitical Compromise, Military Comradeship and the Gender Order in 1930s and 1940s Switzerland, in: Journal of Modern History 82 (2010), p. 101-126.

GRAUS, FRANTISEK, Gewalt und Recht im Verständnis des Mittelalters, Basel 1974.

GROEBNER, VALENTIN, Der Schein der Person. Steckbrief, Ausweis und Kontrolle im Europa des Mittelalters, München 2004.

GUGERLI, DAVID, Redeströme. Zur Elektrifizierung der Schweiz 1880-1914. Zürich 1996.

HARRIES, PATRICK, Butterflies & Barbarians. Swiss Missionaries & Systems of Knowledge in South-East Africa, Oxford 2007.

HENNE, OTTO, Geschichte des Schweizervolkes und seiner Kultur von den ältesten Zeiten bis zur Gegenwart, Erster Band, Leipzig 1865.

JORIS, ELISABETH/WITZIG, HEIDI (Eds.), Frauengeschichte(n). Dokumente aus zwei Jahrhunderten zur Situation der Frauen in der Schweiz, Zürich 1986.

KREIS, GEORG, Der Mythos von 1291. Zur Entstehung des schweizerischen Nationalfeiertags, Basel 1991.

KURY, PATRICK, Über Fremde reden. Überfremdungsdiskurs und Ausgrenzung in der Schweiz 1900-1945, Zürich 2003.

MARCHAL, GUY P./MATTIOLI, ARAM (eds.), Erfundene Schweiz. Konstruktionen nationaler Identität, Zürich 1992.

ID., Schweizer Gebrauchsgeschichte. Geschichtsbilder, Mythenbildung und nationale Identität, Basel 2006.

MATHIEU, JON, Geschichte der Alpen, 1500-1900: Umwelt, Entwicklung, Gesellschaft, Wien et al. 1998.

MATTIOLI, ARAM (ed.), Antisemitismus in der Schweiz, 1848-1960, Zürich 1998.

MATTMÜLLER, MARKUS, Leonhard Ragaz und der religiöse Sozialismus. Eine Biographie, 2 Vol., Zollikon 1957-1968.

MESMER, BEATRIX, Staatsbürgerinnen ohne Stimmrecht. Die Politik der schweizerischen Frauenverbände 1914-197, Zürich 2007.

PFISTER, CHRISTIAN/SUMMERMATTER, STEPHANIE (eds.), Katastrophen und ihre Bewältigung. Perspektiven und Positionen, Bern 2004.

PURTSCHERT, PATRICIA, Postkoloniale Diskurse in der Schweiz. "De Schorsch Gaggo reist uf Afrika", in: Widerspruch. Beiträge zu sozialistischer Politik 54 (2008), p. 169-180.

ROSSFELD, ROMAN, Schweizer Schokolade. Industrielle Produktion und kulturelle Konstruktion eines nationalen Symbols 1860-1920, Baden 2007.

SARASIN, PHILIPP, Reizbare Maschinen. Eine Geschichte des Körpers 1765-1914, Frankfurt am Main 2001.

SCHAFFNER, MARTIN (ed.), Brot, Brei und was dazugehört. Über sozialen Sinn und physiologischen Wert der Nahrung, Zürich 1992.

SIEGENTHALER, HANSJÖRG, Regelvertrauen, Prosperität und Krisen. Die Ungleichmässigkeit wirtschaftlicher und sozialer Entwicklung als Ergebnis individuellen Handelns und sozialen Lernens, Tübingen 1993.

SPUHLER, GREGOR et al. (ed.), Vielstimmiges Gedächtnis, Beiträge zur Oral History, Zürich 1994.

STUDER, BRIGITTE et al., Das Schweizer Bürgerrecht. Erwerb, Verlust, Entzug von 1848 bis zur Gegenwart, Zürich 2008.

TANNER, JAKOB, Fabrikmahlzeit. Ernährungswissenschaft, Industriearbeit und Volksernährung in der Schweiz, 1890-1950, Zürich 1999.

ID., "Das Grosse im Kleinen". Rudolf Braun als Innovator der Geschichtswissenschaft, in: Historische Anthropologie 18 (2010), p. 140-156.

VALLOTTON, FRANÇOIS/NATCHKOVA, NORA, Entre éclat et repli. L'Historie culturelle en Suisse, in: L'histoire culturelle: un "tournant mondial" dans l'historiographie?, ed. by PHILIPPE POIRRIER, Dijon 2008, p. 93-109.

WALTER, FRANÇOIS, Les Suisses et l'environnement: une histoire du rapport à la nature du XVIIIe siècle à nos jours, Carouge-Genève 1990.

ID., Catastrophes: une histoire culturelle: XVIe-XXIe siècle, Paris 2008.

WEHLER, HANS-ULRICH, Synthesekonzepte heute, in: Was ist der Mensch, was Geschichte? Annäherungen an eine kulturwissenschaftliche Anthropologie, Jörn Rüsen zum 65. Geburtstag, ed. by FRIEDRICH JAEGER/JÜRGEN STRAUB, Bielefeld 2005, p. 233-240.

WIRZ, ALBERT, Die Humanitäre Schweiz im Spannungsfeld zwischen Philantropie und Kolonialismus. Gustave Moynier, Afrika und das IKRK, in: traverse 5, 2 (1998), p. 95-110.

ZIMMER, OLIVER, In Search of Natural Identity. Alpine Landscape and the Reconstruction of the Swiss Nation, in: Comparative Studies in Society and History 40 (1998), p. 637-665.
ID., A contested nation. History, memory and nationalism in Switzerland, 1761-1891, Cambridge 2003.

http://www.swissmade.com, 09.03.2010
http://www.zgw.ethz.ch, 21.09.2010
http://www.mediality.ch, 21.09.2010;
http://www.eikones.ch, 21.09.2010
http://www.asienundeuropa.uzh.ch, 09.03.2010
http://www.chronos-verlag.ch/php/traverse-new.php?lang=Deutsch, 09.03.2010
http://www.sgg-ssh.ch/de/szg/search.php, 09.03.2010
http://www.geschichtstage.ch, 10.03.2010

What's new about the *New Cultural History*?
An exemplary survey of the Austrian academic community

CHRISTINA LUTTER

1. Theoretical and methodological approaches

A main goal of this volume, and the conference preceding it, was to take some kind of comprehensive inventory of academic activities, of "institutions—themes—perspectives", to quote the conference's subtitle, filed under *Cultural History/Kulturgeschichte*. This is doubtless an ambitious and important endeavour. Still, before being able to give you the exemplary survey of the current situation in Austria I was asked to contribute in this essay, it seems worthwhile and even necessary to pause for a moment and think about some of the seminal definitions of *Cultural History*, or else of some premises to which the paradigm of *Cultural History*, esp. the *New Cultural History* is committed—for these are not necessarily, and for some of us even categorically *not*, organized in and around institutions and specific thematic topics.

I will shortly return to this issue. But let me first give you an overview of my contribution: In the first part of this essay I will briefly present my personal approach to what might be conceived of as (new) cultural history. I will do that by commenting on some important theoretical principles and methodological approaches, following some texts on *The New Cultural History* that may be regarded as formative for and seminal both in the Anglo-American and the continental academic community and important for my own formation as a scholar of cultural history: *The New Cultural History*, edited in 1989 by Lynn Hunt, and Roger Chartier's important selection of essays published the same year under the title of *Cultural History between Representations and Practices*.[1]

---

1 HUNT, 1989; CHARTIER, 1989a. For a recent overview taking into account a wide range of international contributions, see TSCHOPP, 2009, and the contributions in POIRRIER,

Drawing on these theoretical and methodological considerations I will in the second part move to giving you a short and exemplary survey of some trends and tendencies of the Austrian academic community in the field of *Cultural History*. The central question to establish the respective data was how to define criteria and indicators, which are by no means self-evident, to search for and find *Cultural History/Kulturgeschichte* in research and teaching in a national research environment.[2] Finally, I will close with some remarks about what my preliminary diagnosis might mean for the perspectives of a *(New) Cultural History* in Austria, but also beyond, especially in the European context.

By now it has become a commonplace that the *New Cultural History* is in fact not that *new* any more, but at least more than two decades old. It was at the end of the 1980s that it became visible throughout a range of different disciplines and in various countries. The 1990s then saw the humanities and social sciences substantially *turned* by culture.[3] More than 20 years ago, Lynn Hunt in her introduction to *The New Cultural History* already mapped out some of the key paradigms and legacies, methods and aspects connected with the term that still are valid today.[4] It has to be noted, though, that her issue and those of the other contributors' are not institutions, and only few research themes or topics which are only used to exemplify methodological tasks. In fact, some scholars referred to in the introduction, e.g. François Furet and Robert Darnton, even articulate explicit and strong criticisms of a cultural history defined in terms of its topics of inquiry.[5]

Hunt takes social history and its explanatory roots in Marxism and the *Annales* school as a starting point, but also as a means of differentiation between social and cultural history, as particularly since the 1980s "Marxists and Annalistes alike have become increasingly interested in the history of culture"[6] with "the most striking instance" [of their] "turn toward culture [being] their growing

---

2008. Important German introductory volumes on *Kulturgeschichte* are e.g. DANIEL, 2001; LANDWEHR/STOCKHORST, 2004; LANDWEHR, 2009; MAURER, 2008; TSCHOPP/ WEBER, 2007.

2 I am grateful to Christina Linsboth for the basic data collection and procession that formed part of the background for the observations presented in this essay.
3 A comprehensive discussion of the most important paradigmatic shifts in the humanities, social sciences and cultural studies during the last decades, often labeled as "turns" is provided by BACHMANN-MEDICK, 2006.
4 HUNT, 1989, p. 1-22.
5 ID., p. 9, with reference to FURET, 1983, p. 405, and DARNTON, 1980, p. 364.
6 HUNT, 1989, p. 4.

interest in language."[7] As a consequence, with the criticism of economic and social history and their master narratives, models and theories to explain history and society and with the turns to language and discourse, symbols and meanings, texts and pictures, the crucial question addressed "culture's relationship to the social world".[8] Thus, the debate in the Anglo-American academy has always been more concerned about the relations between social and cultural issues and their complementarity than in the German speaking countries, where a rather strong opposition between social and cultural history prevailed for a long time.[9]

Out of the different models to answer these questions, the anthropological model, mostly connected with the name of Clifford Geertz, was one of the most influential, both in the English speaking world and beyond it.[10] Deciphering of meaning instead of causal laws of explanation became one of the central tasks of Cultural History, after a while followed by a harsh criticism of the notion of a fixed, coherent and common meaning that one would allegedly be able to hermeneutically find within the text.[11]

Drawing on Frederic Jameson, Hunt asserts that for the New Cultural History, in line with newer literary criticism, the question is less what a text *means*, but rather, how it *works*.[12] Hunt takes this argument further by drawing on her own research on the impact of revolutionary discourse in the French revolution: "The point of the endeavour was to examine the ways in which linguistic practice, rather than simply reflect social reality, could actively be an instrument of (or constitute) power. [...] Words did not just reflect social reality; they were instruments for transforming reality."[13]

---

7   ID., p. 5. For a German anthology on the *Annales* school see MIDDELL, 1994.
8   HUNT, 1989, p.10.
9   See e.g. WEHLER, 1998 and 2001. For reconciliating voices e.g. TSCHOPP, 2009; LANDWEHR 2009, as well as his contribution to this volume.
10 Most influential in the German speaking world are probably GEERTZ, 1975 and 1983. On the theoretical and methodological issue of meaning as constitutive for a cultural historical perspective and thus its importance for the paradigm of *Kulturgeschichte* in the German speaking academy see LANDWEHR, in this volume, as well as the respective chapters in DANIEL, 2001, on different related traditions both in historiography and in other disciplines.
11 HUNT, 1989, p. 12-14.
12 JAMESON, 1981, quoted in HUNT, 1989, p. 15.
13 HUNT, 1989, p. 17. This constructionist argument was also developed and became highly influential in the field of gender studies and gender history, SCOTT, 1986, and BUTLER, 1990 and 2004.

This argument leads to Roger Chartier, who figures prominently in Hunt's introduction and also contributed a paper to the volume.[14] He programmatically titled the introduction to his own beautiful book *Die unvollendete Vergangenheit. Geschichte und die Macht der Weltauslegung* (first published in French, 1989, and translated the same year into German) "Kulturgeschichte zwischen Repräsentationen und Praktiken" — "Cultural history between Representations and Practices".[15]

> "The struggles in the realm of representations are not less important than economic struggles, if one wants to understand the mechanisms, through which a group establishes or tries to establish its own vision of the social world, its values and its hegemony."[16]

So, within structures and relations of power culture does not play less important a role than economy or politics, and neither do economic and social relations determine cultural issues. They are themselves fields of cultural practice and production, or in Chartier's words: "The representations of the social world themselves are the constituents of social reality".[17]

Cultural History therefore always is a Cultural History of the Social. That is one of the most important convictions of a *New Cultural History* which can by now be assumed to be shared by most of its representatives.

Drawing on Michel Foucault, Chartier analyzes discourses as *discursive practices*. He does not read them as media of a global ideology, but is interested in their practical layout, their rhetorical interconnections and their strategies of argumentation and evidence. This leads to looking for the relations between texts and their readers, and the production of meaning.[18] Thus, two central questions are:
- Under which circumstances a text becomes *valid* for the reader's specific situation?
- How can a narrative configuration effect a re-figuration of one's own experience?

---

14 CHARTIER, 1989b.
15 CHARTIER, 1989a.
16 ID., p. 12: translation.
17 Quoted in HUNT, 1989, p. 7, footnote 20. For similar arguments elaborated in the German debates see e.g. LANDWEHR, 2003, STOLLBERG-RILINGER, 2005.
18 CHARTIER, 1989a, p. 18-19.

Accordingly, Chartier's notion of appropriation stresses the variety of the uses of texts and the heterogeneity of ways of reading, the meaning of which is exactly *not* set within the text nor determined by it. Cultural History thus is concerned with representations, practices and modes of appropriation:
- representations as classifications, inclusions and exclusions, through which the social world is organized as a historical product;
- practices generating meaningful representations;
- modes of appropriation confirming and opposing, negotiating, modifying, and adjusting them.[19]

2. Cultural History in Austria

In how far would one find these concepts and principles or at least some of them integrated in current *Cultural History* endeavours in Austria[20]? I will start genealogically and take a look back to the 1990s, the *high tide* of *Cultural History/ Kulturgeschichte* and *Cultural Studies/Kulturwissenschaften* and its main reception in the German speaking world. I therefore want to introduce two large-scale initiatives that played a seminal role in the advancement of the cultural turn in the humanities and Cultural Studies in Austria. One of them was a thematic research programme, the other a funding programme, both explicitly including cultural historical approaches as sketched above within their theoretical and methodological framework.

---

19 ID., p. 21. A comparable approach is represented by Stuart Hall in his seminal model on the Encoding/Decoding of meaning, cf. HALL, 1980. For Halls impact on British Cultural Studies see e.g. HALL, 2000; GILROY, 2000; also TURNER, 1996; MARCHART, 2007; LUTTER/REISENLEITNER, 2008.

20 On Austrian Science Fund (FWF), Austria's most important funding organization for basic research, and esp. its funding projects see http://www.fwf.ac.at/de/projects/ sfb.html; for details on the SFB *Modernity: Vienna and Central Europe around 1900* see http://www-gewi.kfunigraz.ac.at/moderne/; as well as http://www-gewi. uni-graz.at/fomop/home.html presenting a follow-up network based on the research undertaken within the SFB; all websites visited on 07.09.2010.

2.1 Special Research Programme (SFB) Modernity: Vienna and Central Europe around 1900

The first programme was a long term *Special Research Programme* (SFB) funded by the Austrian Science Fund (FWF) between 1994 and 2004 titled *Modernity: Vienna and Central Europe around 1900*.[21] It was the first SFB-project in the humanities ever funded in Austria, based at the University of Graz. It included projects from about seven disciplines and employed some 40 research fellows, a lot of them post graduates (both PhD students and post docs) and junior fellows. Its aim was to research and discuss modernity as a "cultural phenomenon, a process which is linked to economic and social transformations that started in the 17th and 18th century [including significant] fundamental socio-economic, socio-political and socio-cultural changes"[22].

Unlike in many traditional approaches, *Vienna Modernity* (Wiener Moderne) was not conceived of in terms of a reductive notion of culture confined to art and cultural production/creativity, but the very concept included social crises and conflicts connected with phenomena such as nationalisms, anti-Semitism, xenophobia, and struggles of identity.[23]

The SFB was organized around specific research topics concentrating on Vienna and Central Europe, but it also highlighted its explicit problem-oriented and trans-disciplinary orientation represented in five research groups working under the headlines of
- isms and ideologies,
- aesthetics of modernity—modernistic aesthetics,
- culture and society,

---

21 http://www-gewi.kfunigraz.ac.at/moderne/edok.htm, 07.09.2010.
22 For a comprehensive list of publications from the research output of the SFB see http://www-gewi.kfunigraz.ac.at/moderne/edok.htm, 07.09.2010. An even further reaching critique of the traditional "Vienna Modernity" paradigm is provided by MADERTHANER/MUSNER, 1999, see also p. 184 below.
23 On the current research policy and programmes of the ministry see http://www.bmwf. gv.at/startseite/forschung/national/programme_schwerpunkte/forschungsprogramme_ schwerpunkte_ueberblick/, 10.09.2010. Information on older research programmes is not available on this website any more. The website of the FSP *Cultural Studies/Kulturwissenschaften* that provided a platform for the emerging research network from 2000 to 2005 (http://www.culturalstudies.at) had to go offline due to a lack of funding.

- cultural transfers,
- identities.

2.2 Research Programme (FSP) Cultural Studies/ Kulturwissenschaften

The second initiative was the research programme *Cultural Studies/Kulturwissenschaften*, which I had the pleasure to develop and head. It was implemented in 1998 as one of the central research initiatives within the department of Social Sciences of the Austrian Ministry of Science and Research. From then until 2003, more than 50 research projects were funded, and as the *Modernity*-SFB did, we were able to develop a far-reaching research network.[24]

The main conceptual issue was to develop and work on a scholarly yet also political notion of culture as well as to historically investigate the different traditions of Cultural Studies and Kulturwissenschaften, however not only concentrate on conceptual differences, but also make visible their convergences, intersections and the possibilities of integrating different approaches.[25] Strategically, the program aimed at stimulating trans-disciplinary research both on a national and international level. But it was also and explicitly committed to the specific Cultural Studies lineage of the *Birmingham-Tradition*, an intellectual practice describing how everyday life is defined in and by culture—as well as offering strategies for mastering and changing it.[26]

The research projects, a lot of them with a historical perspective, therefore comprised a variety of different topics, such as
- migration, minorities and issues of multiculturalism,
- gender issues,
- (post-)colonialism and the construction of identities,
- ethnicity and nation,
- economic and media globalization,
- culture, nature, and science.

---

24 See LINDNER, 1998, LUTTER/MUSNER, 2002 and 2003; cf. also the contributions in GÖTTLICH et al., 2001, esp. LUTTER, 2001 and WAGNER, 2001. On the interrelations of British Cultural Studies and Cultural History see BURKE, 2004 and 2008, cf. also LUTTER/REISENLEITNER, 2002.

25 For introductions and anthologies see e.g. TURNER, 1996; HOFMANN et al., 2006; LINDNER, 2000, MARCHART, 2007; LUTTER/REISENLEITNER, 2008; see also GROSSBERG, 2010.

Both programs—with all their differences—shared the features that they were basically strategically and methodologically oriented (rather than focusing on specific topics), and that they rested to a large extent on flexible networks, organized around workshops and conferences, summer schools and international exchange—but were predominantly *not* rooted in the established academic, esp. university institutions.

2.3 Internationales Forschungszentrum Kulturwissenschaften (IFK)

This quality of not being a traditional inner-academic institution is also characteristic of the *Internationales Forschungszentrum Kulturwissenschaften* (IFK). It was founded in 1993 and has by now developed into one of the most visible institutes of advanced study both on a national and international level, concentrating on trans-disciplinary research and studies of culture. Its approach is made very clear by the mission statement on the IFK's website:

> "[...] cannot be grasped merely historically as the memory of a society but is equally understood as a realm of discourse regarding society's future prospects. Culture may be understood as a *dynamic process* that produces and interprets meanings and is *shaped by political, social, and economic contexts*. Culture as the sum of life-forms and life-styles of human beings, *differently determined according to place, society, and history*, is not self-referential but articulates societal processes as well."

> "Thus the task of cultural studies is not only to analyse the 'interior' of given aesthetic, literary and popular practices, but also to assay their external conditions. Consequently, cultural studies can be understood as a project of deciphering *cultures as textures of the social*." [26]

The institute's research and administrative practice thus relies on some basic features:[27]

---

[26] http://www.ifk.ac.at/about-en.html, 16.09.2010: excerpt, my choice and highlights. See also the mission statement at the institute's most recently relaunched website at http://www.ifk.ac.at/cms/index.php/mission_en.html, 20.09.2010.

[27] http://www.ifk.ac.at/cms/index.php/ifk_senior-fellow_en.html; http://www.ifk.ac.at/cms/index.php/certainty-undermined.html; http://www.ifk.ac.at/cms/index.php/alle-

What's new about the *New Cultural History?*

- structures built upon the open exchange between *senior* and *junior fellows* from different countries, research environments, and disciplines;
- this dialogue, though, is led within a number of *research foci* changing over time and designed to strengthen the institute's profile;
- lectures, workshops and *conferences, graduate schools* and postgraduate research, as well as
- *publications* to promote the common problem-oriented and trans-disciplinary issues.

Today the IFK has become the very institution in Austria where form and content (as laid out above), both in terms of *Cultural Studies/Kulturwissenschaften* and of *Cultural History*, merge in a very innovative, yet sustainable way. It does not—and cannot—provide research-based undergraduate and graduate teaching, which is evidently the task of the universities.

2.4 Academic institutionalization of Cultural History?

This takes me to my last topic, the exemplary survey of the current state of Cultural History in the Austrian academic community. The leading questions for my short survey that can only be preliminary in this context and are by no means intended to be comprehensive, were the following:
- Which *institutions* document research and teaching in Cultural History (universities, *extra-universitarian* institutions)?
- How are existent activities in Cultural History *organized*? Can they be described as *institutionalized*, i.e. rooted within their home institutions (e.g. institutes; research or studies' programmes), or are they rather organized around research projects and project clusters, book series, conferences?
- Are the theoretical and methodological *notions and concepts* of *Cultural History* or *Cultural Studies/Kulturwissenschaften* underlying these initiatives made explicit or defined in terms of mission statements, research profiles etc.?
- To which extent are activities in Cultural History explicitly related to *research traditions* such as *Cultural Studies, Kulturwissenschaften*, or specific trends in historiography?
- Are there any *specific topics* or *thematic clusters* to be traced?

---

termine.html; http://www.ifk.ac.at/cms/index.php/ifk-series-parabasen.html, all 20.09.2010.

First of all it is important to notice that—in contrast to the situation ten years ago—there are no specific public or private funding initiatives to support *Cultural History* and/or *Cultural Studies/Kulturwissenschaften* in Austria. The most important public funders such as the national research fund (FWF), the Vienna fund for science and technology (WWTF), or the Austrian Academy of sciences (ÖAW) are all funding projects in the Humanities, Social Sciences and Cultural Studies and are also—inter- and trans-disciplinary—but not specifically *Cultural History* or *Cultural Studies/Kulturwissenschaften*.[28]

If we turn to universities and focus on departments of humanities and cultural studies, and particularly on historically oriented disciplines, we will find that five of the six major Austrian universities—Graz, Innsbruck, Klagenfurt, Salzburg, Vienna –, as well as one of the newly restructured Art Universities, the *University of Applied Arts* in Vienna[29], clearly feature activities in *Cultural History* and *Cultural Studies/Kulturwissenschaften*.

The University of Vienna provides a somewhat typical example for the structural situation at the beginning of the new century: With the implementation of the new university legislation after 2002,[30] the traditional Faculty of Humanities was split in two, each covering more than a dozen departments of different scale and even more chairs:[31]

- *Historisch-kulturwissenschaftliche Fakultät*
- *Philologisch-kulturwissenschaftliche Fakultät*

The statement of the *Historisch-kulturwissenschaftliche Fakultät* in the university's development plan[32] names a number of exciting *Themenfelder* (topical areas) and *Forschungsschwerpunkte* (research priorities), using the term *Cultural History* or a related notion of *culture*, such as

---

28 See http://www.fwf.ac.at/de/projects/index.html; http://www.wwtf.at/programmes/; http://www.oeaw.ac.at/deutsch/stipendienpreise/index.html, all 16.09.2010.

29 http://www.dieangewandte.at/jart/prj3/angewandte/main.jart?rel=en&reservemode=active, 16.09.2010.

30 For an overview see http://www.univie.ac.at/organisation/, 16.09.2010. Details at http://www.univie.ac.at/dekanat-hist-kult/ and http://phil-kult.univie.ac.at/, both 16.09.2010.

31 The text is available at http://kommentare.rdb.at/kommentare/s/ug/htdocs/start.html, 16.09.2010.

32 http://public.univie.ac.at/fileadmin/user_upload/rektorat/Aktuelles/Entwicklungsplan/UW_Entwicklungsplan_2009.pdf, p. 63-69, 16.09.2010.

- *Kulturen des euromediterranen Raumes und Altertumswissenschaften (topical area),*
- *Historisch-kulturwissenschaftliche Europawissenschaften (topical area),*
- *Visuelle Kulturgeschichte—Kulturen und Medien des Visuellen (research priority),*
- *Wissenschaftsgeschichte—Wissenskulturen—Wissensgesellschaften (research priority).*

Still, of all the chairs within the faculty, only three have an explicit reference to Cultural History, none of the positions have so far been filled and only one has already been advertised.

The statement of the *Philologisch-kulturwissenschaftliche Fakultät* in the development plan and the concrete measures taken show even fewer claims, far-reaching or sustainable activities relating to Cultural History.[33]

Still, one will find a number of research initiatives on different levels in both faculties, e.g. large scale funded research projects and networks that bridge different institutes, but also departments (and faculties) such as the National Research Network *Kulturgeschichte des westlichen Himalaya seit dem 8. Jahrhundert.*[34]

A particular initiative is represented by the *interdisciplinary Cultural Studies working group* (since 1998), assembling teachers and researchers from different disciplines and departments to institutionalize research and teaching in Cultural Studies at the University of Vienna that also cooperates with institutions outside the university.[35] Its mission statement does not only show a clear commitment to inter- und transdisciplinarity, but also refers to some of the central approaches and methodological principles mentioned above:

> "We share a scientific commitment that eschews traditional boundaries between academic disciplines. Our aim is to focus on the cultural process (i.e. the motivations, orientations, and regulations which permeate all areas of work and life), and also to analyse cultural production."[36]

Moreover, one can find both overarching thematic priorities on the level of several departments, such as *media cultures* and a *cultural history of knowledge*

---

33 ID., p. 69-75.
34 http://kunstgeschichte.univie.ac.at/forschung/ifk-2-31/, 20.09.2010.
35 http://www.univie.ac.at/culturalstudies/netw/kooperation.htm, 16.09.2010.
36 http://www.univie.ac.at:80/Geschichte/htdocs/site/arti.php/90057, 16.09.2010.

at the history department,[37] and a number of individual research projects of the institutes' members, a lot of them including internal and external as well as international cooperation.

The same basically applies to other Austrian universities, if mostly—on a smaller scale—due to their general size. The most *institutionalized* of these initiatives are

- *Zentrum für Kulturwissenschaften* (University of Graz)[38]
- *Ludwig-Boltzmann-Institut für Gesellschafts- und Kulturgeschichte* (University of Graz)[39]
- *Zentrum für jüdische Kulturgeschichte* (University of Salzburg)[40]

All of these universities feature different activities in Cultural History, mostly on a very low level of *institutionalization* and, perhaps most importantly, with only two study programmes in cultural studies in the whole country:
- BA and MA *Applied Cultural Studies* (*Angewandte Kulturwissenschaften*) at the University of Klagenfurt—this is the only *full* teaching programme according to the *Bologna*-architecture;[41]
- Interdisciplinary *Erweiterungscurriculum Kulturwissenschaften/Cultural Studies* at the University of Vienna—i.e. it has *only* the status of a cluster/module that can be combined with several BA or MA studies.[42]

---

37 http://www.univie.ac.at:80/Geschichte/htdocs/site/arti.php/90057, 16.09.2010.
38 http://www.kulturwissenschaften.at/index.php, 20.09.2010.
39 http://www.lbg.ac.at/en/humanities/lbi-history-society-and-culture, 20.09.2010.
40 http://www.uni-salzburg.at/portal/page?_pageid=244,136522&_dad=portal&_schema=PORTAL, 20.09.2010.
41 http://www.uni-klu.ac.at/main/inhalt/4704.htm; among others the Austrian Ministry of Science and Research and the University of Vienna provide a dossier with general information, links and documents on the *Bologna process*, the initiative of the European Union to build a European higher education area: http://bmwf.gv.at/startseite/studierende/studieren_im_europaeischen_hochschulraum/bologna_prozess/ and http://bologna.univie.ac.at/index.php?id=aktuelles0, both 20.09.2010.
42 http://www.univie.ac.at/culturalstudies/studium.htm, 20.09.2010. On the scarcity of curricula in cultural history see also PRELIMINARY CONCLUSIONS, p. 185 below.

Moreover there are so-called *Wahlmodule* (elective modules) *Kulturgeschichte*, e.g. for MA at the University of Vienna.[43]

On the other hand, a particular feature of the Austrian academic community not only in the field of Cultural History, but in the whole area of the Humanities, Social Sciences and Cultural Studies is a very strong presence of *extra-universitarian* academic institutions operating outside the universities, with the IFK being the most prominent in the field of Cultural Studies. Among them one can roughly differentiate those having *Cultural History* and/or *Kulturwissenschaften/Cultural Studies* as the main task, such as the *Institut für Kulturwissenschaften und Theatergeschichte* (IKT)[44] at the Austrian Academy of Sciences (ÖAW) or the already mentioned *Internationales Forschungszentrum Kulturwissenschaften* (IFK); and others that work in these fields only within particular projects and research initiatives, such as the

- *Institut für Wissenschaft und Kunst* (IWK)[45]
- *Institut für die Wissenschaften vom Menschen* (IWM)[46]
- *Institut für jüdische Geschichte in Österreich* (INJÖST)[47]

Another specificity of the situation in Austria is the number of strong and productive inter-personal networks and project clusters that reach far beyond the home institutions of their participants, often integrate independent scholars, and establish links—both on a theoretical and thematic level—between the initiatives of the 1990s and the current endeavours, esp. those in the extra-universitarian scene and the project oriented initiatives within the universities. A representative example provides the network of Roman Horak (Univ. of Applied Arts, Vienna), Helmut Konrad (Univ. of Graz; *FSB Modernity*), Lutz Musner (IFK, Vienna), Wolfgang Maderthaner (*Labour History Society*, Vienna), Siegfried Mattl (Univ. of Vienna; *Ludwig-Boltzmann-Institut für Geschichte und Gesellschaft*, Vienna) which has conducted several major research projects employing junior researchers mostly based in Vienna, but also within an international network covering, among others, the University of Berkeley that resulted in a series of important publications in *Cultural Studies* and *Cultural History*.[48] The theo-

---

43 http://www.pri.univie.ac.at:80/activecc/geschichte/index.php?m=D&t=mageschichte &c=show&CEWebS_what=BA~32~Kulturgeschichte, 20.09.2010.
44 http://www.oeaw.ac.at/ikt/, 20.09.2010.
45 http://www.univie.ac.at/iwk/, 20.09.2010.
46 http://www.iwm.at/, 20.09.2010.
47 http://www.injoest.ac.at/institut/das_institut/, 20.09.2010.
48 E.g. MADERTHANER/MUSNER, 1999; HORAK et al., 2001 and 2004.

retical approaches of this research group can be described as rooted in *Cultural Studies* and *Cultural History*, and some of its most important methodological and thematic foci can be summarized as follows:
- deconstruction of *Wiener Moderne* as an elitist culture,
- labour history and the history of Austria's Social Democratic Party,
- mass culture in Vienna in the 19th and 20th centuries (e.g. football),
- urban cultures, esp. youth cultures in the suburbs,
- communication and consumer cultures and their role in identity constructions.

Another example is provided by the cooperation of Moritz Csáky and Heidemarie Uhl, both institutionally based at the *Institut für Kulturwissenschaften und Theatergeschichte* (IKT) at the Austrian Academy of Sciences (Moritz Csáky was the institute's director between 1997 and 2009), but also within the more informal network of the *SFB Modernity* discussed above.[49]

The theoretical basis of their work clearly lies in the fields of *Kulturwissenschaften* and *Cultural History*, their thematic interests focus on:
- modernity in Vienna and Central Europe around 1900,
- (Austrian) memory and identity,
- identity and memory politics after the "3rd Reich" (in the 2nd republic),
- cultural history of the performative forms of the theatre and the *operetta* in Vienna.

These and comparable interpersonal networks are all characterized by their explicit theoretical approach, their theoretical and methodological diversity, drawing on approaches in the *New Cultural History*, as sketched above, and on a variety of traditions in *Cultural Studies* and *Kulturwissenschaften*. Their notions and concepts of *Cultural History* or *Cultural Studies* are made explicit or are defined in terms of mission statements, research profiles on their project websites, in publications, at conferences, and via other means of academic communication.

On a more institutional level, this kind of explicit commitment to *Cultural History* combined with methodological transparency seems independent from the level of institutionalization:

---

49 Research and publications at http://www.oeaw.ac.at/ikt/forschungen.html, 20.09.2010.

What's new about the *New Cultural History?*

Examples of good practice are:[50]
- *Interdisciplinary Cultural Studies working group* (University of Vienna),
- *Institute for Economic and Social History* (University of Vienna),
- *History Department* (University of Salzburg),
- *Department Cultural History and Humanities* (Univ. of Applied Arts, Vienna),
- *Zentrum für Kulturwissenschaften* (University of Graz),
- *Internationales Forschungszentrum Kulturwissenschaften* (IFK),
- *Institut für Kulturwissenschaften und Theatergeschichte* (ITK, Austrian Academy of Sciences).

Examples of *not so good practice*, however, are specifically given by a considerable part of those university initiatives mostly imposed *from above* by the management during the restructuring of the institutions both on an organizational and on a thematic level. Particularly the example of the large faculties at the University of Vienna—the *Historisch-kulturwissenschaftliche Fakultät* and the *Philologisch-kulturwissenschaftliche Fakultät*—show that often you will find less content behind exciting and far reaching labels and headlines than it might be expected.

3. Preliminary conclusions

Thus, to answer my initial question, a superficial survey of the Austrian landscape would mostly not tell you what is *new about new cultural history endeavours* as defined above; it will rather give you an idea of managerial research and knowledge politics at the beginning of the 21st century.

However, this does not necessarily mean that the very researchers and students, working in the smaller entities of the large structures and involved in the endeavours developed therein in a more *grassroots* oriented research and teaching practice, would not be committed to *Cultural History*. On the contrary: If one takes a closer look at the levels of particular departments, research projects—funded and unfunded alike –, networks and project clusters, one discovers a lot of exciting activities thoroughly committed to the theoretical and methodological principles of (*New*) *Cultural History* and covering a wide range

---

50 I cannot go into any details here, but the excerpts from the mission statement of the IFK and the Cultural studies working group at the University of Vienna quoted above from their websites are exemplary for the practice of the initiatives mentioned below. For more information see the weblinks quoted in the footnotes above.

of diverse topics from Antiquity and the Middle Ages to Contemporary History and from Area Studies to Global History.

Therefore, the existence and prosperity of *Cultural History* definitely does not seem a matter of specific thematic topics. The major problem—especially within the European framework—is rather, that current forms of managerial politics tend to highlight plans and big labels instead of *real* activities and to thereby make invisible and sometimes even impossible the continuous background *work*, which draws on structures and research traditions developed in and before the 1990s.

One problematic result specific to Austria is the lack of solid study programmes in *Cultural History* and *Cultural Studies/Kulturwissenschaften*.[51] Another more general issue is the necessity for researchers to devote much time to adjusting their projects to the current rhetoric and organizational frames without many possibilities to sustainably link them to existing endeavours.

Literature

BACHMANN-MEDICK, DORIS, Cultural Turns. Neuorientierungen in den Kulturwissenschaften, Reinbeck bei Hamburg 2006.

BURKE, PETER, What is Cultural History, Cambridge 2004.

ID., "Pas de culture, je vous prie, nous sommes britanniques": L'histoire culturelle en Grande-Bretagne avant et après le tournant, in: L'histoire culturelle: un "tournant mondial" dans l'historiographie?, ed. by PHILIPPE POIRRIER, DIJON 2008, p. 15-25.

BUTLER, JUDITH, Gender trouble. Feminism and the Subversion of Identity, New York/London 1990.

ID., Undoing Gender. New York/London 2004.

CHARTIER, ROGER, Die unvollendete Vergangenheit. Geschichte und die Macht der Weltauslegung, Berlin 1989a.

ID., Texts, Printing, Readings, in: The New Cultural History, ed. by LYNN HUNT, Berkeley et al. 1989b, p. 154-175.

DANIEL, UTE, Kompendium Kulturgeschichte. Theorien, Praxis, Schlüsselwörter, Frankfurt/Main 2001.

---

51 For similarities and differences in Switzerland and Germany see the contributions of DEJUNG and LANDWEHR in this volume.

DARNTON, ROBERT, Intellectual and Cultural History, in: The Past before Us: Contemporary Historical Writing in the United States, ed. by MICHAEL KAMMEN, Ithaca, NY 1980, p. 327-354.
FURET, FRANÇOIS, Beyond the *Annales*, in: Journal of Modern History 55 (1983), p. 389-410.
GEERTZ, CLIFFORD, The Interpretation of Cultures. Selected Essays, London 1975.
ID., Dichte Beschreibung. Beiträge zum Verstehen kultureller Systeme, Frankfurt/Main 1983.
GILROY, PAUL, Without Guarantees. In Honour of Stuart Hall, London 2000.
GÖTTLICH, UDO et al. (eds.), Die Werkzeugkiste der Cultural Studies. Perspektiven, Anschlüsse und Interventionen, Bielefeld 2001.
GROSSBERG, LAWRENCE, We gotta get out of this place: Rock, die Konservativen und die Postmoderne (Cultural Studies 8), Vienna 2010.
HALL, STUART, Encoding/Decoding, in: ID. et al. (eds.), Culture, Media, Language. Working Papers in Cultural Studies, 1972-79, London 1980, p. 128-138.
ID., Ein politisches Theorieprojekt. Ausgewählte Schriften 3, Hamburg 2000.
HOFMANN, MARTIN LUDWIG et al. (eds.), Culture Club: Klassiker der Kulturtheorie, vol. 1, 3rd ed.; vol. 2, 1st ed., Frankfurt/Main 2006.
HORAK, ROMAN et al. (eds.), Stadt, Masse, Raum. Wiener Studien zur Archäologie des Populären. (kultur.wissenschaften 2), Wien 2001.
ID., (eds.), Randzone. Zur Theorie und Archäologie von Massenkultur in Wien 1950-1970 (kultur.wissenschaften 10), Wien 2004.
HUNT, LYNN, The New Cultural History, Berkeley et al. 1989.
JAMESON, FREDERIC, The Political Unconscious. Narrative as a Socially Symbolic Act, London et al. 1981.
LANDWEHR, ACHIM, Diskurs—Macht—Wissen. Perspektiven einer Kulturgeschichte des Politischen, in: Archiv für Kulturgeschichte 85 (2003), p. 71-117.
ID., Kulturgeschichte, Stuttgart 2009.
ID./STOCKHORST, STEFANIE, Einführung in die Europäische Kulturgeschichte, Paderborn 2004.
LINDNER, ROLF, Kulturanalyse, Kulturwissenschaft, Cultural Studies, in: Ästhetik & Kommunikation 100 (1998), p. 105-109.
ID., Die Stunde der Cultural Studies, Vienna 2000.
LUTTER, CHRISTINA, Baustellen in Wien. Ein kulturwissenschaftlicher Werkstattbericht, in: Die Werkzeugkiste der Cultural Studies. Perspektiven, Anschlüsse und Interventionen, ed. by UDO GÖTTLICH et al., Bielefeld 2001, p. 63-84.
ID. et al., Kulturgeschichte—Fragestellungen, Konzepte, Annäherungen (Querschnitte 15), Innsbruck 2004.

ID./MUSNER, LUTZ, Austrian Cultural Studies (Cultural Studies. Theorizing Politics, Politicizing Theory, ed. by LAWRENCE GROSSBERG et al., Special Issue 16, 6 (2002).

ID. (eds.), Kulturstudien in Österreich, Vienna 2003.

LUTTER, CHRISTINA/REISENLEITNER, MARKUS, Introducing History (in)to Cultural Studies. Some Remarks on the German-Speaking Context, in: Cultural Studies 16, 5 (2002), p. 611-630.

ID., Cultural Studies. Eine Einführung, 6th ed., Vienna 2008.

MADERTHANER, WOLFGANG/MUSNER, LUTZ, Die Anarchie der Vorstadt. Das andere Wien um 1900, Frankfurt/Main 1999.

MARCHART, OLIVER, Cultural Studies, Konstanz 2007.

MAURER, MICHAEL, Kulturgeschichte. Eine Einführung, Köln et al. 2008.

MIDDELL, MATTHIAS (ed.), Alles Gewordene hat Geschichte. Die Schule der "Annales" in ihren Texten 1929-1992, Leipzig 1994.

POIRRIER, PHILIPPE (ed.), L´Histoire culturelle: Un "tournant mondial" dans l´historiographie? Dijon 2008.

SCOTT, JOAN, Gender. A Useful Category of Historical Analysis, in: American Historical Review 91 (1986), p. 1053-1075.

STOLLBERG-RILINGER, BARBARA (ed.), Was heißt Kulturgeschichte des Politischen? Berlin 2005.

TSCHOPP, SILVIA SERENA, Die Neue Kulturgeschichte—eine (Zwischen-)Bilanz, in: Historische Zeitschrift 289 (2009), p. 573-605.

ID./WEBER, WOLFGANG e.J. Grundfragen der Kulturgeschichte, Darmstadt 2007.

TURNER, GRAEME, British Cultural Studies: An Introduction, 2nd ed., London/ New York 1996.

WAGNER, BIRGIT, Denken (und Schreiben) in Netzwerken: Antonio Gramsci, Walter Benjamin und Antonio Machado, in Die Werkzeugkiste der Cultural Studies. Perspektiven, Anschlüsse und Interventionen, ed. by UDO GÖTTLICH et al., Bielefeld 2001, p. 223-243.

WEHLER, HANS-ULRICH, Die Herausforderung der Kulturgeschichte, München 1998.

ID., Das Duell zwischen Sozialgeschichte und Kulturgeschichte. Die deutsche Kontroverse im Kontext der westlichen Historiographie, in: Francia 28 (2001), p. 103-110.

http://www.fwf.ac.at/de/projects/sfb.html, 07.09.2010
http://www-gewi.kfunigraz.ac.at/moderne/, 07.09.2010
http://www-gewi.uni-graz.at/fomop/home.html, 07.09.2010
http://www-gewi.kfunigraz.ac.at/moderne/edok.htm, 07.09.2010

What's new about the *New Cultural History?*

http://www.bmwf.gv.at/startseite/forschung/national/programme_schwerpunkte/
forschungsprogramme_schwerpunkte_ueberblick/, 10.09.2010
http://www.ifk.ac.at/about-en.html, 16.09.2010
http://www.ifk.ac.at/cms/index.php/mission_en.html, 20.09.2010
http://www.ifk.ac.at/cms/index.php/ifk_senior-fellow_en.html, 20.09.2010
http://www.ifk.ac.at/cms/index.php/certainty-undermined.html, 20.09.2010
http://www.ifk.ac.at/cms/index.php/alle-termine.html, 20.09.2010
http://www.ifk.ac.at/cms/index.php/ifk-series-parabasen.html, 20.09.2010
http://www.fwf.ac.at/de/projects/index.html, 16.09.2010
http://www.wwtf.at/programmes/, 16.09.2010 http://www.oeaw.ac.at/deutsch/stipendienpreise/index.html, 16.09.2010
http://www.dieangewandte.at/jart/prj3/angewandte/main.jart?rel=en&reserve-mode=active, 16.09.2010.
http://kommentare.rdb.at/kommentare/s/ug/htdocs/start.html, 16.09.2010.
http://www.univie.ac.at/organisation/, 16.09.2010.
http://www.univie.ac.at/dekanat-hist-kult/, 16.09.2010
http://phil-kult.univie.ac.at/, 16.09.2010.
http://public.univie.ac.at/fileadmin/user_upload/rektorat/Aktuelles/Entwicklungsplan/UW_Entwicklungsplan_2009.pdf, p. 63-69, 16.09.2010.
http://kunstgeschichte.univie.ac.at/forschung/ifk-2-31/, 20.09.2010
http://www.univie.ac.at/culturalstudies/netw/kooperation.htm, 16.09.2010.
http://www.univie.ac.at/culturalstudies/engl.htm, 16.09.2010.
http://www.univie.ac.at:80/Geschichte/htdocs/site/arti.php/90057, 16.09.2010.
http://www.kulturwissenschaften.at/index.php, 20.09.2010.
http://www.lbg.ac.at/en/humanities/lbi-history-society-and-culture, 20.09.2010.
http://www.uni-salzburg.at/portal/page?_pageid=244,136522&_dad=portal&_schema=PORTAL, 20.09.2010.
http://www.uni-klu.ac.at/main/inhalt/4704.htm, 20.09.2010 http://bmwf.gv.at/startseite/studierende/studieren_im_europaeischen_hochschulraum/bologna_prozess/, 20.09.2010
http://bologna.univie.ac.at/index.php?id=aktuelles0, 20.9.2010
http://www.univie.ac.at/culturalstudies/studium.htm, 20.09.2010. http://www.pri.univie.ac.at:80/activecc/geschichte/index.php?m=D&t=mageschichte&c=show&CEWebS_what=BA~32~Kulturgeschichte, 20.09.2010
http://www.oeaw.ac.at/ikt/, 20.09.2010
http://www.univie.ac.at/iwk/, 20.09.2010
http://www.iwm.at/, 20.09.2010
http://www.injoest.ac.at/institut/das_institut/, 20.09.2010
http://www.oeaw.ac.at/ikt/forschungen.html, 20.09.2010

We've only just begun
Cultural history in Germany

ACHIM LANDWEHR

A Young Scholar's Guide to Cultural History in Germany

While preparing this essay, I thought briefly about giving it a different subtitle. Sitting in front of my computer, I said to myself (or to my computer?) that I should rather call it "A young scholar's guide to cultural history in Germany". This heading suddenly seemed to be more appropriate to me because it would reflect on the different audiences this conference volume (and my essay in it) is addressing.

Asking myself "Whom are we talking to as cultural historians?", four groups or public spheres came to my mind: Firstly, the wider public whom we are trying to convince about the necessity and quality of our work. Secondly, the academic field of the arts in general, whom we are trying to convince as well. Thirdly, we are talking to ourselves in the sense of shaping our own identity as an academic subfield. Fourthly, we are talking about our future—indeed, we are talking *to* our future, and this future is the young scholar thinking about working in the field of cultural history. Now, if this young scholar would come up to me, what would I tell her about cultural history? What should she do (because statistically this young scholar rather is female)—and what should she rather avoid? Are there any chances to making a career in cultural history? And which steps are to be taken of reach that aim? Thus, I am trying to present some (hopefully helpful) rules for that young scholar to help her to find her way through the field of cultural history, including some *dos and don'ts*.

According to the general objective of this conference volume I will roughly split my paper into two parts and try to give you an impression of the institutional framework of cultural history in Germany before I turn to the contents of this field of research.

1. The institutionalization of cultural history in Germany

Let's start with some very basic and practical questions like: Where is cultural history happening in Germany, where can it be studied and where are the institutions specialized in that field of research?

In the last years several courses were established at German universities with a wider or a rather concentrated focus on cultural history[1]

1. Bachelor-Level
- BA *Antiquity in Europe* (*Die Antike in Europa*), University of Marburg
- BA *Cultural History of Christianity* (*Kulturgeschichte des Christentums*), University Erlangen-Nürnberg
- BA *European Cultural History* (*Europäische Kulturgeschichte*), University of Augsburg
- BA *Cultural Studies* (*Kulturwissenschaft*) with a focus on cultural history, University of Bremen
- BA *Cultural Studies* (*Kulturwissenschaften*) as well with a focus on cultural history, University of Frankfurt/Oder
- BA *Folklore Studies/Cultural History* (*Volkskunde/Kulturgeschichte*), University of Jena

Table 1

---

1   This information was gathered from: http://www.hochschulkompass.de/studium.html, 01.03.2010.

2. *Master-Level*
- MA *European Cultural History* (*Europäische Kulturgeschichte*), University of Frankfurt/Oder
- MA *European Cultural History* (*Europäische Kulturgeschichte*), University of Augsburg
- MA *European Cultural History* (*Europäische Kulturgeschichte*), University of Magdeburg
- MA *Interdisciplinary Medieval Studies* (*Interdisziplinäre Mittelalterstudien*), University of Münster
- MA *Cultures of Central and Eastern Europe* (*Kulturen Mittel- und Osteuropas*), Humboldt-University of Berlin
- MA *Cultural and Medieval Studies* (*Kulturgeschichtliche Mittelalterstudien*), University of Regensburg
- MA *Cultural Foundations of Europe* (*Kulturelle Grundlagen Europas*), University of Constance
- MA *Cultural Studies of Antiquity* (*Kulturwissenschaft der Antike*), University of Constance
- MA *Folklore Studies/Cultural History* (*Volkskunde/Kulturgeschichte*), University of Jena
- MA *Renaissance and Reformation Studies* (*Renaissance- und Reformationsstudien*), University of Osnabrück
- MA *Enlightenment—Religion—Knowlegde* (*Aufklärung—Religion—Wissen*), University of Halle

Table 2

Table 3

It would obviously be easier for our student to specialize on cultural history on the Master-Level, while the possibilities to concentrate on that field on a Bachelor-Level are not really overwhelming. Nonetheless, one could say that there are sufficient possibilities to turn to cultural history at a very early stage.

However, taking on specific courses on cultural history is only one way to tackle that field. In addition, there is the possibility to consider some chairs in universities specialized mainly or at least partly in cultural history. Here is a short list that may serve as an overview:
- Chair for European Cultural History (*Europäische Kulturgeschichte*), University of Augsburg
- Within the Faculty of Cultural Studies (*Fakultät für Kulturwissenschaften*) at the Viadrina-University of Frankfurt/Oder there is a whole branch of chairs for cultural history
- Chair for Cultural History (*Fach Kulturgeschichte*), University of Jena

Furthermore there are some research institutes concentrating exclusively on cultural history or have at least a special focus on that field of research. You will not be surprised at the metion of *usual suspects*, who are already familiar to you now:
- Institute of European Cultural History (*Institut für Europäische Kulturgeschichte*, IEK) University of Augsburg

- Institute of Cultural Studies (*Kulturwissenschaftliches Institut*), Essen
- Historical Cultural Sciences (*FSP Historische Kulturwissenschaften*), University of Mainz
- Interdisciplinary Institute for the Cultural History of the Early Modern Period (*Interdisziplinäres Institut für die Kulturgeschichte der Frühen Neuzeit*, IKFN), University of Osnabrück
- Research-Centre for the Early Modern Period (Zentrum zur Erforschung der Frühen Neuzeit), University of Frankfurt/Main
- Interdisciplinary Centre for European Enlightenment Studies (*Interdsziplinäres Zentrum für die Erforschung der Europäischen Aufklärung*, IZEA), University of Halle

Table 4

If we look a little closer at these university courses as well as on the research institutions it is quite obvious that medievalists and early modernists are prevailing in the field of cultural history. Thus, in Germany we have more or less the same situation as in France or in the United Kingdom, whereby scholars concentrating on these periods are much more attracted by cultural history. Even institutions, which do not explicitly concentrate on the Middle Ages or the early modern period, do so at least implicitly, as in the case of the Institute in Augsburg. Of course, this combination of older periods and cultural history does not occur by accident. Being an early modernist myself, I could make it easy by just stating that scholars concentrating on the history prior to the French Revolution are simply the *avant-garde*. But that would indeed be too easy. The reason why medievalists and early modernists feel attracted to cultural history is the need to shed new light on old problems and sources. Historians concentrating on modern history might not always see the necessity to ask new questions in this way.

But to prevent a possible misunderstanding: This quite impressive list of research institutions does not mean that the cultural history in Germany is swimming in an ocean of funds, stipends, positions, or money in general. In fact, many of these institutes have no money at all, are nothing else but a combination of researchers interested in cultural history. Thus, these are relatively small institutions, organizing conferences, smaller research projects, sometimes offering PhD positions, etc. But it would be bad advice for our young scholar, were she to put her hopes in these institutions. There are other possibilities I will mention soon. But before, the list with important institutionalisations of cultural history has to be closed with some journals. Only one journal in Germany consentrates exclusively on cultural history, the *Archiv für Kulturgeschichte* (Archive for Cultural History), concentrates.[2]

However, in the wider surroundings of cultural history there are several journals which have a special focus on cultural history:
- *Historische Anthropologie* (Historical Anthropology)[3]
- *KulturPoetik* (Cultural Poetics)[4]
- *Zeitschrift für Kulturphilosophie* (Journal of Cultural Philosophy)[5]
- *Saeculum. Jahrbuch für Universalgeschichte* (Saeculum. Yearbook of Universal History)[6]
- *WerkstattGeschichte* (WorkshopHistory)[7]
- *Jahrbuch für Kommunikationsgeschichte* (Yearbook of Communication History)[8]

Apart from these specialized journals, there are contributions to cultural history in all important major journals in the field of history, including the *Historische*

---

2 http://www.historische-anthropologie.uzh.ch/index.html, 01.03.2010.
3 http://www.geschichte.uni-erlangen.de/lehrstuehle/mittelalter/forschung/AKG.shtml, 01.03.2010.
4 http://www.uni-saarland.de/fak4/fr41/Engel/kulturpoetik/welcome.htm, 01.03.2010.
5 http://www.meiner.de/zkph, 01.03.2010.
6 Unfortunately there is no Saeculum homepage. Information can be gathered at the homepage of the publisher: http://www.boehlau.de, 01.03.2010.
7 http://www.werkstattgeschichte.de, 01.03.2010.
8 http://www.steiner-verlag.de/JbKG, 01.03.2010.

Zeitschrift[9] as the most traditional and still most important. Articles on cultural history can also be found in the broader field of literary, cultural, visual studies and so on. That there seems to be no further need to establish specialized journals on cultural history in their own right is — I believe — rather a good indication. It shows that the new cultural history in Germany, after it has been confronted with resentment and even hostility for a while, has established itself in the centre of the field of academic history.[10] Cultural-historical approaches certainly do not only have friends (but then: who wants to be friends with everybody?), but now the pursuit of this approach no longer requires justification.

On the contrary, in some areas of historical research cultural issues have become quite dominant. Numerous theses, dissertations and so on refer explicitly to cultural history as the dominant perspective. Apparently many young scholars are expecting to open an innovative potential from cultural history up new perspectives and answer old questions in a different way. Accordingly it is not very surprising that publishing houses respond very positively to this cultural trend. Additional indicators give hints in this direction: The very influential internet platform *H-Soz-u-Kult* (Humanities Social and Cultural History)[11] awards a prize for the best historical books in different categories every year. That this prize is taken very seriously, evident by the fact that the publishing houses are advertising the results quite frequently. I will only give you a few examples of books with a focus on cultural history, which have been awarded with that prize in 2008 and 2009:

- Barbara Stollberg-Rilinger about *The emperor's old clothes. The history of constitution and language of symbols in the early modern German Empire*[12]
- Karl Ubl about *Incest taboo and legislation. Construction of a crime 300-1100*[13]
- Jakob Vogel about *A shimmering crystal. A history of knowledge about salt in early modern and modern times*[14]
- Karl Schlögel about *Terror and dream: Moscow 1937*[15]

---

9 http://www.historische-zeitschrift.de, 01.03.2010
10 The respective discussion has been drawn together by TSCHOPP/WEBER, 2007.
11 http://hsozkult.geschichte.hu-berlin.de, 01.03.2010.
12 STOLLBERG-RILINGER, 2008.
13 UBL, 2008.
14 VOGEL, 2008.
15 SCHLÖGEL, 2008.

- Sabine Doering-Manteuffel about *The occult. A success story in the shadow of the Enlightenment*[16]
- Marian Füssel about *The culture of scholars as symbolic practice: Rank, ritual, and conflict in early modern universities*[17]
- And again Barbara Stollberg-Rilinger about *The cultural history of the political*[18]

2. The possibilities of funding for cultural history

Well, that's all nice: Offering courses at universities, establishing research institutes without any or only low funding, publishing journals and books some people will hopefully read—but what about the serious stuff, what about money? The relative success of cultural history in Germany really can be seen here. If one looks at the projects supported by the largest research funding organization by far in Germany, the *Deutsche Forschungsgemeinschaft* (DFG), one finds that cultural history plays quite a prominent part. If you search the database of projects funded by the DFG for *cultural history* there are no less than 135 results.[19] There you will find everything from the cultural history of the human experiment to a cultural history of the diagram. But let us concentrate on the really big projects, like the so called clusters of excellence (*Exzellenzcluster*), mainly intended for the natural sciences with an almost disappearing part for the humanities. But cultural history cannot be overlooked in that small section: There is a cluster on processes of cultural exchange between Asia and Europe (Heidelberg),[20] a cluster on the formation and transformation of space and knowledge in cultures of antiquity (Berlin),[21] a cluster on religion and politics in pre-modern and modern times (Münster),[22] and a cluster on the cultural foundations of integration (Konstanz).[23] All of them refer explicitly to cultural history. And just to make sure of what we are talking about: Every one of these clusters is getting funded with 3 to 8 million Euros every year. Thus for instance,

---

16 DOERING-MANTEUFFEL, 2008.
17 FÜSSEL, 2006.
18 STOLLBERG-RILINGER, 2005.
19 http://gepris.dfg.de/gepris, 02.03.2010.
20 http://www.asia-europe.uni-heidelberg.de/en/home.html, 01.03.2010.
21 http://www.topoi.org, 01.03.2010.
22 http://www.uni-muenster.de/religion-und-politik, 01.03.2010.
23 http://www.excl6.de, 01.03.2010.

right now it is quite easy for our young scholar to get funding for a dissertation. Indeed, some of these clusters really had problems to fill all the positions that were established during the so called *initiative of excellence*. It is quite obvious that there will also be some serious problems in the long run. Our young scholar will finish her dissertations with dozens, if not hundreds of other cultural historians—but the possibilities to find an adequate position at a university afterwards are still quite bad and they will get even worse when these clusters of excellence will release a flood of highly qualified young people.

However, the clusters of excellence are only the tip of the iceberg. Apart from that there are several graduate schools, research groups and priority programmes, all of them with a respectable part of cultural history. (Not to forget that the DFG is also funding this conference.) And apart from the DFG there are still more organizations funding research projects, such as the Henkel-, the Thyssen- or the Volkswagen-foundation to name just the majors.

But let us not forget that the success of cultural history in terms of raising funds really is a double-edged sword. On the hand it is great to see that cultural history obviously is able to receive support even with huge projects and large amounts of money. On the other hand we still have our young scholar sitting in front of us, thinking about her future in cultural history—and we have to face her with the hard facts that there is a *normal* academic life which is not getting funded. And that the possibilities to get a position, even on a tenure-track basis, are difficult and probably will become even more difficult. But our young scholar quite is convinced that she will be able to make an academic career and she is convinced that cultural history is the field in which she has something to say— and her enthusiasm is slowly convincing us. Thus, what we need now are some ideas on a subject she would be interested in and that would—at best—open up new perspectives for cultural history. Which topic should she choose?

3. Past, present and the future of cultural history in Germany

That was the easy part. Now that we assured ourselves that the institutional conditions of cultural history in Germany are not that bad—at least not that worse than in other fields of research in the humanities and that in some respects the situation is even better—and before we can give our young scholar really good advice about her research topics, we have to turn to a much more difficult question: What is being discussed in Germany under the heading of *cultural history*? What are the main subjects, with whom is cultural history cooperating, who are the main opponents? These aspects must be clarified before we can really say anything about promising fields of research for the future. No doubt, these questions are important for our young scholar, because mistakes should be avoided if you want to make a living of cultural history; at the same time the aim should be to establish new topics and to open up new perspectives. What can we tell our young scholar, which advice can be given? Maybe the best way to answer these questions is to concentrate on the *problems* of cultural history, because that is probably the best way to learn about the strengths and weaknesses of an academic discipline. I would like to look at two perspectives: Firstly, look at the problems cultural history is posing to others, second, the problems cultural history has with itself—or should have with itself.

3.1 The problem cultural history poses to others

When we turn to the problems cultural history is posing to others, we have mentioned one since the turn of the century: its success cultural history profits, from a large popularity, not only in terms of research funding. Stroll through any bookstore, take a look at the growing number of popular magazines with historical content and switch on any of the history programmes on television—cultural history will show an inestimable presence. However, cultural history not only enjoys increased attention in the media and in the broader public but—as we all know—also in the community of professional historians since the beginning of the 1990s.[24]

A second problem is tightly connected with the first one; it is the question of the status of cultural history. For quite a while now there are debates going on about the aims, the basis and—generally speaking—the meaning of cultural history. These discussions very often circle around the problem of self-definition of cultural history. What is cultural history all about? Since it follows a broad term of culture—one not restricted to an understanding of culture as arts, everyday life, material culture, etc.—it is difficult to make clear what it really wants to know. Sometimes cultural history appears as an approach that evokes the impression to know everything and to be able to explain everything—and for that reason—many critics say—cultural history in fact knows and explains nothing

---

24 The birth date of the new cultural history is marked by the publication of the volume of HUNT, 1989.

anymore. The problem arises: Is cultural history really such a vague field of research?[25]

To make one thing clear: I think that it is very positive and very productive that cultural history raises all these questions. It helps not only to shape its own programme, but it makes everybody in the field of historical research think about their work, about their preconceptions and their bases. Thus, cultural history in general is a challenge, maybe even a provocation—and that is very important!

That cultural history functions as a productive provocation can be seen by the fact that problems with that approach are often being brought forward by those who are *not really* in favour of it. Sometimes it is even said that, because of its character, cultural history is representing a massive threat for the academic conception of history.[26] And of course, there is a point. Even within cultural history regret is being expressed from time to time, that it has not been made sufficiently clear what this approach is all about and that it is the concept of culture in particular which leads to considerable blurs and uncertainties.

Looking at the state of art of cultural history, it is not surprising that this approach is confronted with the argument to do everything and nothing at the same time. Regarding the topics being tackled in this field, one indeed has the impression that no aspect of past life is left aside. There are the *classical* subjects like the histories of body, sex and gender, identity and alterity, communication and media, knowledge and science as well as the arts or the importance of memory for past and present societies. But one also finds cultural histories of politics, economy, technology etc.

Anyway, the question has to be asked if the critics are not right: Isn't this approach really too all-encompassing? Doesn't it mean that cultural history can do nothing anymore, because it wants to do everything? Against the background of the variety of topics, is it possible that cultural history remains in the state of a dilettante in all these possible fields of research? Is it possibly that cultural history produces nothing but *fashionable nonsense*?

One reason for these discussions, and even for these misunderstandings, is the fact that cultural history in Germany neither as a concept nor as an approach is a radical innovation; on the contrary, it can look back at a very long tradition. For this reason there are always certain preconceptions regarding cultural history, preconceptions which quite often turn out to be misunderstandings. Cultural history, as it is being practiced (again) for about two decades, has certain

---

25 I worked on this topic to a larger extent in LANDWEHR/STOCKHORST, 2004; LANDWEHR, 2005; LANDWEHR, 2009.
26 WEHLER, 1998; Id., 2001.

ties to older traditions, but shows a profile of its very own altogether. This profile sometimes contradicts general ideas about cultural history.

Let me just briefly mention a few of the influences that paved the way for the *new cultural history* in Germany. Firstly, there is the tradition of the historiography of the enlightenment with names like Johann Christoph Adelung, Johann Gottfried Herder and many others.[27] Secondly, there is the branch of cultural historians working in the late 19th and early 20th century, with the Swiss Jacob Burckhardt being very influential in Germany, but also with scholars like Karl Lamprecht, Eberhard Gothein, or Kurt Breysig. These traditions, especially the second, still influence the perception (or rather misperception) of cultural history in the wider public and even among historians not really in favour of cultural history.[28] However, *the usual suspects* of the international discussion have been much more influential for the new cultural history in Germany, e.g. all the debates about postmodernism and poststructuralism, probably even more so the tradition of German cultural philosophy and cultural sociology of Max Weber and Ernst Cassirer. During the 1980s the discussions about historical anthropology, micro-history and the history of everyday life (*Alltagsgeschichte*) directly influenced the new cultural history.[29] Something that has not been too important in Germany was the Cultural Studies.[30]

Thus, we have quite a long tradition of cultural history, but at the same time an actual practice of cultural history which contradicts these traditions in many ways. For some people cultural history therefore does not seem to require explanation, because it appears so self-evident, because everybody seems to *know* what cultural history (traditionally) is all about—and because of all these aspects an explanation is all the more necessary. The most problems caused in the preoccupation with cultural history is the fact that it takes a different path of self-definition.

The present-day cultural history does not seek the easy way to characterize itself, because it does *not* define a certain area of life as *culture* to which it dedicates itself. If culture would be conceived as a residual, the aim would be

---

27 Silvia Serena Tschopp recently drew attention to the wide range of cultural historians in the German enlightenment, TSCHOPP, 2009, p. 584.
28 About the history of cultural history in Germany: JUNG, 1999; HAAS, 1994; SCHLEIER, 2003.
29 See the respective chapters in DANIEL, 2001.
30 Therefore the Cultural Studies in the German speaking countries refer mainly to the British tradition: LUTTER/REISENLEITNER, 2008; MARCHART, 2007; GÖTTLICH et al., 2001.

determined by delimiting the concept of culture compered to other concepts such as nature, civilization or society. Another (far too simple) solution chosen frequently in the past is the understanding of culture as *totality*. A certain conglomerate, determined either ethnically, nationally or religiously, is said to produce certain values, norms and artefacts which transform culture into a unity.[31]

The new cultural history—that now is really not *that new* anymore—pursues a considerably different approach. It conceives culture as production of meaning and therewith puts the perspectives of different observers at the centre and propagates this certain cultural perspective on all objects of human life as its core element. Thus it is not the object of research but the perspective that forms the central element of cultural history.[32]

To take hold of cultural history and to characterize it more precisely sometimes appears to be difficult, because it does not submit itself to the usual ways of self-definition used in historical approaches. Usually, a historical approach is expected to define itself via its object: While economic history is dealing with economy, political history with politics, legal history with the law etc., one would expect that cultural history with culture. Far from it! Cultural history chooses explicitly another way by rejecting a defined object of observation. To put it clearly: Cultural history doesn't have any (specific) object at all, but turns to all historical phenomena, be it the theatre of the 18th century, rural clothes in the Alps, warfare in antiquity, procedures in the stock exchange market or programs of communist parties. There is no specific area of life called *culture* that could neatly and tidy be separated from other areas of human life (and in fact there never has been one). Thus, one has to say that culture surely is not everything—but culture is everywhere.

What is this perspective of cultural history? It is the question of systems of meaning with which societies of the past have equipped their world to transform it into a sensible and meaningful world. Cultures therefore can be understood as systems of meaning and distinction in other words as specific forms of interpretation of the world, which are produced, continued and transformed in the historical process. Cultures therefore cannot be reduced to the status of a superstructure vaulting the *real society*. Cultures are symbolic forms to organize reality without which individuals and social groups simply could not exist as they represent the necessary and constitutive background to all social practices. With this specific perspective it is surely not possible for cultural history to recognize everything, but it can focus on towards everything.

---

31 That is the direction of the argument in MAURER, 2008.
32 LANDWEHR/STOCKHORST, 2004; LANDWEHR, 2009.

At this point our critical young scholar raises her voice. She asks: If cultural history is concerned with the production of meaning in past societies, is it then not in danger to do exactly what it's critics say? Is cultural history not the (more or less) successive attempt to evoke the belief that cultural historians know everything and can do everything?

Yes and no (a typical answer for a cultural historian, one might say: neither fish nor fowl...). Cultural history is not an approach for and about everything, because it freely accepts its own restrictions. It cannot produce statistics of mortality nor does it collect economic data and it does not analyse the constitution of social strata. But, of course, cultural history is interested in statistics of mortality, in economic data and in the constitution of social strata, and therefore happily works together with all the experts in the respective fields of history. And in this sense, cultural history of course is an approach for and about everything because it leaves no aspect of history aside. It is concerned with economy, law and politics as well as the arts or the everyday life of people. Thus, cultural history is not everything, but it is everywhere. That's what a certain perspective does: You cannot see everything, but you can look everywhere.

What are the consequences of this understanding of cultural history? It results in a more radical way of historicization that leaves nothing aside. Cultural history has to show that all objects of past and present realities, especially those taken for granted and those that seem to be self-evident, have no other basis than their historical contingency. That is true even of the idea of fundamental historicity of social reality.

A first consequence is the special attention that has to be paid to the relations between observer and observed, between historian and history. The subject of practicing cultural history cannot be separated from the object called *cultural history*.[33]

A second consequence primarily arises from the circumstance of the *historical* perspective on cultural objects, and that is the fundamental contingency of historical developments and the openness and uncertainty of human experiences. The analysis of reciprocal relations between practices and structures not only shows their mutual dependence and historicity, but also dismantles every form of teleology still characteristic for approaches of modernization theory.

A third consequence is the multiplication of historical approaches and objects. If culture can be understood no longer as a homogeneous thing, then this applies also to *reality* and *history*. We inevitably have to deal with a multitude of realities and histories. The great task consists of making this circumstance

---

33 GOERTZ, 2001.

manageable both theoretically and methodologically. One of the greatest projects of cultural history therefore would not only be to establish something that could be called the non-unity of history,[34] but make clear at the same time that this non-unity is not a loss in clarity but a gain in complexity. As Einstein once said: Everything should be made as simple as possible—but not simpler.

A last—and I think, very important—consequence arises directly from the social dimension of the broad concept of culture, being the insoluble connection between culture and power. Culture is a social product, therefore it is neither innocent nor unproblematic, but it is inevitably controversial and disputed. Individuals and collectives are interested in establishing their specific form of the system of meaning as generally binding. Speaking with Pierre Bourdieu, one could call this the question of who manages to win the dominance of interpretation about reality a problem of symbolic power[35].

Cultural history has to offer a fresh perspective on past life. It does not reinvent the past nor does it completely renew history. At best it can offer new questions and puzzle us with different problems.

3.2 The problems cultural history has with itself

So far we were concerned with the problems cultural history is posing to others, but we shall not forget the problems cultural history has with itself. I spoke a lot about the possibilities of cultural history, the chances it has—but it is not at all clear if this approach is able to accept all these options and if cultural history really will be as promising as we all hope. So let us not forget our young student, eager to work in the field of cultural history: What can we tell her about the dangers and problems of cultural history? Which mistakes should be avoided?

A first possible difficulty the new cultural history could one day face is the restriction to certain set topics, that is: to maintain the status quo. As I mentioned briefly before, there is a set of well-established research topics of cultural history in Germany, mainly the history of memory, of body, sex, and gender, the history of the sciences, of everyday life, of media and communication, and certainly a few more. To prevent a possible misunderstanding: All of these topics are and were enormously important and certainly should not be left aside. But I think that it would be dangerous if cultural history voluntarily restrict itself to these topics. If what I said before about cultural history being characterized by a particular perspective directed to all aspects of past life is true, then it would

---

34 HAUSEN, 1998.
35 BOURDIEU, 1989.

be dangerous if cultural history would if only take into account a certain set of these aspects.

There are a few things and some blind spots coming to one's mind: In Germany there has been quite an intensive discussion about a cultural history of the political during the last years.[36] This has been quite fruitful and I think that it should be continued with respect to other fields of historical research and past life. In Germany there are the first hints of cooperation between cultural and economic history.[37] This would without doubt be a very interesting field for future research. But there are some enormously important subjects completely left aside so far. We have quite an intensive discussion about the cultural history of the sciences, but what about the history of technology? What about legal history that—to my knowledge—has not yet seen a cultural turn? In the field of military history, the history of war and violence there have been made some efforts as well,[38] but there is still a lot to do. As far as I can see there is no cultural history of society at all.[39] I could go on with this list, but what I am trying to say is obvious: Cultural history cannot and must not restrict itself; it has to broaden the range of its topics.

That is also true for another field of research sometimes (incorrectly) called *culture and its other*. It is meant to establish a contrast between culture and materiality or between culture and nature. From a theoretical point of view it is hardly understundable how and why there should be an opposition. Speaking as a cultural historian it is clear that materiality and nature are parts of historical cultures just as everything else. And of course there has been considerable work done by cultural historians in that field. But what we see right now is something like a *material turn* (although I've really had enough at the word *turn* anymore) and cultural history has to pay attention to play its part in that field.

Now allow me to make a last theoretical point. One really could not say that cultural history is not aware of its theoretical basis. On the contrary, there is a wide discussion of a group of theoretical authors important to cultural history as well as to other disciplines in the wide field of cultural studies. I already mentioned Max Weber and Ernst Cassirer as specific German influences, Niklas Luhmann surely has to be added, and then there are of course Pierre Bourdieu, Michel Foucault, and Michel de Certeau and many, many others. I think that

---

36 STOLLBERG-RILINGER, 2005; MERGEL, 2002; LANDWEHR, 2003.
37 BERGHOFF/VOGEL, 2004; HILGER/LANDWEHR, (forthcoming).
38 PRÖVE, 1999.
39 Although there are the important arguments of JOYCE, 2010.

these discussions are enormously important, because cultural history has to reflect theoretically on what it is doing empirically.
But aren't there any theoretical offerings cultural history has to make itself? Why should we leave theoretical thinking to philosophy, sociology and the like? It is not just possible, but I believe necessary, to take the empirical results of cultural history and turn them into a theoretical approach in its own right. Cultural history also has to make theoretical contributions, thus, a theory of cultural history (by cultural historians) really would be a task for the future.

4. Conclusion

If by now our engaged and courageous student is not completely confused by this *tour de force*, what might her overall impression be of the present state of cultural history in Germany? She probably might think that the situation is sufficiently paradox. On the one hand cultural history in Germany is well established: cultural historians successfully obtain university positions, the subjects of cultural history are present in the academic sphere as well as in the public and the media, impressive research programmes are concentrating on cultural history. At the same time one has to note that: cultural history in Germany is not too well institutionalised, some thematic (self-) restrictions are becoming obvious, and cultural history is sometimes seen as a mere short-term fashion. While leaving the office, she might say to herself: Cultural history still has to prove its ability to open new perspectives, it has to do so again and again—we've only just begun.

Literature

BERGHOFF, HARTMUT/VOGEL, JAKOB (eds.), Wirtschaftsgeschichte als Kulturgeschichte. Dimensionen eines Perspektivenwechsels, Frankfurt a.M./New York 2004.
BOURDIEU, PIERRE, Social space and symbolic power, in: Sociological Theory 4 (1989), p. 14-25.
DANIEL, UTE, Kompendium Kulturgeschichte. Theorien, Praxis, Schlüsselwörter, Frankfurt a.M. 2001.
DOERING-MANTEUFFEL, SABINE, Das Okkulte. Eine Erfolgsgeschichte im Schatten der Aufklärung. Von Gutenberg bis zum World Wide Web, München 2008.

FÜSSEL, MARIAN, Gelehrtenkultur als symbolische Praxis. Rang, Ritual und Konflikt an der Universität der Frühen Neuzeit. Darmstadt 2006.

GOERTZ, HANS-JÜRGEN, Unsichere Geschichte. Zur Theorie historischer Referentialität, Stuttgart 2001.

GÖTTLICH, UDO et al. (eds.), Die Werkzeugkiste der Cultural Studies. Perspektiven, Anschlüsse und Interventionen, Bielefeld 2001.

HAAS, STEFAN, Kulturforschung in Deutschland 1880-1930. Geschichtswissenschaft zwischen Synthese und Pluralität, Köln et al. 1994.

HAUSEN, KARIN, Die Nicht-Einheit der Geschichte als historiographische Herausforderung. Zur historischen Relevanz und Anstößigkeit der Geschlechtergeschichte, in: Geschlechtergeschichte und allgemeine Geschichte. Herausforderungen und Perspektiven, ed. by HANS MEDICK/ANNE-CHARLOTT TREPP, Göttingen 1998, p. 15-55.

HILGER, SUSANNE/LANDWEHR, ACHIM (eds.), Wirtschaft—Kultur—Geschichte, Stuttgart (forthcoming).

HUNT, LYNN, The New Cultural History, Berkeley et al. 1989.

JOYCE, PATRICK, What is the social in social history, in: Past and Present 206 (2010), p. 213-248.

JUNG, THOMAS, Geschichte der modernen Kulturtheorie. Darmstadt 1999.

LANDWEHR, ACHIM, Diskurs—Macht—Wissen. Perspektiven einer Kulturgeschichte des Politischen, in: Archiv für Kulturgeschichte 85 (2003), p. 71-117.

ID./STOCKHORST, STEFANIE, Einführung in die Europäische Kulturgeschichte, Paderborn 2004.

ID., Kulturwissenschaft und Geschichtswissenschaft, in: Kulturwissenschaft Interdisziplinär, ed. by KLAUS STIERSTORFER/LAURENZ VOLKMANN, Tübingen 2005, p. 39-57.

ID., Kulturgeschichte, Stuttgart 2009.

LUTTER, CHRISTINA/REISENLEITNER, MARKUS, Cultural Studies. Eine Einführung, 6th ed. Wien 2008.

MARCHART, OLIVER, Cultural Studies, Konstanz 2007.

MAURER, MICHAEL, Kulturgeschichte. Eine Einführung, Köln et al. 2008.

MERGEL, THOMAS, Überlegungen zu einer Kulturgeschichte der Politik, in: Geschichte und Gesellschaft 28 (2002), p. 574-606.

PRÖVE, RALF, Gewalt und Herrschaft in der Frühen Neuzeit. Formen und Formenwandel von Gewalt, in: Zeitschrift für Geschichtswissenschaft 47 (1999), p. 792-806.

SCHLEIER, HANS, Geschichte der deutschen Kulturgeschichtsschreibung. Bd. 1: Vom Ende des 18. bis Ende des 19. Jahrhunderts, Waltrop 2003.

SCHLÖGEL, KARL, Terror und Traum. Moskau 1937, München 2008.
STOLLBERG-RILINGER, BARBARA (ed.), Was heißt Kulturgeschichte des Politischen? Berlin 2005.
ID., Des Kaisers alte Kleider. Verfassungsgeschichte und Symbolsprache des Alten Reiches, München 2008.
TSCHOPP, SILVIA SERENA, Die Neue Kulturgeschichte—eine (Zwischen-)Bilanz, in: Historische Zeitschrift 289 (2009), p. 573-605.
ID./WEBER, WOLFGANG E.J., Grundfragen der Kulturgeschichte, Darmstadt 2007.
UBL, KARL, Inzestverbot und Gesetzgebung. Die Konstruktion eines Verbrechens (300-1100), Berlin 2008.
VOGEL, JAKOB, Ein schillerndes Kristall. Eine Wissensgeschichte des Salzes zwischen Früher Neuzeit und Moderne, Köln 2008.
WEHLER, HANS-ULRICH, Die Herausforderung der Kulturgeschichte, München 1998.
ID., Das Duell zwischen Sozialgeschichte und Kulturgeschichte. Die deutsche Kontroverse im Kontext der westlichen Historiographie, in: Francia 28 (2001), p. 103-110.

http://www.hochschulkompass.de/studium.html, 01.03.2010
http://www.geschichte.uni-erlangen.de/lehrstuehle/mittelalter/forschung/AKG.shtml, 01.03.2010
http://www.historische-anthropologie.uzh.ch/index.html, 01.03.2010
http://www.uni-saarland.de/fak4/fr41/Engel/kulturpoetik/welcome.htm, 01.03.2010
http://www.meiner.de/zkph, 01.03.2010
http://www.boehlau.de, 01.03.2010
http://www.werkstattgeschichte.de, 01.03.2010
http://www.steiner-verlag.de/JbKG, 01.03.2010
http://www.historische-zeitschrift.de, 01.03.2010
http://hsozkult.geschichte.hu-berlin.de, 01.03.2010
http://gepris.dfg.de/gepris (March 2nd, 2010), 01.03.2010.
http://www.asia-europe.uni-heidelberg.de/en/home.html, 01.03.2010
http://www.topoi.org, 01.03.2010
http://www.uni-muenster.de/religion-und-politik, 01.03.2010.
http://www.exc16.de, 01.03.2010

Cultural History in Spain
History of Culture and Cultural History: same paths and outcomes?*

CAROLINA RODRÍGUEZ-LÓPEZ

An overview

Cultural history is currently a booming topic in Spain. Cultural history is now flourishing and certain areas have distinguished themselves as autonomous fields of study: the history of cultural politics, reading and printing, and medical cultural practices, for example. However, what is defined as *cultural history* in current Spanish historiography is not an easy issue. Like the rest of European (even American) historiographies, Spanish historiography has gone through an extensive and interesting process, shifting from social to cultural history. The process has not been exempt from problems and misunderstandings and has determined not only the ways in which cultural history has traditionally flowed but also the kinds of research and scientific works that have been labeled with the *cultural history* title.

This chapter offers a brief overview of what I have just mentioned above. In order to do so, it is divided into three sections. The first one deals with the historical and historiographical contexts when the first research and debates in Spain focused on cultural history. In the second section, I introduce the research groups, institutions, academic programs and publishing house projects that have encouraged and are currently organizing Spanish cultural history knowledge and production. And last but not least, I present a first and tentative list of exact-

---

* I am grateful to Elena Hernández Sandoica for detailed suggestions and to Patricia Berasaluce and Elisabeth Klein for accurate reading of this chapter's first version.

ly what Spanish historians have written on the field of cultural history. In other words, I offer a first and non-exhaustive portrait of Spanish cultural history production: the most significant titles and the subfields of Spanish cultural history.

Historical and historiographical context: When and how? When did new *cultural history* appear in Spain?

Before the Spanish Civil War, there was a budding and interesting debate on the history of ideas and thoughts about the kind of historiography historians could write. The entire debate was based on one idea: could historians reach a newer and more modern historiography by including specific issues such as cultural trends and movements? Would they be able to explore, in some Spanish historical processes, paths recently opened by the French *Annales* School? Was it possible to concentrate on specific traits of *Spanish civilization* by studying cultural expressions and experiences? More importantly, would these new kind of studies contribute a whole modernization process, which was claimed for a long time by Spanish society?[1]

This debate was abruptly interrupted by the Spanish Civil War and its aftermath. Exile and the ideological barrenness of the postwar period opened political, ideological and intellectual doors to neo-Catholic and fascist forms of historiography. However, Franco's regime unwittingly left some gaps, which were used by historians for their own intellectual production. Thus, since the 1950s, Spanish historians received varied and fruitful information about what French historians were doing within the framework of *Annales,* due mainly to quite significant historians of the early modern period such as Pierre Vilar. British books and others related to the study of French *civilization* were used by Spanish historians searching for new historical approaches, which allowed them to depart from the traditional political perspective. José M. Maravall and José M. Jover were undoubtedly the most important historians of that time.

A new panorama started to appear during the 1960s and 1970s.[2] British social history, inspired by Marxist principles, offered a new, transnational direction for Spanish historiography, mainly focused on modern times. In 1971, Spanish historians could read for the first time a Spanish translation of Rudé's book *The Crowd in History: A Study of Popular Disturbances in France and England, 1730-1848.* In 1977, they could read the first Spanish translations of E.

---

1 ALTAMIRA, 1909-1911; ID., 1913, ID.; 1928-1930.
2 JOVER, 1961; HERNÁNDEZ SANDOICA, 1997.

P. Thompson's research and in 1978 the co-authored Rudé & Hobsbawm book *Captain Swing: A Social History of the Great English Agricultural Uprising of 1830* appeared in its Spanish version for the first time.

What was happening in Spanish historiography and in the rest of Spanish political and cultural life during the 1960s and 1970s is quite significant in understanding the process previously mentioned. The end of Franco's dictatorship, the beginning of an intense and fruitful cultural movement in the subsequent transition period—defining the framework for democratic practice—and the arrival of new and different historiographical approaches deeply contributed to the development of two consecutive and parallel processes. On the one hand, encouraged by resistance to the Spanish dictatorship, Spanish historians—mainly the youngest and those who traveled abroad and read foreign languages—embarked on new research focused on the Spanish workers' movement, trade unions and other similar movements during the Spanish Civil War. Specifically, there was the fertile work of a varied group of foreign researchers specialized in Spanish history and culture (the *Hispanists*) often coming from France, England, Germany and the US.[3]

On the other hand, by focusing their research on workers and trade unions, Spanish historians *discovered* a new path to bring other kinds of culture to light. These dealt with culture practiced, made, and lived (experienced) by subaltern groups and individuals. In other words, by paying attention to and discovering the forms of popular, subaltern and workers' culture they delved into their research topics in depth and, at the same time, compared and confronted popular and elite cultures.

It was generally assumed that former ways of research in the field of cultural history (or, rather, *history of culture*) outlined the importance of the so-called *high culture*. The ideological perspectives from which these new approaches to culture were observed—sometimes tacitly; sometimes explicitly—led to the former production about the topic being defined as conservative and elitist. Research, which only pointed out trends in art, music, literature, leaving aside popular and subaltern culture expressions, gradually ran the risk of being considered both an old and an incomplete history of culture.[4]

---

3 P. Vilar, J. F. Botrel, S. Saläun, C. Serrano, J. L. Guereña among the French; M. Tuñón de Lara—a Spanish historian living in France as an exile and returning to Spain after Franco's death—; P. Preston, J. Lynch, J. Elliott, among the British; W. Bernecker among the Germans or S. Payne and S. Ellwood, among the Americans.
4 URÍA, 1984a; ID., 1984b; ID., 1991a; ID., 1991b.

We can sum up the two main paths along which the first Spanish cultural history flowed: on the one hand, it connected with social history, sociology — anthropology arrived later in this process — and focused on common, trendy and *Marxist* concepts like *association movements, workers' movements* and, even, *everyday life*.[5] This sort of cultural history is strongly related to women's history.[6] On the other hand, it was intellectual history and the history of ideas, which was practiced without any contact social history. These two different — usually contrasting — approaches to Spanish cultural history characterized not only the scientific productions focused on the topic, but also the cultural and ideological context in which this debate took place.

Most Spanish historians who considered social history as the main focus of all historical research often thought that intellectual history and the history of ideas were the natural ways in which historicism continued working (remember that for historicist trends all history was naturally a history of ideas including decisions, desires, purposes, and feelings). Moreover, they recognized that traditional political history was quite close to this kind of history of culture. Only the new perspectives in the field of social history were considered appropriate to achieve good and new studies dealing with cultural history. The rest of the works concerning intellectual history and the history of ideas remained as classic history productions.[7]

What did Spanish historians understand as *culture*? What kinds of cultural expressions did they consider worth studying? If we really want to understand what *culture* meant to Spanish historians in the 1970s, we need to identify the trends that influenced them. French historiography has traditionally had an influence on Spanish historians. From the 1950s to the 1970s we can easily identify the impact of the *Annales* French historiography school.

Influenced by the Marxist British thoughts and the impacts from the new trend focused on the proximity of history to the rest of social sciences, Spanish historians were interested in *everyday life*, mainly of workers, usually the main emphasis of their research. By considering intellectual history and the history of ideas as the study of exceptional and exclusive culture, everyday life studies emerged as a perfect medium to know the most representative aspects of cultural human life. So, culture adopted a variety of meanings — attitudes, shared values, symbols and cultural expressions — which combine to form a way of life.

---

5   CASTELLS, 1985; ID., 1987; ID., 1990; ID., 1993; ID., 1995a; ID., 1999.
6   CID, 2006.
7   HERÁNDEZ SANDOICA, 2004, p. 378.

It is easy to see that these changes and strategic perspectives were not simple, especially since the two sides in *conflict*, high (intellectual) and popular culture became quite closely identified by the eclectic historians. History constituted, at this point, a comprehensive exercise where elements coming from intellectual history, anthropology perspectives, and from the history of ideas and thought went hand in hand.[8]

Little by little this whole group was assimilating anthropological perspectives. Sociology and Marxism were pushed into the background and historians chose to practice new socio-cultural perspectives: work history and workers' and peasant culture, among others, were in the center of new and fruitful cultural histories. These dealt with a socio-anthropological history now interested mainly in language and communication. In some aspects, this new history approach was indebted to social sciences and especially to the most outstanding historical trends: the two just mentioned and the French School of *Annales*. They were changed by concepts like *sociability* borrowed from Maurice Agulhon and by the neo-Marxist British perspective.[9]

In sum, Spanish historians who considered the history of culture as a reminder of elitist behavior, left this aside and started to draw nearer to another kind of cultural history by understanding culture as a part of social history. There is a third group: historians who achieved a sort of middle ground. They studied intellectual history from a cultural perspective by justifying their choices in these words: intellectuals are a social group who make cultural products. In this latter group, are the first cultural history texts quite close to literary reviews, semiotics, linguistic, and anthropology. Only through a little but fruitful contact with social sciences could history complete its change process in the 1970s.

The 1980s can be characterized as the time when social and cultural history disputed their own spaces in the Spanish historiography panorama. It was when political history did not waste its time and reorganized its interests and perspectives index. The former way in which historians used to practice history of

---

8   ID., p. 382. These comprehensive history readings included: history of ideas, history of thought, intellectual history (informal thought, opinion trends, literary movements…), social history of ideas (ideas transmission and ideologies), culture from an anthropological perspective (collective mentalities…) or intellectual sociology. The names of Robert Darnton, Roger Chartier, Hans-Robert Gauss, Quentin Skinner, Stefan Collini, Richard Tuck, John Dunn, Istvan Dunn or Clifford Geertz can be related to all these history approaches and were well-known among a number of Spanish historians.

9   URÍA, 2008c.

culture was consolidated in to what is now called *intellectual* history.[10] C*ultural studies* have optimistically encouraged the growth of historiography in this field. From the first year of the 21st century socio-cultural studies on the one hand and intellectual history on the other outlined the axes of this growth. Because of intellectual history's recent development, new texts, materials and documents are available. Due to its interest in understanding behaviors and productions of the intellectual elites, intellectual history became close to cultural studies. Its utilization of methods and techniques typical of cultural studies (like discourse analysis or elites' sociability) enabled intellectual history to be gradually immersed in cultural history and perspectives.

Following the previously described process, the first Spanish production in the field of cultural history was designed from the perspective of *micro* studies and focused on language, thanks to its closeness to linguistic anthropology. The utilization of oral sources[11] became important and enabled Spanish historiography to include topics such as experience and identity among its interests.[12]

All these elements worked together and produced the concept of Spanish cultural history, which continued being confronted by both political (i.e., the kind of political history not influenced by social sciences) and social history (i.e., the form of social history focused on structures and quantification).

The most ambitious studies were those related to *everyday life*. That focus made it easy to use analysis tools from quantitative and urban sociology, ethnology and social class analysis; all of them enabled these studies to be framed at a *micro* and a *local* perspective. In this context, regional Spanish historiographies started to differ from each other. Studies focusing on Catalonian and Basque issues could easily be found which focused; Asturias and Castilian studies whose topics and perspectives were quite close to sociology and *sociability*; Valencia studies, which started from political approaches and went deeply into Valencia everyday life during the Spanish Civil War period, to mention just a few examples. These everyday life studies included material culture, ideas and beliefs, ways of life, and social practices and behaviors. One more interesting step brings us directly to *women's history*.

Spanish historiography started to outline its own cultural history fields from the 1980s. Starting with the use and study of literary sources, education history and book history were recognized as two pioneering topics. In the 1990s, Spanish cultural history rose to the challenge of integrating the proposals of

---

10 HERNÁNDEZ SANDOICA, 2001, p. 59.
11 See The Journal, *Antropología y Fuentes Orales* from its first issue in 1989.
12 CABRERA, 2001a; ID., 2001b; ID., 2007; ID., 2003; OLÁBARRI/CAPISTEGUI, 1996.

Ginzburg, Chartier, Nora and Agulhon. As a result, various and fruitful studies appeared. We will take up this topic again in the fourth section.

What has been going on in institutions, publishing houses and academia in the field of cultural history?

Some academic and scientific institutions were created with the aim of supporting cultural history research. Several publishing houses developed their own projects in order to bring these research outcomes to light. Furthermore, academic programs were designed in order to include cultural history among the university subjects.

Concerning research groups and institutions, GEHCI was one of the first research groups in the field of cultural history created in Spain.[13] The meaning of this acronym—currently used by the group—is quite relevant: Group for Cultural and Intellectual History Study. Starting with its first meeting in 1989, the group, based at Barcelona University, identified among its tasks establishing a discussion meeting point for cultural history issues, where young students can start their PhD dissertations. From the very beginning their main topic of interest was the study of *intellectuals'* roles, functions and characteristics. That was the rationale behind determining the order of the group's first name: *Group for Intellectual History Study*.

One of the first activities of this Group was the design of the first academic program including subjects related to Cultural History in Modern Europe (1870-1930). This subject was taught for the first time in the academic year 1990-1991.

The Group clearly sought contacts with other groups and Spanish universities as well as with foreign institutions among its targets. The French University Paris VIII held the first international seminar which put the Spanish group in contact with the *Group de Recherche sur l'Histoire des Intellectuels* directed by Michel Trebitsch. The group designed a data base, which included details concerning intellectuals' activities, cultural strategies, contacts with popular culture and cultural relationships in the region of Catalonia.

In 1995, the group changed its name to Group for Cultural and Intellectual History Studies. In 1998, the first issue of *Cercles (Cultural History Review)*—the group's journal—appeared. *Cercles* is a yearly journal which aims to create a meeting point for encouraging debates and research on cultural history and for fostering interdisciplinary exchanges.

---

13 CASASSAS I YMBERT, 2004.

By studying the group's subject evolution, we can easily a picture of a part of Spanish cultural historiography's progress. From intellectual history perspectives, GEHCI expanded its view to incorporate cultural history including themes dealing with cultural expressions and everyday life. Catalonia is the regional-local framework where the group's studies take place, making it easier to have a local, regional and *micro* perspective.

The analysis of *Cercles* allows us a similar exercise. By checking the journal's index during the past decades we can easily identify its fields of interest. These indexes include articles on historiography analysis and review;[14] historians and historiography analysis;[15] urban history from socio-cultural perspectives;[16] biographies of intellectuals;[17] cultural expressions and spaces;[18] identity and national thought;[19] iconography and symbols;[20] ideology, thought and philosophy;[21] high-culture institutions;[22] history of books;[23] history of intellectuals;[24] and working-class culture.[25]

An interesting circle of research groups is related to one of the most significant research fields within cultural history, namely *written culture history* and *book and reading history*. Following the methodological and theoretical proposals offered by French historians, mainly Jean François Botrel and Roger Chartier, two interesting groups were created in the late 1990s: *Litterae: Group for Cultural History Studies* at Carlos III University of Madrid, and *SIECE—Interdisciplinary seminar for written culture studies*—at Alcalá de Henares University. Both groups share similar aims and activities.

Litterae was created in 1997 to research, debate, study and support cultural history, as well as to work on and publish outcomes in this field. *Litterae's* fields of interest include: social history of written culture, reading history, university

14 CASASSAS I YMBERT, 1998a; LIAKOS, 2000.
15 OSTENC, 1999.
16 FUENTES, 1998.
17 IZQUIERDO BALLESTER, 1998; LLORENS I VILA/CASASSAS I YMBERT, 1998.
18 HOFFMAN, 1999; GHANIME, 2002; LLORENS I VILA, 2002; FUENTES, 2003; LOFF, 2003.
19 GUIRAO, 2002; XIFRÓ Y COLLSANATA, 2002; CASASSAS I YMBERT, 2006.
20 FUENTES, 2002.
21 SIMÓN I TARRÉS, 1999; D'AURIA, 2000; IZQUIERDO BALLESTER, 2006.
22 PÉREZ LEDESMA, 2004.
23 GÓMEZ, 2002; IZQUIERDO BALLESTER, 2002.
24 GÓMEZ, 2003.
25 Issue 8 of it is entirely devoted to this topic.

history, women's history, iconography in written culture, religion and religiosity in written history, urban history (mainly Madrid history), and international cultural exchanges. Litterae has a yearly journal: *Litterae. Written Culture Journal.*[26]

SIECE's first activities started in 1995 with the aim of promoting research, teaching and popularization of the role of reading and writing in History. Similarly to Litterae, SIECE organizes scientific meetings, conferences and seminars to discuss and disseminate research results in its field. SIECE also publishes a journal called *International Written Culture and Society Journal.*[27]

A group on Printed Culture History in Modern Spain mentioned in Complutense University of Madrid's research group catalogue focuses on a quite similar field.

Girona University holds a seminar for political and cultural studies which joins two different groups simultaneously: *Research Group for Cultural Studies* and *History, Memory and Identities Group*. Both share interests, aims and fields. Concerning cultural studies, their main subfields are: written history, urbanization processes, images and meanings in architectural buildings, political, social, and sexual and gender identities, social consensus and repression forms, political uses of memory, and artistic and cultural heritage in the Girona region. This Catalan group not only organizes conferences and seminars, but also publishes its journal: *Studium medievale: visual and written culture Journal.*[28]

The University History field is one of the most perused by historians interested in cultural history and in high culture institutions. Since the 1990s, several research groups have been working on projects that consider the university as an institution which not only supports scientific knowledge and subjects, but also where scholarly and academic sociability is developed. Valencia University created CESHU (Center for University History Studies) in 1995. Using the university as starting point, the main focus was on teaching and on knowledge dissemination. CESHU's main aim is to study science production and dissemination in European and American universities. Most of its activities (research and dissemination support, publishing projects, discussion seminars and international

---

26 Litterae. Cuadernos sobre cultura escrita to date, has published four issues: no. 1 (2001); no. 2 (2002); no. 3-4 (2003-2004).
27 Revista internacional de Historia social de la Cultura Escrita. The Journal is published twice a year. The first issue appeared in September 2005 and the latest one (no. 9) in September 2009.
28 Studium medievale. *Revista de cultura visual-cultura escrita*. Only one issue was published in 2008.

conferences) have focused on laws and internal organization of universities and on the evolution and historical planning of legal subjects and fields. In addition, CESHU's main research has paid attention to Valencia University's history.

The Alfonso IX Center of Salamanca University History started to operate in 1997. The Center is focused on the study of Salamanca University's history and is concerned with the four main aspects of research, teaching, publishing and organizing seminars and conferences. The Center publishes an annual Journal (*Miscelánea*) and has often collaborated in the edition of some collective volumes about Salamanca University's history. Its most innovative activity concerns teaching: from the very beginning the Center has offered an annual course on *Spanish Universities in the Early Modern Age: academic culture and student life*. The aim of this course is to study the evolution and role of Spanish universities in Spanish culture and politics. This course focusses on the to academic and student's life at Salamanca University.

Whereas the Valencia and Salamanca Centers are focused mainly on the history of their own universities, the Antonio de Nebrija Institute for University Studies—IAN—(at Carlos III University of Madrid) has a broader view of University history. Created in 1997, IAN includes among its aims: to promote scientific research about history and current university processes alike; to publish the most outstanding results of current research about this topic; to organize teaching and dissemination activities; and to compile a bibliographical collection about university history and studies. From its very beginning, IAN publishes a yearly Journal (*Antonio de Nebrija Institute Journal*)[29] and also has a publishing house which produces new books and monographs dealing with university history.[30]

It is also worth mentioning a recently consolidated group: the Group for Modern Spain Cultural History Studies at Complutense University of MadrID. This Group began its activities in 2006 and has five main research fields: political cultures; university and cultural institutions' history; everyday life; women's history and intellectuals and intellectual life. The group seeks to combine the most interesting, current and fruitful fields in cultural history studies. Among its

---

29 The first issue appeared in 1999. The last one, number 12, came to light in 2009.
30 PESET/NAVARRO, 1999; MERINO, 1999; RIVIÉRE GÓMEZ, 2000; MARTÍNEZ NEIRA, 2001; COMAS CARABALLO, 2001; RODRÍGUEZ LÓPEZ, 2002; AZNAR I GARCIA, 2002; VILLALBA PÉREZ, 2003; CRUZ MUNDET, 2003; MORA, 2004; MARTÍNEZ NEIRA ET AL., 2004; MORA CAÑADA/RODRÍGUEZ LÓPEZ, 2004; BERMEJO CASTRILLO, 2004; GUIJARRO GONZÁLEZ, 2004; ONCINA COVES, 2008; MARTÍNEZ NEIRA/PUYOL MONTERO, 2008; PERALES BIRLANGA, 2008; ARAGONESES, 2009; LÓPEZ VEGA, 2009; CARONI, 2010.

aims are: to support research in cultural history; to update international cultural history outcomes; to organize scientific meetings and seminars; and to collect a bibliography on cultural history issues.[31]

History departments and institutes are not the only places where people have been working on cultural history projects. University departments of literature and languages have usually been supporting research projects in a similar way. For example, the Group for Culture, Publishing and Literature Studies in Hispanic World (CSIC) are investigating: culture history during the 19th century; heterodox literature publishing in the 19th century; reading and publishing history; writers' professional work and the legal status of copyrights. Other entities include the *Group for Literary and Cultural Exchanges between Spain and Slavic Countries* (Complutense University of Madrid—UCM); the *Group for Literary and Cultural Exchanges between Spain and German-speaking Countries* (at UCM too) and *Jewish Cultural Heritage in Spain*.

The history of historiography has gradually been included within cultural history in recent Spanish historiography. The status of this kind of study, located half-way between intellectual, academic and thought history, allows us to mention it in this compilation. Carlos III University of Madrid hosts, since 2005, the Julio Caro Baroja Historiography Institute focused on the study not only of the history of historiography, but also of past and current trends in historical writing. The Institute is dedicated to Julio Caro Baroja, a versatile Spanish historian whose fields of interest ranged from history to anthropology, ethnology and literature as well. The Historiography Institute, like other similar institutions, organizes seminars and conferences, has its own book collection and publishes a journal *Journal of Historiography*.[32]

Nowadays, most Spanish university programs include subjects concerning cultural history. The title and perspectives regarding these subjects are various and very interesting. We do not intend to be exhaustive but a quick look at university programs reveals the following data:

---

31 This group is still working at its website: http://www.ucm.es/info/culturalhistory/main.php, 10.09.2010

32 First issue in 2004; last issue (no. 10) in 2009.

University	Degree	Subjects
Alcalá University	BA	Social history of written culture
Political thought history	Cultural history of the Middle Ages	Written culture history
Cultural history in the Middle Ages	Autonoma University of Madrid	Current BA
	Writing and society	Cultural history
Archive and library history and procedures	Written culture history	From Codex to printing
Culture and religion in Early Modern Spain	Aristocracy and culture in Early Modern Spain	Culture formation in Modern Times (from the 15th to the 18th century)
Culture and political ideas in Early Modern and Modern Spain	History of Mediterranean Cultures (from the 16th to the 21st century)	Elite culture and popular culture in Early Modern Spain
Catholic culture and Protestant culture in the Early Modern Age	Carlos III University	Current BA
Classical culture	Antiquity and classical heritage	Cultural history
Economic thought history	Theatre history	Complutense University of Madrid
Former BA	Thought and intellectual activity in the Middle Ages	Culture and mentality in the Early Modern Age
Introduction to early modern culture history	Culture history in America	Culture and everyday life in the Middle Ages
European science and technology	Madrid history	Extremadura University
Former BA	History of scientific and technological processes	Granada University
Former BA	Archeology and material culture in the Middle Ages	Writing history: documents and manuscripts
History, society and everyday life in Early Modern Europe	Medieval culture history	Huelva University
Former BA	Book history	Civilization and culture in America
Latin documents and writing history	Philosophic and scientific thought history	Classical culture
Culture history in the Early Modern World	Humanism and culture	Society, culture and mentality in the Middle Ages
Jaén University	Former BA	Classical culture
History of religion in Antiquity	Social anthropology	La Laguna University

Cultural History in Spain

Former BA	Indigenous Canary Islands culture	American cultures
Cultural anthropology	Mediterranean science and culture history	History of political ideas in the Modern World
Urban history	Everyday life in the Middle Ages	Mentalities and sensitivities
Women's history	History of mentalities in the Early Modern Age	
Las Palmas de Gran Canaria University	Current BA	
		Former BA
History of political ideas and social movements	Women, history and culture	
History of political ideas	Society and culture in the Greek and Roman World	Written culture history
History of mentalities in the Middle Ages	History of mentalities in the Ancient Regime	History of ideologies and religions in the Ancient World
Museums: history, meanings and content	La Rioja University	Former BA
Social movements and ideas in the Modern Age	Social Anthropology	Thought and culture history in the Middle Ages
History of religion	Book history and culture dissemination	León University
Current BA		
Former BA	Ideologies and mentalities in the Early Modern and Modern World	
Science and Technology history	Málaga University	Former BA
Mentality and everyday life in Early Modern Europe	Material culture and European dissemination in Early Modern Europe	Murcia University
Current BA		
Former BA	Territory, society and culture in the Early Modern Age	
Everyday life in the Middle Ages	Medieval civilizations	Mentality and culture in the Early Modern Age
Oviedo University	Former BA	Mentality and culture in Early Modern Spain
Culture history in the Middle Ages	History of religion and mentality in the Middle Ages	Urban history in the Middle Ages
Ideology and religion in the Ancient Mediterranean		Seville University
Current BA		Former BA

223

Cultural anthropology		Manuscript history
Political and social thought in the 20th century	Political and social thought in the 19th century	Social and cultural anthropology
Printed book history	History of intellectual movements'	From Humanism to Enlightenment: political thought
History of writing in the Early Modern Age	Medieval Document History	Early Modern and Modern Document History
History of writing in colonial America	Cultural anthropology in America	Culture history in Spanish America
Culture history in Modern America	Zaragoza University	Former BA
Thought History	Material culture in the Middle Ages	Mentality and culture in the Middle Ages
Mentality and culture in the Early Modern Age		

Table 1: Cultural History in some spanish University Programs

Recently, some publishing houses have included the publication of numerous titles concerning cultural history. Perspectives and analyses depend on the author's intention and on their targeted audience in 2005. J. Serna and A. Pons published a volume collecting the last seventy years' productions, trends and perspectives in cultural history research. As the title suggests, the book's aim is to sum up the debates, types, and outcomes of cultural history not only in Europe but also in America.[33] So, they paid attention to cultural history forms in Europe (starting with France and England) and in America, the main authors and perspectives, the results of each perspective and the current status of this kind of historiographical production.

Finally, other publishing house projects have integrated the cultural aspect into their general book collection in order to offer readers a general panorama of historical periods. For example, take a look at the *Síntesis* collection. This publishing house promoted a new project called *España tercer milenio* (Third Millennium Spain) where they published three different volumes concerning every Spanish history period. In dealing with Modern Spanish history, they issued *The End of the Ancient Regime* whose first volume was devoted to economic aspects. The second dealt with politics and the third with culture and everyday life.[34] The rest of the history processes follows the same structure. Regarding the Spanish liberal period, we can find three volumes: on economic issues (the

---

33 SERNA/PONS, 2005.
34 SAIZ PASTOR/VIDAL OLIVARES, 2001; SERRANO GARCÍA, 2001.

first), politics (the second) and on culture and everyday life (the third).[35] This scheme is followed for the rest of Spanish history periods: the Modernization period (1917-1939),[36] Franco's Regime (1939-1975)[37] and the Democratic period (1975-2000).[38] The most suggestive titles, in our opinion, are those written by Gracia & Carnicer and by Uría.

Historiographical production: paths and types of Spanish *cultural history*

This section, concerning the birth and the evolution of Spanish Cultural history, helps us identify the most significant research outcomes on this topic. The most prolific cultural history field, since the 1980s is book history. Due to the work of some *Hispanists*, mainly French[39] who were working in this field and focused their research on the Spanish *milieu,* Spanish book history became a productive research field.[40]

Like book history, one more research field appeared in Spain during the 1980s: science and scientific political history.[41] Historians who specialized in these fields were concerned not only with legal and institutional perspectives, but also included an anthropological perspective.[42] In most cases, research in this field began with an exclusive social perspective and gradually expanded to explore cultural aspects related to scientific practices, scientific exchanges, and scientific transfers. The latter is today undoubtedly one of the most prolific research fields.

Other classic traditions continued to be practiced by Spanish historians. However, these new paths for cultural history were opened, producing a more and more complex Spanish cultural history panorama. Concepts borrowed from literary reviews, linguistics, and semiotics as well as from sociology and anthro-

---

35 BERNAL/PAREJO BARRANCO, 2001; SUÁREZ CORTINA, 2006; URÍA, 2008a.
36 PAREJO BARRANCO/SÁNCHEZ PICÓN, 2007; BARRIO ALONSO, 2004; AGUADO/RAMOS, 2002.
37 BARCIELA ET AL., 2001; MORADIELLOS, 2000; RUIZ CARNICER/GRACIA, 2001.
38 RUIZ, 2002; DÍAZ BARRADO, 2006.
39 BOTREL, 1988; SALAÜN/SERRANO, 1991.
40 MARTÍNEZ MARTÍN, 1991.
41 HERNÁNDEZ SANDOICA, 2000.
42 GONZÁLEZ BLASCO ET AL., 1979; MILLÁS VALLICROSA, 1987; ELENA/ORDÓÑEZ, 1988; GIRÓN SIERRA, 1996; SÁNCHEZ RON, 1999.

pology (i.e., *perception and representation*) were integrated into cultural history perspectives.

Whereas cultural history was gradually becoming more complex, intellectual history continued defining its own space in historiography. Cultural history, history of culture, and intellectual history each occupied their own space by reflecting the social context in which cultural expressions occurred. In this way, the history of intellectuals (from social, cultural, intellectual, anthropological and even sociological perspectives) made more sense than ever.[43] This so-called intellectual history connects the three different aspects of society, politics and intelligentsia by locating individuals and their rapport with others in the research centre.

There are additional projects concerning intellectual history. Starting with classic intellectual history approaches, in a parallel process, a historian like V. Cacho Viu devoted his research to study the profile, biography, and role of the most prominent Spanish intellectuals. In his case, each individual biography and thought offered very positive data, which was helpful to explain how national and collective identity were created.[44]

As a pioneering historian, Cacho opened this intellectual field to the study of biographies[45] and significant philosophical trends such as *krausism*. Cacho and Marxist historians like M. Tuñón de Lara[46], for example, shared the same research topics even though each of them started from quite different points of view.

Cacho was also interested in knowing which high culture institutions were connected with these intellectual projects.[47] Most studies devoted to high culture institutions have pointed to a special and concrete period in Spanish history, the 1930s. The so-called *Silver Age of Spanish Culture* has been an extraordinary stage for Spanish historians searching for modern and positive intellectual projects and solutions.[48] It is well known that most modern cultural projects developed during the 1930s were drastically interrupted by the Spanish Civil War, mainly by the subsequent Franco dictatorship. The long duration of Franco's

---

43 CASSASAS I YMBERT, 2009; ID., 2005; ID., 1997; ID., 1990; ID., 1989; ID., 1986; ID., 2006a; ID., 1999; ID., 1998a; ID., 1998 b; ID., 1995; ID., 1993; ID., 1992; ID., 1983; ID., 1978.
44 CACHO VIU, 1962a; ID., 1984; ID., 1997a.
45 ID., 1985; ID., 1997b; ID., 2000.
46 TUÑÓN DE LARA, 1974.
47 CACHO VIU, 1962b.
48 MAINER, 1999.

regime forced some of the most prominent Spanish intellectuals to leave the country in search for new destinations. Repression and exile once again played a part in the Spanish cultural panorama. Historians, interested in recovering the *Silver Age of Spanish Culture* heritage and in studying the ways in which these intellectuals were able to reorganize their lives and careers, eventually published some interesting books.[49]

Individual biographies finally found another way to be present in Spanish cultural history. They fall within the field of historiography history and include historians' biographies. Publishing houses such as Urgoiti and Fernando el Católico Institution are examples of institutions that publish this kind of work.[50]

There is no doubt that the reconstruction of personal, intellectual, and professional networks is nowadays a profitable subfield within *cultural history* studies. On the one hand, we can easily find studies focused on personal profiles which make biography one of their most fruitful subfields[51] and, on the other hand, these studies are gradually paying attention to cultural transfers among national and international intellectuals. This means that the networks and rapports among intellectuals foster idea transfers, international connections (both individual and academic as well as political), and international support institutions and relationships.[52]

Both the history of the university and of high culture institutions have become accepted within the framework of education history. University history studies, though, came from a traditional perspective which focused its starting point on legal and institutional conditions for the birth an organization of these institutions'. Therefore, university history has been consolidated as a mixed type of intellectual history (i.e., by studying scientific outcomes, historiography production and professional thought), cultural history (i.e., by focusing on experiences, activities and sociability among students and professors) and political and institutional history (i.e., by studying university internal regulations and governmental politics concerning university activities).[53]

---

49 SÁNCHEZ-CUERVO, 2008; SORIANO, 1989; ALTED VIGIL, 2005; ABELLÁN, 1983.
50 Among others: PÉREZ BUSTAMANTE, 2009; FERNÁNDEZ ALMAGRO, 2008.
51 RUIZ-MANJÓN CABEZA, 2007; MORENTE, 2006, only to mention some of them.
52 NIÑO RODRÍGUEZ, 1988; ID., 2001; ID., 1989; NIÑO RODRÍGUEZ/DELGADO, 1990; DELGADO GÓMEZ-ESCALONILLA, 1992; ID., 1988.
53 See note 24. VVAA, 1983; PALOMARES IBÁÑEZ, 1989; RODRÍGUEZ CRUZ, 1990; ÁLVAREZ DE MORALES, 1993; PESET, 1999; ID., 2000a; ID., 2000b; BARREIRO, 2000; ID., 2003; RODRÍGUEZ SAN-PEDRO BEZARES, 2002; ID., 2004a; ID., 2004b; URÍA et al., 2008b.

New perspectives and approaches have been practiced by Spanish historians in the last decade. This was the period when new subfields appeared and when some earlier interests about culture and society in Spanish historiography began to be considered in several research programs.

From the very beginning, Spanish historians were concerned with political culture[54] which means cultural origins and expressions of every political trend mainly during the first decades of the 20th century. Regional perspectives gradually became consolidated as the most preferential approach for this kind of study. We are thinking, for example, about studies focused on cultural expressions of republicanism[55] or anarchism,[56] mainly in the Catalonian context.[57] Other examples are popular and working class studies,[58] which connected this kind of historiography productions with the early origins of Spanish debates about cultural history.

Everyday life studies are currently the arena where cultural history and cultural studies find an appropriate place.[59] In the Spanish case, this kind of research has focused on *popular culture and leisure time*[60] and on *everyday life* during the first three decades of the 20th century[61] (mainly during the Spanish Civil War).[62]

Concept history as a middle ground between cultural and political history also needs to be mentioned. New historiography trends have defined this field as a sort of new history of ideas field where both political concepts and sociocultural context have equal value.[63]

---

54 MORÁN, 1999; CAPISTEGUI, 2004; BERAMENDI, 1998; BURDIEL/ROMEO, 1996; CRUZ/ PÉREZ LEDESMA, 1997; DE DIEGO ROMERO, 2006.
55 MORALES MUÑOZ, 2006; PEYROU, 2002; DUARTE/GABRIEL, 2000; SUÁREZ CORTINA, 2000.
56 BERNALTE VEGA, 1991.
57 FRADERA, 1992; MARFANY, 1995; CANALS VIDAL, 2006; DUARTE, 1992; ID., 1993.
58 RADCLIFF, 1996; ELORZA, 1990; BARRIO, 1991; PÉREZ LEDESMA, 1993; GONZÁLEZ, 2000; BARRIO, 2000; PANIAGUA et al., 1999.
59 CASTELLS, 1995b.
60 URÍA, 1996.
61 ARAGÓN GÓMEZ, 2005.
62 ABELLA, 2004.
63 FERNÁNDEZ SEBASTIÁN/FUENTES, 2004; ID., 2002; FUENTES, 2009.

Conclusion

Cultural history and cultural issues are recently moving in circles, which are constantly appearing, developing and overlapping. New approaches, new fields and subfields emerge and complete not only the cultural history panorama but also the historiography reflection which is a basic tool for understanding cultural history purposes, aims and epistemology paths. In the Spanish case, an interesting turn is evident concerning studies focused on times when cultural history was the starting point. In other words, in recent Spanish historiography, the period between 1975 and 1985 is considered, as the period of political, social and cultural transition from a dictatorial to a democratic era. This period also opened a new process enabling historiography reflection and new historiography products. Nowadays, these new times and cultural perspectives are in fact a new field at which historians working on cultural issues focus their research. Cultural history currently continues to be a booming topic.[64]

Literature

ABELLA, RAFAEL, Historia de la vida cotidiana durante la guerra civil, Barcelona 2004.

ABELLÁN, JOSÉ LUIS, De la guerra civil al exilio republicano (1936-1977), Madrid 1983.

AGUADO, ANA/RAMOS, MARÍA DOLORES, La modernización de España (1917-1939). Cultura y vida cotidiana, Madrid 2002.

ALTAMIRA, RAFAEL, Historia de España y de la civilización española, Barcelona 1909-1911.

ID., Historia de España y de la civilización española, Barcelona 1913.

ID., Historia de España y de la civilización española, Barcelona 1928-1930.

ALTED VIGIL, ALICIA, La voz de los vencidos: el exilio republicano de 1939, Madrid 2005.

ÁLVAREZ DE MORALES, ANTONIO, Estudios de historia de la Universidad española, Madrid 1993.

ARAGÓN GÓMEZ, JAIME, La vida cotidiana durante la Guerra de la Independencia en la provincia de Cádiz, Cádiz 2005.

ARAGONESES, ALFONS, Un jurista del Modernismo. Raymond Saleilles y los orígenes del derecho comparado, Madrid 2009.

---

64 GRACIA/RÓDENAS DE MOYA, 2009.

AZNAR I GARCIA, RAMÓN, Cánones y leyes en la universidad de Alcalá durante el reinado de Carlos III, Madrid 2002.

BARCIELA, CARLOS et al., La España de Franco (1939-1975). Economía, Madrid 2001.

BARREIRO, XOSÉ MANUEL (ed.), Historia de la Universidad de Santiago de Compostela. Vol. 1, De los orígenes al siglo XIX, Santiago de Compostela 2000.

ID. (ed.), Historia de la Universidad de Santiago de Compostela. Vol. 2, El siglo XIX, Santiago de Compostela 2003.

BARRIO ALONSO, ÁNGELES, Cultura del trabajo y organización obrera en Gijón en el cambio de siglo, in: Historia Contemporánea 5 (1991), p. 27-51.

ID., Historia obrera en los noventa. Tradición y modernidad, in: Historia Social 37 (2000), p. 143-160.

ID., La modernización de España (1917-1939). Política y sociedad, Madrid 2004.

BERAMENDI, JUSTO, La cultura política como objeto historiográfico. Algunas cuestiones de método, in: Culturas y civilizaciones. III Congreso de la Asociación de Historia Contemporánea, ed. by CELSO ALMUIÑA, Valladolid 1998, p. 73-94.

BERMEJO CASTRILLO, MANUEL (ed.), Manuales y textos de enseñanza en la universidad liberal, Madrid 2004.

BERNAL, ANTONIO MIGUEL/PAREJO BARRANCO, ANTONIO, La España liberal (1868-1913). Economía, Madrid 2001.

BERNALTE VEGA, FRANCISCA, La cultura anarquista en la república y la guerra civil: los ateneos libertarios en Madrid, Madrid 1991.

BOTREL, JEAN FRANÇOIS, La diffusion du livre en Espagne (1868-1914): les librairies, Madrid 1988

BURDIEL, ISABEL/ROMEO, MARÍA CRUZ, Historia y lenguaje. La vuelta al relato dos décadas después, in: Hispania 192 (1996), p. 433-446.

CABRERA, MIGUEL ÁNGEL, Historia, lenguaje y teoría social, Madrid 2001a.

ID., Historia y teoría de la sociedad: del giro culturalista al giro lingüístico, in: Lecturas de la historia. Nueve reflexiones sobre historia de la historiografía, ed. by CARLOS FORCADELL/IGNACIO PEIRÓ, Zaragoza 2001b, p. 255-272.

ID., La crisis de la historia social y el surgimiento de la historia postsocial, in: Ayer 51 (2003), p. 201-234.

ID., La historia postsocial: más allá del imaginario moderno, in: Por una historia global: el debate historiográfico en los últimos tiempos, ed. by TERESA MARÍA ORTEGA LÓPEZ, Zaragoza 2007, p. 41-72.

CACHO VIU, VICENTE, Las tres Españas de la España contemporánea, Madrid 1962a.
ID., La Institución Libre de Enseñanza. Vol. 1, Orígenes y etapa universitaria (1860-1881), Madrid 1962b.
ID. (ed.), Els modernistes i el nacionalisme cultural: 1881-1906, Barcelona 1984.
ID. et al., Presencia de Ortega: Joaquín Costa-José Ortega y Gasset: "tres cartas inéditas", Madrid 1985.
ID., Repensar el 98, Madrid 1997a.
ID., Revisión de Eugenio D'Ors: (1902-1930); Seguida de un Epistolario inédito, Barcelona, 1997b.
ID., Los intelectuales y la política: perfil público de Ortega y Gasset, Madrid 2000.
CANALS VIDAL, FRANCISCO, Catalanismo y tradición catalana, Barcelona 2006.
CAPISTEGUI, FRANCISCO JAVIER, La llegada del concepto de cultura política a la historiografía española, in: Usos de la Historia y políticas de la memoria, ed. by CARLOS FORCADELL, Zaragoza 2004, p. 167-185.
CARONI, PÍO, La soledad del historiador del derecho. Apuntes sobre la conveniencia de una disciplina diferente, Madrid 2010.
CASASSAS I YMBERT, JORDI, La configuració del sector "inte.lectual-professional" a la Catalunya de la Restauració (a propòsit de Jaume Bifill i Mates), in: Recerques: Història, economia i cultura 8 (1978), p. 103-131.
ID., Els quadres del regionalisme. L'evolució de la Joventut Nacionalista de la Lliga fins el 1914, in: Recerques: Història, economia i cultura 14 (1983) p. 7-32.
ID., Història de l'Ateneu Barcelonès. Dels orígens als nostres díes, Barcelona 1986.
ID., Intel.lectuals, professionals i politics a la Catalunya contemporània (1850-1920), Sant Cugat del Vallès 1989.
ID., Entre Escil.la i Caribdis. El catalanisme i la Catalunya conservadora de la segona meitat del segle XIX, Barcelona 1990.
ID., Desenvolupament. Territori. Nacionalisme, in: Treballs de la Societat Catalana de Geografia 32 (1992), p. 177-188.
ID., Espacio cultural y cambio político: Los intelectuales catalanes y el catalanismo, in: Espacio, tiempo y forma. Serie V, Historia contemporánea 6 (1993), p. 55-80.
ID., Política i cultura en el primer nou-cents català, in: El contemporani: revista d'història 6-7 (1995), p. 32-39.
ID., El futur del catalanisme, Barcelona 1997.

ID., La historia cultural e intelectual profesional. Una visión personal, in: Revista d'història cultural 1 (1998a) p. 6-11.
ID., Els ambients intel.lectuals a Catalunya a la fi del segle XIX, in: Afers: fulls de recerca i pensament 31 (1998b), p. 557-567.
ID., Institucionalització i acció nacionalista a la Catalunya de la Restauració, in: L'Avenç: Revista de història i cultura 239 (1999), p. 34-38.
ID., Editorial. Quince años. Una biografía intelectual colectiva, in: Cercles. Revista de Historia Cultural 7 (2004), p. 6-11.
ID., El temps de la nació. Estudis sobre el problema polític de les identitats, Barcelona 2005.
ID., La memoria y la identidad. Unas reflexiones sobre la historia cultural, in: Cercles. Revista d'història cultural 9 (2006), p. 7-9.
ID., La domesticación novecentista de la "Renaixença": un problema de cultura política, in: Melanges de la Casa de Velázquez 36/1 (2006), p. 35-48.
ID., La fàbrica de les idees. Política i cultura a la Catalunya del segle XX, Barcelona 2009.
CASTELLS, LUIS, Una aproximación al conflicto social en Guipúzcoa, 1890-1923, in: de historia social 32-33 (1985) p. 261-315.
ID., El desarrollo de la clase obrera en Azcoitia y el sindicalismo católico (1900-1923), in: de historia social 42-43 (1987) p. 151-180.
ID., El comportamiento de los trabajadores en la sociedad industrial vasca (1876-1936), in: contemporánea 14 (1990), p. 319-340.
ID., trabajadores en el País Vasco (1876-1923), Madrid 1993.
ID. (ed.), Historia de la vida cotidiana, Madrid 1995a.
ID., Vida cotidiana y nuevos comportamientos sociales (El País Vasco 1876-1933), in: Ayer 19 (1995b) p. 135-164.
ID. (ed.), El rumor de lo cotidiano: estudios sobre el País Vasco contemporáneo, Bilbao 1999.
CID, ROSA MARÍA, Los estudios históricos sobre las mujeres en la historiografía española. Notas sobre su evolución y perspectivas, in: Aljaba, 10 (2006), p. 19-38.
COMAS CARABALLO, DANIEL, Autonomía y reformas en la Universidad de Valencia (1900-1922), Madrid 2001.
CRUZ, RAFAEL/PÉREZ LEDESMA, MANUEL (eds.), Cultura y movilización en la ESPAÑA CONTEMPORÁNEA, MADRID 1997.
CRUZ MUNDET, JOSÉ RAMÓN (ed.), Archivos universitarios e historia de las Universidades, Madrid 2003.

D'AURIA, ELIO, Una interpretación liberal-demócrata del totalitarismo: el problema del fascismo, in: Cercles. Revista d'história cultural 3 (2000), p. 74-99.

DE DIEGO ROMERO, JAVIER, El concepto de cultura política en ciencia política y sus implicaciones para la historia, in: Ayer 61 (2006), p. 233-266.

DELGADO GÓMEZ-ESCALONILLA, LORENZO, Diplomacia franquista y política cultural hacia Iberoámerica: 1939-1953, Madrid 1988.

ID., Acción cultural y política exterior: la configuración de la diplomacia cultural durante el régimen franquista (1936-1945), Madrid 1992.

DÍAZ BARRADO, MARIO PEDRO, España democrática (1975-2000). Cultura y vida cotidiana, Madrid 2006.

DUARTE, ÁNGEL, Possibilistes i federals. Politica y cultura republicanes a Reus, 1874-1899, Reus 1992.

ID., Republicanos y nacionalismo. El impacto del catalanismo en la cultura política republicana, in: Historia contemporánea 10 (1993), p. 157-177.

ID./GABRIEL, PERE, ¿Una sola cultura política republicana ochocentista en España?, in: Ayer 39, (2000), p. 11-34.

ELENA, ALBERTO/ORDÓÑEZ, JAVIER, Historia de la ciencia, Madrid 1988.

ELORZA, ANTONIO, La cultura de la revuelta en el siglo XIX español, in: Peuple, mouvement ouvrier de 1840 à 1936, Saint-Denis, ed. by JEAN MAURICE et al., Vincennes 1990, p. 127-140.

FERNÁNDEZ ALMAGRO, Manuel, Vida y literatura de Valle-Inclán, Pamplona 2008.

FERNÁNDEZ SEBASTIÁN, JAVIER/FUENTES, JUAN FRANCISCO (eds.), Diccionario político y social del siglo XIX español, Madrid 2002.

ID. (eds.), Historia de los conceptos, Madrid 2004.

FRADERA, JOSEP MARÍA, Cultura nacional en una sociedad dividida. Patriotismo i cultura a Catalunya, 1838-1868, Barcelona 1992.

FUENTES, JUAN FRANCISCO, Madrid ¿paradigma de una historia sociocultural?, in: Cercles. Revista d'história cultural 1 (1998) p. 12-30.

ID., Iconografía de la idea de España en la segunda mitad del siglo XIX, in: Cercles. Revista d'história cultural 5 (2002), p. 8-25.

ID., Prensa y política en el tardofranquismo (1962-1975). La rebelión de las elites, in: Cercles. Revista d'história cultural 6 (2003) p. 6-11.

ID., Pueblo y República, in: Diccionario político y social del mundo iberoamericano, ed. by JAVIER FERNÁNDEZ SEBASTIÁN, Madrid 2009.

GHANIME, ALBERT, Aproximación a los periódicos y a los periodistas de la Barcelona de 1820 a 1939, in: Cercles. Revista d'história cultural 5 (2002), p. 52-78.

GIRÓN SIERRA, ÁLVARO, Evolucionismo y anarquismo en España, 1882-1914, Madrid 1996.

GÓMEZ, PAQUITA, El Diario de Barcelona y el mundo del libro (1840-1854), in: Cercles. Revista d'història cultural 5 (2002), p. 170-173.

ID., Circuitos y grupos intelectuales en la Barcelona del siglo XIX (1854-1868), in: Cercles. Revista d'història cultural 6 (2003), p. 170-173.

GONZÁLEZ, ANTONIO, Los trabajadores y la política en Sevilla. Una aproximación a la cultura política obrera en la Restauración, in: En torno al 98. España en el tránsito del siglo XIX al XX, Huelva 2000, p. 513-527.

GONZÁLEZ BLASCO, PEDRO et al., Historia y sociología de la ciencia en España, Madrid 1979.

GRACIA, JORDI/RÓDENAS DE MOYA, DANIEL, Más es más. Sociedad y cultura en la España democrática, Madrid 2009.

GUIJARRO GONZÁLEZ, SUSANA, Maestros, escuelas y libros. El universo cultural de las catedrales en la Castilla medieval, Madrid 2004.

GUIRAO, ANTONI, El proceso nacionalizador en Cataluña, in: Cercles. Revista d'història cultural 5 (2002), p. 104-115.

HERNÁNDEZ SANDOICA, ELENA, La sustracción del objeto. Sobre historia de la cultura e historiadores en España (1968-1986), in: Problèmaticas em història cultural, Porto 1997, p. 143-164.

ID., ¿Hacia una historia cultural de la ciencia española?, in: Ayer, 38 (2000), p. 263-274.

ID., La historia cultural en España: tendencias y contextos de la última década, in: Revista de Historia cultural, 4 (2001) p. 57-91.

ID., historiográficas actuales. Escribir historia hoy, Madrid 2004.

HOFFMAN, STEFAN, Un escenario cultural para el conflicto franco-alemán: el teatro municipal de Estrasburgo de 1870 a 1919, Revista d'història cultural 2 (1999), p. 59-69.

IZQUIERDO BALLESTER, SANTIAGO, Pere Coromines (1870-1939). Política, cultura i economia, in: Revista d'història cultural 1 (1998), p. 67-72.

ID., El mundo editorial, una reconstrucción necesaria, in: Revista d'història cultural 5 (2002), p. 222-224.

ID., Pensamiento y filosofía en Cataluña en el siglo XX, in: Revista d'història cultural 7 (2006), p. 182-185.

JOVER, JOSÉ MARÍA, Sobre la situación actual del historiador, in: Saitabi XI (1961), p. 231-240.

LIAKOS, ANTONIS, Encounters with Modernity: Greek historiography since 1974, in: Revista d'història cultural 3 (2000) p. 108-118.

LLORENS I VILA, JORDI/CASSASAS I YMBERT, JORDI, Vicente Cacho Viu (1929-1997). In memoriam, in: Cercles. Revista d'história cultural 1 (1998) p. 46-54.

LLORENS I VILA, JORDI, Los escritores catalanes de la Restauración: entre la literatura y la política, in: Cercles. Revista d'história cultural 5 (2002), p. 6-11.

LOFF, MANUEL, Un país visto desde arriba. Revista político-culturales en el Portugal contemporáneo (1820-1974), in: Cercles. Revista d'história cultural 6 (2003), p. 126-156.

LÓPEZ VEGA, ANTONIO, Biobibliografía de Gregorio Marañón, Madrid 2009.

MAINER, JOSÉ CARLOS, La Edad de Plata, (1902-1939): ensayo de interpretación de un proceso cultural, Madrid 1999.

MARFANY, JOAN LLUÍS, La cultura del catalanisme, Barcelona 1995.

MARTÍNEZ MARTÍN, JESÚS ANTONIO, Lecturas y lectores en el Madrid del siglo XIX, Madrid 1991.

MARTÍNEZ NEIRA, MANUEL, El estudio del derecho. Libros de texto y planes de estudio en la Universidad contemporánea, Madrid 2001.

ID. et al., Universidad española, 1889-1939. Repertorio de legislación, Madrid 2004.

ID./PUYOL MONTERO, JOSÉ MARÍA, doctorado en derecho 1930-1956, Madrid 2008.

MERINO, CARMEN (ed.), investigación en la Universidad, Madrid 1999.

MILLÁS VALLICROSA, JOSEP MARÍA, Estudios sobre historia de la ciencia española, Madrid 1987.

MORA, ADELA (ed.), La enseñanza del derecho en el siglo XX, Madrid, 2004.

MORA CAÑADA, ADELA/RODRÍGUEZ LÓPEZ, CAROLINA (eds.), Hacia un modelo universitario: la Universidad Carlos III de Madrid, Madrid 2004.

MORADIELLOS, ENRIQUE, La España de Franco (1939-1975). Política y sociedad, Madrid 2000.

MORALES MUÑOZ, MANUEL (ed.), República y modernidad: El republicanismo en los umbrales del siglo XX, Málaga 2006.

MORÁN, MARÍA LUZ, Los estudios de cultura política en España, in: Revista Española de Investigaciones Sociológicas 85 (1999), p. 97-129.

MORENTE, FRANCISCO, Dionisio Ridruejo: del fascismo al antifranquismo, Madrid 2006.

NIÑO RODRÍGUEZ, ANTONIO, Cultura y diplomacia: los hispanistas franceses y España de 1875 a 1931, Madrid 1988.

ID., El hispanismo científico y los intereses franceses en España a finales del siglo XIX, Madrid 1989.

ID., La europeización a través de la política científica y cultural en el primer tercio del siglo XX, Madrid 2001.

ID./DELGADO, LORENZO, Emigración, enseñanza y nacionalidad en las relaciones hispano-francesas, Bilbao 1990.

OLÁBARRI, IGNACIO/CAPISTEGUI, FRANCISCO JAVIER (eds.), La "nueva" historia cultural: la influencia del postestructuralismo y el auge de la interdisciplinariedad, Madrid 1996.

ONCINA COVES, FAUSTINO (ed.), Filosofía para la universidad, filosofía contra la universidad, Madrid 2008.

OSTENC, MICHEL, François Furet, in: Cercles. Revista d'história cultural 2 (1999) p. 36-45.

PALOMARES IBÁÑEZ, JOSÉ MARÍA (ed.), Historia de la Universidad de Valladolid, Valladolid 1989.

PANIAGUA, JAVIER et al.(eds.), Cultura social y política en el mundo del trabajo, Valencia 1999.

PAREJO BARRANCO, ANTONIO/SÁNCHEZ PICÓN, ANDRÉS, modernización de España (1917-1939). Economía, Madrid 2007.

PERALES BIRLANGA, GERMÁN, estudiante liberal. Sociología y vida de la comunidad escolar universitaria valenciana. 1875-1939, Madrid 2008.

PÉREZ BUSTAMANTE, CIRIACO, Felipe III, semblanza de un monarca y perfiles de una privanza, Pamplona 2009.

PÉREZ LEDESMA, MANUEL, La cultura socialista en el años veinte, in: Los orígenes culturales de la II República, Madrid 1993, p. 149-198.

ID., Precedentes de la biblioteca del Ateneo barcelonés (1800-1860), in: Cercles. Revista d'história cultural 7 (2004), p. 155-170.

PESET, JOSÉ LUIS/NAVARRO, DAVID (eds.), Estado de la Universidad de Alcalá (1805), Madrid 1999.

PESET, MARIANO (ed.), Historia de la Universidad de Valencia. Vol. 1, El estudio general, Valencia 1999.

ID. (ed.), Historia de la Universidad de Valencia. Vol. 2, La Universidad ilustrada, Valencia 2000a.

ID. (ed.), Historia de la Universidad de Valencia. Vol. 3, La Universidad liberal (siglos XIX y XX), Valencia 2000b.

PEYROU, FLORENCIA, El republicanismo popular en España 1840-1843, Cádiz 2002.

RADCLIFF, PAMELA BETH, From Mobilization to Civil War. The Politics of Polarization in Spanish City of Gijón, 1900-1937, Cambridge 1996.

RIVIÈRE GÓMEZ, AURORA, Orientalismo y nacionalismo español. Estudios árabes y hebreos en la Universidad de Madrid (1843-1868), Madrid 2000.

RODRÍGUEZ CRUZ, ÁGUEDA MARÍA, Historia de la Universidad de Salamanca, Salamanca 1990.

RODRÍGUEZ LÓPEZ, CAROLINA, La Universidad de Madrid en el primer franquismo: ruptura y continuidad (1939-1951), Madrid 2001.

RODRÍGUEZ-SAN PEDRO BEZARES, LUIS ENRIQUE (ed.), Historia de la Universidad de Salamanca. I, Trayectoria histórica e instituciones vinculadas, Salamanca 2002.

ID. (ed.), Historia de la Universidad de Salamanca. II, Estructuras y flujos, Salamanca 2004a.

ID. (ed.), Historia de la Universidad de Salamanca. III, Saberes y confluencias, Salamanca 2004b.

RUIZ, DAVID, España democrática (1975-2000). Política y sociedad, Madrid 2002.

RUIZ CARNICER, MIGUEL ÁNGEL/GRACIA, JORDI, España de Franco (1939-1975). Cultura y vida cotidiana, Madrid, 2001.

RUIZ-MANJÓN CABEZA, OCTAVIO, Fernando de los Ríos: un intelectual en el PSOE, Madrid 2007.

SAIZ PASTOR, CANDELARIA/VIDAL OLIVARES, JAVIER, El fin del Antiguo Régimen (1808-1868). Economía, Madrid 2001.

SALAÜN, SERGE/SERRANO, CARLOS (eds.), 1900 en Espagne. Essai d'histoire culturelle, Madrid 1991.

SÁNCHEZ-CUERVO, ANTOLÍN (ed.), Las huellas del exilio, Madrid 2008.

SÁNCHEZ RON, JOSÉ MANUEL, Cincel, martillo y piedra: historia de la ciencia en España (Siglos XIX y XX), Madrid 1999.

SERNA, JUSTO/PONS, ANACLET, La historia cultural. Autores, obras y lugares, Madrid 2005

SERRANO GARCÍA, RAFAEL, fin del Antiguo Régimen (1808-1868). y vida cotidiana, Madrid 2001.

SIMÓN I TARRES, ANTONI, ideología i identitat nacional a la revolució catalana de 1640, in: Cercles. Revista d'història cultural 2 (1999), p. 10-22.

SORIANO, ANTONIO, ÉXODOS: historia oral del exilio republicano en Francia, 1939-1945, Barcelona 1989.

SUÁREZ CORTINA, MANUEL, El gorro frigio. Liberalismo, Democracia y Republicanismo en la Restauración, Madrid, 2000.

ID., La España liberal (1868-1913). Política y sociedad, Madrid 2006.

TUÑÓN DE LARA, MANUEL, Costa y Unamuno en la crisis de fin de siglo, Madrid 1974.

URÍA, JORGE, Cultura oficial e ideología en la Asturias franquista: el IDEA, Oviedo 1984a.

ID., Cultura y comunicación de masas en Asturias (1931-1934), in: Estudios de historia social 31 (1984b), p. 145-168.
ID., Sociedad, ocio y cultura en Asturias (1898-1914), Oviedo 1991a.
ID., La taberna en Asturias a principios del siglo XX. Notas para su estudio, in: Historia contemporánea 5 (1991b), p. 53-72.
ID., Una historia social del ocio: Asturias 1898-1914, Madrid 1996
ID., España liberal (1868-1913). y vida cotidiana, Madrid 2008a.
URÍA, JORGE et al. (eds.), Historia de la Universidad de Oviedo. V. 1, De la fundación a la crisis del Antiguo Régimen (1608-1808), Oviedo 2008b.
ID., La historia social hoy, in: Historia Social 60 (2008c) p. 233-248.
VILLALBA PÉREZ, ENRIQUE, Consecuencias educativas de la expulsión de los jesuitas de América, Madrid 2003.
VVAA, Historia de la Universidad de Zaragoza, Madrid 1983.
XIFRÓ Y COLLSANATA, MARC, Sentimientos identitarios, nacionalismos y uso de la historia. Aportaciones historiográficas recientes, in: Cercles. Revista d'història cultural 5 (2002), p. 198-205.

http://www.ucm.es/info/culturalhistory/main.php, 10.09.2010

Cultural History in Italy

ALESSANDRO ARCANGELI

A late recognition of cultural history as a specific dimension of research and teaching can be taken, roughly speaking, as the Italian approach to our story. On one hand, there is the legacy of an idealistic tradition that regarded all history as cultural, and therefore left limited room for a specific cultural dimension; on the other hand, resistance to theory is widespread and pragmatism does not contemplate paying much attention to international trends and debates. Having said this, a look at many historians' actual production (and familiarity with the work of other colleagues) may reveal a somewhat different picture from the official scepticism. Also, a higher degree of enthusiasm for and awareness of this orientation in historical studies is perceivable among a younger generation of scholars.

Outside the academia, the pursuit and publication of works of cultural history is even harder to pin down—but so is the general readership, in a country where books are, on the whole, a commodity that attracts a limited clientele.

Let us start with the good news. An inter-university Centre of Cultural History (CSC) was launched in March 2009 as the product of a consortium between the universities of Bologna, Padua, Pisa and Venice, with Padua acting as its current base. The Centre has a Directing Council, formed by representatives of all participating institutions, and individual membership, which also admits academics from other universities, or scholars without permanent academic affiliation. The timing of the inauguration of the Centre, which naturally results from a period of preparation, offers here the opportunity to portray a group of Italian scholars who have recently taken the initiative of choosing cultural history both as the best definition of what they are doing and as the ground for setting up an academic network. To be perfectly honest hesitations and distinctions existed even at the launch of the Centre; in particular, a group of colleagues was concerned about the risk of losing sight of the social side of the past and advocated the use of the expression *social history of culture*. As odd as it may seem in that context, this criticism is quite representative of a wider tendency within Italian academia. Unlike Germany—to take the best-known example, as well as the most appropriate on the present occasion—Italy has not experienced a significant clash between the social and the cultural. The former may be largely intended to include the latter: social history is perhaps less connected with economic history than elsewhere, and social historians may be engaged in what others would call cultural history without being fully aware of it.[1]

I will begin the first section of my paper by introducing the themes of research recently covered (and ongoing projects) by the Italian scholars who have more consciously and openly identified themselves as cultural historians. I will subsequently turn to institutions and the profession in general—in an attempt to assess how representative this trend is, what portion of historical studies has opted for similar methodology—and conclude with perspectives.

At the time of writing, the Padua-based Centre lists about 70 scholars, the majority of which appear on the web site[2] with a short CV. The field of expertise of members is Modern History for about 50 of them, Early Modern for just under ten, while ten more are experts in other periods or different disciplines. It is peculiar that the majority of the late modernist bulk do not hold a permanent academic position. Thus, the composition of the Centre reflects the fact that it is partly the product of the work of some research teams, which have their leaderships within the university system, but are staffed by researches who are still largely job seekers. A significant number of them are also participating in a project put forward for ministerial funding as a Research project of national interest (on these, we will soon return) two years ago. The core of the project is the visual culture of the long 19th century history, with the *transformations of the gaze* brought about by the introduction of photography, up to the origins of cinema; a significant number of members of the Centre work on the relationship between history and the media.[3]

The proposed coordinator of the project, Alberto Maria Banti, who sits on the Centre's Directing Council, is also the author of one of the most recent and innovative history textbooks for the Italian secondary school (in particular for

---

1   I wish to thank Federico Barbierato and Miri Rubin for their comments on previous versions of the present contribution.
2   http://www.centrostoriaculturale.unipd.it/, 01.09.2010.
3   Although the 2008 application was not successful, the project was presented again in 2009.

the last three years, age 16+). The manual is published by Laterza—a publishing house whose emphasis on philosophy and history still bears the marks of the past role of Benedetto Croce as its chief advisor—and is as systematic a cultural-historical enterprise as one can possibly expect; its late modern section (the author's main period of expertise) has subsequently been adapted for use by undergraduates. To propose to young students a historical-anthropological approach and selection of topics, complete with methodologically updated textual analyses of sources, is a praiseworthy investment in the formation of younger generations and in the future of our field and style of research. Unfortunately, the current Italian government has subsequently reformed secondary education, and from the academic year 2010/11 there will be less history and hardly any geography at all taught to precisely that age group.

Seminars are one of the Centre's main initiatives. Over the past couple of years, cultural history seminars principally held in the universities affiliated with the Centre have become a regular feature of the national academic life, occasionally inviting internationally renowned speakers. Among those organized in Spring 2010 between Padua and Pisa were the presentation of *Nostalgia. Memory and passages on the Adriatic shores*, a volume edited by one of the Centre's members, Rudolf Petri, and resulting from an international day conference held at the Deutsches Studienzentrum in Venice, which was preceded by a multimedia artistic event; a seminar on History and the Novel; another yet, co-organized with the Italian society of women historians, on soldiers and gender; and a discussion by Michel Vovelle on *L'histoire des mentalités revisitée*.

In collaboration with the Edizioni ETS, the Centre has also launched a new book series (*Cultural studies. Concepts and practices*). The inaugurating volume was a thought-provoking pamphlet by Lynn Hunt on cultural history in the global era, which has not yet been published in English.[4]

Let us now take a look at academic research from the perspective of main projects and public financial support. A core channel of governmental funding for research over the past few years has been provided by Research projects of national interest (the Italian acronym is PRIN). The fields in which the ministerial database allows searching include, beyond the title of the project, descriptions of the research objectives and of the expected innovation in relation with the state of the art. We do not have access in the same way to those projects that were not funded. We can therefore analyse themes and methods of the approved

---

4   HUNT, 2010. Similarly, a book series launched in Verona opened its publications with BURKE, 2009, ahead of its English edition.

projects, not appreciate to what extent these represent a wider orientation among all applicants.

The exact phrase *storia culturale* was found by the search engine in a not insignificant number of projects (32 out of 8000, in all disciplines and over nine years). If we consider that six proponents of the projects in question have been awarded twice (either for significantly different projects, or in a more or less explicit continuation of their previous ones), the number of financed heads of projects that have used our formula goes down to 26.[5] Only in one case, however (in 1999, presented again with a wider chronology in 2002), it prominently appeared within the very (sub)title of a project (on early 20th century women's networks across the Northern Atlantic).

Italian research is organized in 14 macro-areas, and the ones in which the projects in question fall are number 10 (Antiquity, philological-literary and art-historical sciences), 11 (History, philosophy, education and psychology), with one only for area 14 (Political and social sciences), a 2004 project on Power and the word: religion, politics, communication; a less predictable entry from area 2 (Physics) was for a 2005 project on the history of 20th century physics, presented as an important chapter in the cultural and economic history of the country. Among the two most relevant subject areas, the philological hosts by far more winning projects, among the ones searched, than the historical, possibly testifying to a somewhat literary declension of what cultural history is meant to be. 18 literary proponents feature in our list versus six historians (a gap that even widens if one considers the fact that five of the literary scholars were awarded funding a second time). The imbalance may be softened if we take into fuller account some of the peculiarities of the system, such as the fact that ancient historians are counted under the philological umbrella.

It may be worth taking a closer look at the six explicitly historical projects, as they should offer some indications on current research themes. For reasons of brevity, I will identify them by the name and affiliation of the project coordinator, taking for granted that it usually also comprises a series of other units in different locations. In 1999 Gabriele Turi, a Professor of modern history in Florence, led a team working on *Publishing in Italy: the production and distribution of the book from the 18th century*. In the case of the project (funded in the year 2000), on the *Cultural and economic relations in the Western Mediterranean during the late medieval centuries*, *storia culturale* is mentioned within the description of the tasks of the leading unit of research, based in Pisa, in the

---

5   That always the same people won—it should perhaps be added—has been for a long time a point made by many, who challenge the system with allegations of unfairness.

significant role of posing its interconnection with the economy as the qualifying feature of the team's approach (as the general title of the project states clearly enough). The project's coordinator was Marco Tangheroni, a leading medievalist who died in 2004. Still in Pisa, Adriano Prosperi, who recently retired from his chair in early modern history at the Scuola Normale Superiore, coordinated a group on *The Inquisition and the control of dissent and minorities in Catholic Europe during the early modern period* in 2002. The outcome of the research is a major *Historical Dictionary of the Inquisition*, awaiting publication shortly.[6]

Two projects were approved in 2006: one led in Verona by medievalist Gian Maria Varanini and devoted to *Political cultures and documentary practices in communal and seigneurial Italy (XII-XIV centuries)*; the other, in Rome, by early modernist Marina Caffiero, on *The Mediterranean of the three religions: identities, conflicts and hybridizations (XIV-XX centuries)*. The latter project's team, when illustrating its proposed innovative aspects, outlined some methodological preferences in the following terms:

> "In the light of a historiographical present in which the power of symbols and communicative languages have become essential to an understanding of events, the new spheres of inquiry privilege the history of mentalities and representations, cultural history, the anthropological and semiological dimension, and recover the dimension of political history by integrating it within the new vision focusing on languages, discoursive and real practices, the gap between the normative and institutional moment and actual conduct."[7]

Lastly, in 2007, Gian Paolo Brizzi lead a project on *Academic institutions, ideological and cultural models in the formation of the elites and of political and social leadership during the Ancien Régime*.[8]

Having individually examined the projects approved within the area comprising history, I do not intend to underestimate the level of interest we may prove for the majority belonging to the more literary-centred area 10. To mention just a few, Mario Citroni's work on the Hellenistic culture and Roman iden-

---

6   In this case, whose relevance to our discourse is nevertheless undoubted, the project was picked up via the adopted search criteria only because one of the local units (Padua) used the phrase *cultural history* within the description of its aims.
7   http://cercauniversita.cineca.it/php5/prin/cerca.php?codice=2006110234, 01.09.2010 (my translation).
8   Once again, its relevance is out of question, but the actual *storia culturale* phrase was only contributed by the Padua unit.

tity is centered on the Roman intellectuals' awareness of a process of cultural appropriation and of its implications, and makes an explicit plea for a culturalist approach to ancient history. Cultural modernization is studied in different contexts within two other projects—one concerned with post-World War II Spain and Latin America, the other with the oriental city from antiquity onwards. All the above projects, the duration of which is fixed at two years, were funded with resources ranging widely, according to the size of the project and/or the liberality of allocation, from a minimum of € 21,000 to a maximum of € 185,000.[9]

Beyond the occurrence of *cultural history* as a precise phrase, one naturally would like to know which thematic preoccupations and methodological orientations emerge from the approved projects in the most relevant fields. The 2008 awards have been recently announced and are not yet searchable: they are only available in the form of a list of coordinators, titles and allocated funds. Thus, it is not yet possible to get complete picture of their themes and methods. Some titles would suggest patterns of research interesting to our survey.[10]

If we go back to the last year that offers richer documentation, 2007, an examination of the 62 projects approved for the area 11 shows that 20 of them were centred on an expertise in philosophy, 17 in psychology (this category includes both medical and humanistic psychology), 14 in historical sciences, seven in education, three in geography, one in anthropology, none in physical education. Among the historical projects, the early modern period led with five, two each went to the medieval, the late modern, the history of science and palography, one to the history of Eastern Europe, none to bibliography, the history of Christianity or of religions. These indications have to be taken with caution, because the categories I just mentioned are bureaucratic pigeon-holes, but, for instance, the lack of the last two groups (Christianity and religions) does not mean that the study of religious aspects is not present within projects with a different disciplinary label; and the approach to periods which may appear underrepresented could be found inside philosophical, literary and other branches of research. Every single set of data will have its peculiarities, which discourages generalization.[11] If we remember this caveat, a closer look at the 2007 projects—now

---

9 This is money distributed (rather than requested: the standard distance between the two figures has been varying from one year to another).
10 Just to mention one, the expression "rappresentazioni culturali" occurs in the title of a project lead by a Professor of education in Foggia devoted to the elderly.
11 For instance, in 2007 a special quota was reserved for young team leaders, and so one finds, unusually, a number of academics of lower rank as successful coordinators. As well as seeing other proposals turned down, that year also witnessed the

that we are considering all the approved projects, not those selected under any key-word search—may help getting an idea of the spectrum of areas of research interest within the Italian historical profession.

Of the five early modern projects approved in 2007, we have already met— because it mentioned cultural history—Brizzi's research on academic institutions and the formation of the elites. Brizzi specializes in this area and, among other commitments, directs a periodical and Inter-University Centre for the history of Italian universities.[12] The other projects were submitted by Angelo Bianchi (Catholic University of Milan) for a historical atlas of education in 18th and 19th century Italy; by Vincenzo Ferrone (Turin) on the late Enlightenment and the crisis of the Ancien Régime in Europe; by Gigliola Fragnito (Parma) on the 17th century Catholicisms (in the plural) of Italy, France and Spain; by Aurelio Musi (Salerno) on lay and ecclesiastical fiefdoms in Southern Italy, 15th to 19th century. Ferrone's work can be more appropriately labeled as intellectual history; however, the statement of the project's intended innovative aspects includes explicit reference to a dialogue with such international scholars as Robert Darnton and Daniel Roche, whose names are familiar to most of us.

The 2007 approved projects for other periods and historical specialties included the two medieval projects by Paolo Cammarosano (on civic identities and political aggregations in Italy, 11th to 15th century) and Franco Cardini (on the relations between Italy, Jerusalem and the Levant). The former, with comparative research between different Italian areas, repeatedly refers to cultural processes and experiences, thus interpreting institutional history in terms of an inquiry into political and administrative cultures. One of the modern projects, led by Maria Malatesta (Milan), concerns professions and power in Italy in the *longue durée*; the Milan unit is early modern, and among the methodological references of the project one encounters the name of Bourdieu.

Having devoted significant time and attention to one of the main channels of public funding, it should probably be added that discontent with the way the system works is strong; and that, according to some, the criteria by which projects are selected for financing tell us more about the social anthropology of Italian academia (hierarchy, networks, factions and feuds) than about research itself.

---

offering of significantly lower grants against the requested funds, to the extent that the scale of the projects (including the capacity of employing research support staff on a fixed-term basis) had to decrease significantly.

12 Brizzi is also the current head of the Department of history, anthropology and geography at the University of Bologna.

Another type of governmental support is provided by FIRB (Fund for the investment in strategic research—in Italian, *ricerca di base*; later renamed as FIRST, Fund for the investment in scientific and technological research). As it is often the case with private resourcing for research, like that provided by the cultural foundations associated with banks, they may be advertised with one or more general topics which encourage applications, while limiting the range of subjects admitted. Thus, in 2001 one of these calls for projects was on Heritage and perspectives in the human sciences and invited to consider history, art and literature as tools for a dialogue between Mediterranean, Middle-European and Atlantic cultures. Compared with PRIN, FIRB are fewer in number but last three years and can be substantial in the amount of resources allocated. In 2008, to take the most recent and relevant, there was funding in the human sciences, with the approval of projects proposed by Mauro Antonelli on historical archives of Italian psychology, Paola Barocchi on artistic and literary culture between 19th and 20th century, Anna Maria Bellina on librettos for opera, Lina Bolzoni for a digital archive of words and images from 16th century manuscripts, Claudio Leonardi for an archive of medieval manuscripts in the European cultural tradition, Enrico Pattaro on medieval juristic manuscripts, Angelo Stella on the manuscript tradition of modern writers, Loris Sturlese on medieval German philosophy. These eight projects were cumulatively granted the sum of €4,200,000. As the list suggests clearly enough, the emphasis here is in making a variety of sources more widely available (one on literary archives of the Italian 20th century had been launched two years earlier), surely a vital precondition for their further study and interpretation.

Beyond these types of national projects, naturally, the bulk of academic research consists of locally funded (and, more often than not, individually pursued) initiatives, which are far more difficult to monitor, unless one looks at them from their result, that is, considers the profession's whole output of publications (that again is easier said than done). A combination of prolonged financial restraint with attempts to improve the system and encourage academic excellence has put pressure for an increasingly selective distribution of research funds and for the adoption of peer review schemes largely inspired by the British Research Assessment Exercise. This will have inevitable, though not entirely predictable, consequences on the nature and framework of future work.

Among institutions other than universities, the National Council of Research should at least be mentioned. Of its eleven departments, one deals with Cultural identity, another with Cultural heritage, with ten and six ongoing projects respectively. The subjects of the projects assembled under the heading of Identity include historical memory, the history of ideas (with particular focus on the philosophical terminology—this is the institute that produces the volumes of the *Lessico intellettuale europeo* series), the vocabulary of law, the Italian language, migrations and multiple identities. Under *Heritage* we find landscape, the conservation and fruition of heritage, the artefact as historical and material monument. Although I have no reason to suggest that a clear sign of a cultural-historical turn is perceivable in the CNR's activities, the above initiatives may be worth mentioning as somehow related to our line of inquiry.

Italy also has a rich tradition of local and regional institutions promoting the study of history and producing publications that frequently give prominence to culture, although they may not be the most methodologically up-to-date places. Local government—from city to regional level—tends to engage in promoting or supporting ephemeral cultural events, rather than invest in lasting structures and human resources. Private (or semi-private) foundations that promote initiatives of interest for this audience include, among others: the Fondazione Benetton in Treviso (with programs on landscape and architectural history, and in the history of sports and games, as well as on its region); in Venice, the Fondazioni Cini and Levi (the latter, entirely devoted to music); in Turin, the Fondazioni Einaudi and Firpo, respectively concerned with socio-economic research and with the study of political thought; in Milan, the Fondazioni Feltrinelli (again with a core in the history of political movements and ideas) and Mondadori (for the history of publishing); in Prato, the Istituto Datini, for the economic history of the pre-industrial era; in Spoleto, the Italian centre for the study of the High Middle Ages. During the Summer of 2010 the state funding of all these institutions was the subject of hot discussions in the public opinion, following threats of complete withdrawal as the result of budget cuts.

The Italian academic system does not contemplate at any level degree programs entirely dedicated to cultural history, courses such as the ones we heard of in this conference (Aberdeen, Turku and the German degrees) or the recently announced program in Utrecht. Nevertheless, teaching modules and exams have recently appeared with the specific denomination of *storia culturale*. They are mostly sized at six credits, occasionally at twelve (as most other European countries, Italy sets students the target of acquiring 60 credits per year). During the academic year 2009/10, seven universities (all in Northern Italy) offer a modul on cultural history. They are normally taught by specialists in the early or late modern period (in at least one case, Genoa—where the course denomination is preceded by the clause "genres of historiography", thus offering cultural history as an example—with the contributing teaching role of a medievalist). In Bologna, the cultural history module is combined with a more philosophically oriented history of ideas, to compose a twofold program entitled, "cultural history and history of the systems of thought" following Foucault. In Milan a chronological delimitation is explicit in the title, *cultural history of the early modern period* (here, as for recruiting and careers, it may be worth mentioning that most of the teaching of history within the Italian academia falls, at least formally, into period-specific labels, and only by adopting them officially but ignoring them practically it possible to teach themes and methods across chronological barriers). Even more specifically, in the Faculty of Education of the University of Modena and Reggio Emilia, a course on offer concerns the cultural history of education (here combined with a module on education theories and methods); while in Verona, a topic taught by a colleague of mine is the cultural and social history of medicine. All taught courses belong to master degrees (the +2 of the Bologna and Sorbonne system), in the current Italian denomination, *corsi di laurea magistrale*. The contexts, however, differ considerably, ranging from history degrees, to literary-philological ones (Bologna), or others devoted to the study of the performing arts (Padua), languages and publishing (Milan), as well as the afore-mentioned education. The ministry's web site shows a similar pattern for last year, although, an undergraduate course of cultural and social history was then also offered at the University of Florence (within a degree program on psychology).[13]

The more traditional—and methodologically less relevant to us—wording *storia della cultura* (history of culture) is a clause used for many more teaching courses, this time spread throughout the country (with a significant presence in the Centre-South), although often in combination with adjectives that define them as belonging to particular fields and educational programs: the latter range from specific languages and literatures (history of the English or Anglo-American, French, German, Portuguese, Russian or Spanish cultures—in Venice, still within the faculty of modern languages, a specific course is also devoted to the theory and history of postcolonial cultures), to the culture and literature of the region hosting the university (Abruzzo at Chieti-Pescara). Anthropologists teach modules on the history of material culture, within degree courses in the humanities (at Cagliari, in Calabria, and Venice, where the level is postgraduate and the module description also includes reference to ethnographic museology). Less common is the more generic history of culture, which is attested at the Faculty of Political sciences of the small university of Teramo, where it is taught with a late modern syllabus; while, in the same faculty, an early modernist teaches a module specifically entitled history of the *European* culture. The Third Uni-

---

13 With sabbatical leaves and other circumstances that may affect the yearly offer, such slight variations are only to be expected.

versity of Rome offers a course on the history of culture in the early modern period; Salerno has one each for the medieval, early and late modern periods (within the faculty of languages); Milan one for the late modern, another for the history of classical culture and philology (of the classical culture and tradition is the phrase used in Pisa, instead). The history of Roman culture is taught in Perugia. At Padua, the teaching of medieval culture is combined with that of the same period's mentalities. In Naples, the Faculty of Sociology has a course on the philosophy and history of culture (taught by a philosopher). At Genoa, the Faculty of Law offers a module on the history of the European legal culture, the Faculty of Humanities one on sources and methods for the history of scientific culture. At Cassino, the *genius loci* has suggested a specific course on the history of Benedictine culture.[14]

As with the case of research projects, though, it may prove too nominalistic to stop at the open denomination of *cultural history* courses: in order to assess the impact of the cultural turn, it would be even more relevant to judge how much of an influence it has exercised on the teaching of general history and on the determination of any other specific historical subject. To value and measure this, of course, is much less simple. The structure of professors' and lecturers' formation and career is reflected in the teaching, which usually puts an emphasis on individual periods, and leaves little room for general introductions, as well as for thematic or methodological approaches that span a wide chronology. Thus, textbooks on the history of the different periods and reading lists should be examined for an answer. Generally speaking, over the past ten years the Italian publishing system has produced a significant number of up-to-date teaching aids, which help willing academics to offer a fairly realistic and reasonably attractive image of the discipline. The orientation of authors and choices of teachers will obviously vary; however, it would be unusual today to complete a course without some exposure to the constructivist emphasis on history as an inevitably subjective discourse; to analyses such as the ones proposed by Norbert Elias or Michel Foucault as challenging keys to a deeper interpretation of the past; or to works by Peter Burke, Roger Chartier, Robert Darnton, Carlo Ginzburg or Natalie Zemon Davis—just to mention the most obvious names—

---

14 One could further speculate over the status of all these teaching modules by taking into account the academic rank of professors and lecturers in charge of them—but this would move us towards the tentative field of a sociology of academia on which I do not intend to improvise here (even if I wanted to, there seems to be a certain hierarchical balance in this case, not a clear-cut attribution of assignments to colleagues with more or less experience, in higher or lower positions).

as options within lists of recommended reading. The *histoire événementielle* is no longer the main menu. Having said this, it would be unwise to hide the fact that this is not everyone's favourite dish, and substantially different approaches will have to cohabit for the foreseeable future.

A few of the academic and general publishers most active in the field of history are worth a glance. Il Mulino has a history catalogue subdivided in sections, partly thematic partly chronological. It currently lists 45 titles under the subcategory *storia della cultura*, a label that certainly includes also (although understandably not only) works with a cultural-historical orientation, as testified by several volumes by Peter Burke. (There are inevitable exceptions, but in general the Italian publishing system is receptive of the international output, and the main figures in the Anglo-Saxon or French cultural history tradition easily find their way to the Italian reader.) Laterza adopts slightly narrower headings —among them the history of the book and of libraries (50 items), of women and gender (circa 50 more), of food (about 20 titles, many of which by medievalist Massimo Montanari). A smaller but specialized history publisher as Viella has special categories, as well as on traditional chronological basis, on gender and religious history.[15]

Almost entirely lacking from the panorama of Italian publishing is—with few and fairly recent exceptions—the university press. This substantial difference from the standard international situation has inevitable consequences: publishing is subject to market pressures; academics may be required to cover publishing expenses; consequently, when this is guaranteed by recourse to financial support from their institutions, publishers may turn a blind eye to the quality of what is passed on to them. The peer review procedures in progress I mentioned earlier are going to have an impact on all this world; it has already been suggested that where you publish—as well as what—will be taken into fuller consideration in assessing the quality of research, and resources we distributed accordingly. Thus, individual and group strategies in writing and submitting work, in editing and publishing are likely to change significantly.

The dedicated Italian periodical possibly presenting closer family resemblances with our field is *Cultural studies*, now in its seventh year. Although, properly speaking, it clearly belongs to the neighbouring field indicated by its title, one historian sits in its direction,[16] and it has hosted articles written by renowned historians, like John Brewer. *Cromohs* (Cyber Review of Modern His-

---

15 Bruno Mondadori is another publisher with a dynamic editorial policy in cultural history; the Edizioni Sylvestre Bonnard are specialized in the field of bibliology.

16 Paolo Capuzzo (Bologna), also a member of the CSC.

toriography), the outcome of a project by scholars of the Universities of Trieste and Florence and the first entirely electronic review devoted to the history of modern historiography (first issued in 1995), also displays a general orientation very much in tune with cultural history.[17]

In most other cases, relevant material can be found within history periodicals either more generalist in their subject matter or methodological preferences, or dedicated to more specific issues that, however, may leave room to a culturalist approach. *Le carte e la storia*, *Cheiron*, *Genesis*, *Giornale di storia*, *Passato e presente*, *Quaderni di storia*, *Rivista di storia e letteratura religiosa*, *Rivista storica italiana*, *Società e storia*, *Studi storici*, as well as the multilingual *Storia della storiografia*, are among the periodicals in which both articles of original research and methodological discussions relevant to our discourse can be found in recent years.

Quaderni Storici is the internationally better-known periodical that, in the recent past, has acted as the flagship of Italian *new history*. It has continued to be a vital venue of research and discussion on questions that matter to us, as testified by some topics of monographic issues of recent years, from *Postcolonial societies* (2008), to *Slavery and conversions in the Mediterranean* (2007) and *Cultural objects and exchanges* (2006). Since the periodical was traditionally twinned to the theory and practice of micro-history, it may offer us here the opportunity to remember what, was a characteristic way of doing history a generation ago, and that, while never conquering the entire nation, has inspired a significant number of scholars with its distinctive style, which paid due attention to the cultural side of the stories it retold.

A comparatively more recent periodical whose style and approach deserve special citation is *Storica*. Its special issue celebrating the first 15 years of publishing (2009) included essays on symbols of politics, on historians and emotions, and on gender and world history.

Contributions by Italian scholars to foreign and international publications would pose some further issues in order to be assessed (as it is the case with books published abroad by Italian scholars, it would also cause significant problems of identification); however, on this point it may be worth registering that a member of the editorial board of *Quaderni Storici*, Angelo Torre, has recently contributed to a methodological discussion on *Histoire et paysage* on the French *Annales*.[18] On the other hand, the reader of *Quaderni Storici* would also remem-

---

17 One of its two directors, Guido Abbattista (also managing director of *Storia della storiografia*), is a member of the CSC too.

18 TORRE, 2008.

ber that, back in 1995, the same Italian historian had accused Roger Chartier of abandoning the study of practices — and of *reality* altogether — for that of (mere) representations. The French historian had the opportunity to reply on *Quaderni Storici* and offer a lesson in theory and method; the episode, however, testified to a certain resistance from the Italian academia in accepting a culturalist approach, too quickly and unproblematically identified with postmodernism.[19]

Cultural historians in Italy do not have a specific professional association (other than the newly founded Centre). Few of them are members of international associating. Rather, they belong to established period-specific associations, namely, the Società Italiana per lo Studio della Storia COntemporanea (SISSCO), the Società Italiana per la Storia dell'Età Moderna (SISEM) and the Società Italiana degli Storici MEDievisti (SISMED); the latter two have special connections, but do not coincide, with the associations respectively running the web portals http://www.stmoderna.it and http://www.retimedievali.it/ — both currently in the process of moving to the Verona University server. There are also, of course, more specific institutions devoted to the study of local or thematic issues, which may be relevant to cultural history: The fact remains that, partly because all Italian academic historians are recruited and progress in their careers within distinct period-specific disciplinary sectors, the above-mentioned associations and related web sites reflect better than any other their activities and (individual as well as group) self-image. It is within their ranks that we will try to identify traces of a cultural-historical turn.

The http://www.stmoderna.it portal has a register of scholars (*anagrafe*). Since the site is undergoing substantial restructuring, the criteria under which the research interests of individuals are indicated will also be revised. The previous (current) list does not include a specific culture-historical box one can tick. One of the closest could perhaps be *storia delle idee*, although everyone can easily understand that it may refer to a more traditional, philosophically-oriented intellectual history. Still, it will be interesting to know that, in a context in which profiled historians had the opportunity to indicate their expertise by ticking one or multiple boxes if appropriate (or else had them chosen for them, if their entry was created editorially) a significant number of them — over 200 out of just under 1700 — expressed interest in the history of ideas (alone or in combination with others of the ten thematic fields on display).

---

19 TORRE, 1995; CHARTIER, 1996.

A key-word search through the SISSCO web site[20] gives 15 scholars adopting *storia culturale* as a phrase within their CVs, either to describe their research interests or their teaching assignments.

Although the web site of the SISMED lists two hundred members, it does not currently allow searches throughout their CVs. Potentially interesting facilities as a list of ongoing and recent PhD research projects are also under construction. *Reti medievali*, though—a portal (also, an online periodical) providing information in English, French and Spanish, as well as Italian—collects a wide range of material of interest for the medievalist. Although a search on the exact phrase *storia culturale* gave a poor result, there is no doubt that many scholars on the field are operating in full awareness and tune with international trends. Nevertheless, perhaps they have a lesser tendency to identify the cultural as their main mark of identity, or refrain from joining dedicated organizations, if we have to draw conclusions from the fact that only one Italian medievalist is a member of the Padua Centre, another one of the ISCH.[21]

An Italian specialist of Antiquity has also joined the International Society.[22] To bring together scholars of Antiquity, there is not quite an equivalent structure to the ones we have seen active for later periods, although the Association Internationale d'Épigraphie Greque et Latine (AIEGL) and Terra Italia ONLUS (Associazione per lo sviluppo e la diffusione degli studi sull'Italia romana) are prominent institutions in the field that help coordinating research.

I will now move to perspectives. In my opening remarks on the Padua Centre, I have pointed out that a significant group of relatively young late modernists—whose work is partly showcased on the Centre's own web site—are now consistently operating, with strong methodological awareness and convictions, according to a culturalist agenda.

Among early modernists, a glance to possible future developments is allowed by the fact that our association (SISEM) has launched the project of holding, a yearly, three-day seminar especially intended to offer younger scholars the opportunity to showcase their ongoing research projects and discuss them with colleagues commencing September 2010. The twenty teams that have applied the first time tell us a slightly different story from the more cautious one we are able to read among the established profession. For a start, many of the applicants (the panel coordinators, as well as the remaining speakers) have high profiles

---

20 http://www.sissco.it, 15.03.2010.
21 Respectively, Cristina La Rocca (Padua) and Marina Montesano (Genoa, where she also collaborates to the above mentioned teaching module).
22 Gabriella Valera Gruber (Trieste).

of study and research. Holding a doctorate or a comparable qualification was a requirement; but what we have here is several young scholars who have pursued an international career, and are currently holding, in several cases, fixed-term research positions abroad. The age threshold of 40 may strike representatives of other countries as fairly high to qualify as *young*, but is justified—let alone Italian demographic and social structure, with an entrenched late departure from family nests—by the continuing poor level of recruiting in the university system.

What I meant to point out, though, are themes and methods that characterize the panels proposed for the seminars to be held in Arezzo in 2010. A cluster of them still holds on to a fairly traditional focus on the history of institutions. The large majority, on the other hand, could very easily fit under a cultural-history umbrella, either for their proposed topic, or for methodological and bibliographical points of reference, or furthermore for the featuring of culturalist key words or names in the candidates' CVs and self-presentations. Thus, there are proposed themes that present obvious family resemblances for us, such as the history of the book, cultural translation, discourses on travel and discoveries, the circulation of scientific knowledge (with science interpreted as a communication practice). Political history too appears several times with a culturalist approach, and emphasis on symbols, rituals, languages, behavioural practices, ideas and texts; economic history from the point of view of consumption; military history, as circulation of models. Other proposals concern community history, or the history of gender, religious and ethnic groups.

On the whole, therefore, if this is a reasonable sample of what the next generation of Italian scholars is up to, the perspectives of cultural history look fairly promising. The challenge is, rather, whether the national academic system will be able to recruit them and offer them a stimulating environment for teaching and research. Considering that the Italian government, as many others, has been consistently cutting university funding; that currently even the replacement of the turnover is blocked, and in the near future it will be allowed only as a limited percentage, thus actually reducing the size of the sector; that the country devotes to research and development a portion of the GDP dramatically lower than most other industrialized countries (1.09% versus a European average of 1.85%, in the most recent available figures, with France, Denmark, Germany and Austria above 2%, Finland and Sweden above 3%)[23]—there are few grounds for optimism. The "brain drain" of Italian researchers is likely to continue; wherever

---

23 http://ec.europa.eu/research/era/pdf/key-figures-report2008-2009_en.pdf, 01.09.2010, p. 22. Data referring to 2006.

they may find employment, though, it is comforting for us to register an increasing interest for the approach to history which was the focus of this conference.

Literature

ARCANGELI, ALESSANDRO, L'histoire culturelle en Italie, in: L'histoire culturelle: un "tournant mondial" dans l'historiographie?, ed. by PHILIPPE POIRRIER, DIJON 2008, p. 41-50 (revised Italian edition in press, Verona 2010).

BURKE, PETER, Ibridismo, scambio, traduzione culturale. Riflessioni sulla globalizzazione della cultura in una prospettiva storica, trans. A. Arcangeli, Verona 2009.

CHARTIER, ROGER, Rappresentazione della pratica, pratica della rappresentazione, in: Quaderni storici 92 (1996), p. 487-493.

HUNT, LYNN, La storia culturale nell'età globale, Pisa 2010.

TORRE, ANGELO, Percorsi della pratica, 1966-1995, in: Quaderni storici 90 (1995), p. 799-829.

ID., Un "tournant spatial" en histoire? Paysages, regards, ressources, in: Annales. Histoire, Sciences Sociales 63 (2008), p. 1127-1144.

http://www.centrostoriaculturale.unipd.it/, 01.09.2010
http://cercauniversita.cineca.it/php5/prin/cerca.php?codice=2006110234, 01.09.2010
http://www.sissco.it, 15.03.2010
http://ec.europa.eu/research/era/pdf/key-figures-report2008-2009_en.pdf, 01.09.2010

Contributors

Alessandro Arcangeli is Associated Professor of Early Modern History at the Department of Tempo, Spazio, Immagine e Società (TeSIS), University of Verona, Italy. His main research interests are cultural history of the body in Europe, 1400-1700: moral, medical and political discourses on dance, leisure and recreation, and cultural history methods and historiography (Italian and global).
Contact: alessandro.arcangeli@univr.it.

Christof Dejung is Senior Lecturer and Researcher at the University of Konstanz, Germany. His current research project examines the social and cultural foundations of global trade in the 19th and 20th century by example of the Swiss trading house Volkart Bros.
Contact: christof.dejung@uni-konstanz.de.

Anne Erikson is Professor of Cultural History, University of Oslo, Norway. She specializes in popular religion, collective memory, the concept of history and heritage.
Contact: anne.eriksen@ikos.uio.no.

Nick Fisher was Director of the Institute for Cultural History (1995-98, since 1999 early retirement), University of Aberdeen, Scotland (UK). His current research interest is the Great Exhibition of 1851, Hyde Park, London.
Contact: n.fisher@abdn.ac.uk.

Ludmilla Jordanova is Professor of Modern History, King's College, London. She specializes in the cultural history of science and medicine, on gender and the family and on visual and material culture.
Contact: ludmilla.jordanova@kcl.ac.uk.

Igor Kąkolewski is Research Assistant at the German Historical Institute, Warsaw. His research interests are religious, social and ethnic stereotypes and mutual perceptions in pre-modern Poland, German and Polish social, economic and political history in the early modern period.
Contact: kakolewski@dhi.waw.pl.

Achim Landwehr is Professor of Early Modern History, Heinrich-Heine-Universität Düsseldorf, Germany. His main research interests are Cultural History of the 17th century, concepts of time in the Early Modern Times, Theories and Methods of historiography
Contact: landwehr@phil-fak.uni-duesseldorf.de

Christina Lutter is Professor for Austrian History at the University of Vienna. Her research interests are Medieval and Early Modern Cultural and Gender History; Cultural Theory and Cultural Studies, Gender Studies.
Contact: christina.lutter@univie.ac.at.

Mārtiņš Mintaurs is free-lance Lector at the University of Latvia and chief specialist at the Museum of the River Daugava, Latvia, Salaspils. He specializes in Heritage Studies, Material Culture and Architectural History.
Contact: mintaurs@hotmail.com.

Andrea Pető is Associate Professor at the Department of Gender Studies at the Central European University, Budapest, Hungary. Presently she is working on gender and history of World War II.
Contact: petoand@t-online.hu.

Carolina Rodríguez-López is Assistant Professor of History at Universidad Complutense de Madrid, Spain. Herr current research interest belongs to the history of Spanish and European Universities during the 20th century.
Contact: carolinarodriguez@ghis.ucm.es.

Jörg Rogge is Professor of History, Middle Ages, at the University of Mainz, Germany. He is also Spokesperson of the Special Research Group Historical Cultural Sciences, Mainz. His main research interests are methods and theory of historical cultural sciences and politics and culture in Late Medieval Europe.
Contact: rogge@uni-mainz.de.

Hannu Salmi is Professor of Cultural History, University of Turku, Finland. He specializes in the history of Wagner and Wagnerism, the cultural history of the 19th century and the history of time travel.
Contact: hansalmi@utu.fi.